ART & SOUL

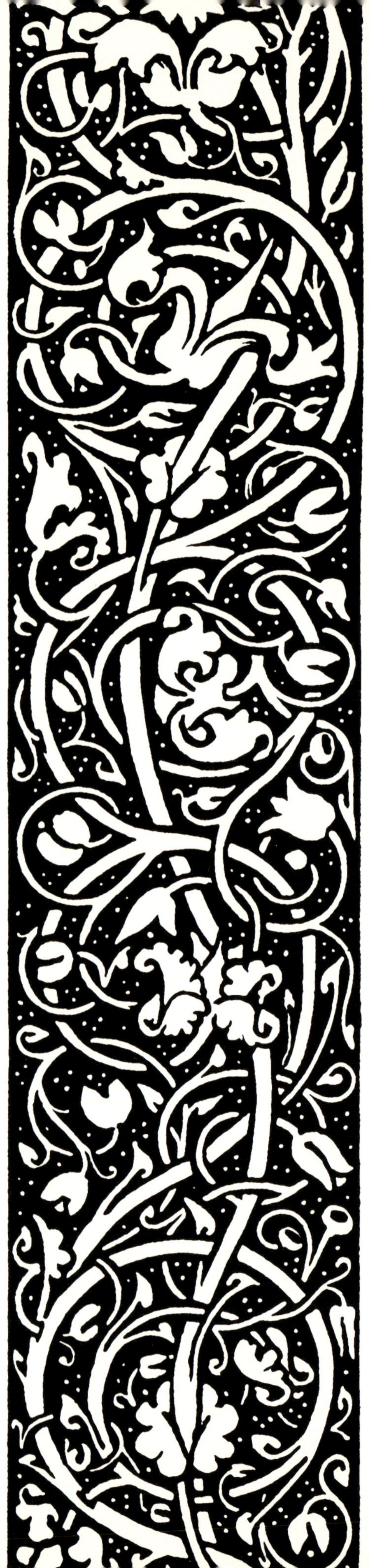

ART & SOUL

VICTORIANS AND THE GOTHIC

Joanne Parker & Corinna Wagner

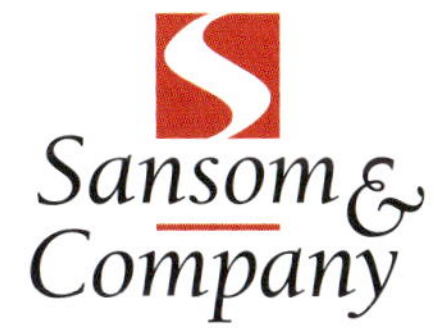

Sansom &
Company

in association with

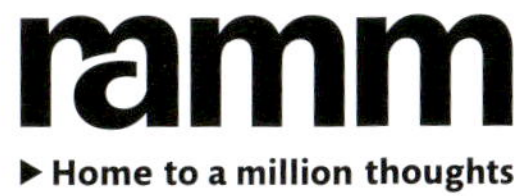

First published in 2014 by Sansom & Co. an imprint of Redcliffe Press Ltd
81G Pembroke Road, Bristol BS8 3EA

info@sansomandcompany.co.uk
www.sansomandcompany.co.uk

ISBN 978-1-908326-65-2

Published to accompany the exhibition 'Art and Soul: Victorians and the Gothic'
at the Royal Albert Memorial Museum & Art Gallery, Exeter, 22 November 2014–12 April 2015

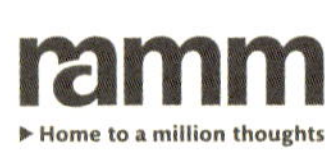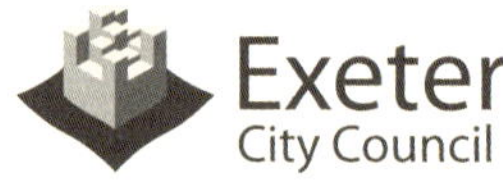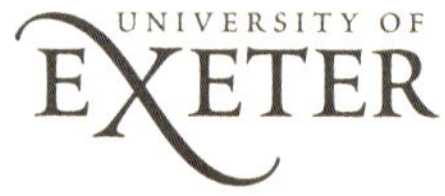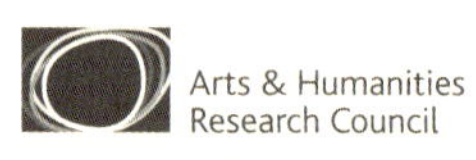

British Library Cataloguing-in-Publication Data
A catalogue record for this book is available from the British Library

Designed and typeset in Doves Type and Goudy Old Style (italic) by E&P Design.
Doves Type was created c.1900 and used in all of the Doves Press publications. Alas, following
a business dispute in 1916, the matrices and blocks of type were deliberately 'drowned' in the Thames.
Thankfully, it has recently been 'salvaged' by typographers working from original source material.

Printed by Zenith Media

CONTENTS

FOREWORD

CAMILLA HAMPSHIRE
Museums Manager
Royal Albert Memorial Museum & Art Gallery

An exhibition focused on Victorian Gothic, or more pragmatically Victorian medievalism, was first mooted by colleagues at the University of Exeter in 2010. This book and the accompanying exhibition at the Royal Albert Memorial Museum & Art Gallery (RAMM), from 22 November 2014 to 12 April 2015, represent the culmination of four years' collaboration between the two institutions. Research was led by the university in a project entitled 'Identity, Community and Victorian Medievalism in the South West'. RAMM's curators have worked closely with the academic team to bring together paintings, books, textiles, furniture, silver, glass and medals which express the enormous impact of the movement on our region, set within the national context.

What gives this exhibition particular relevance for RAMM is its exploration of the revival of all things medieval as played out in the south west of England. As visitors to RAMM will recognise immediately, the museum building is a landmark of the Gothic revival style of the 1860s, much influenced by John Ruskin: architectural commentators have described it as a Venetian casket that sits on Exeter's Queen Street. There is a strong and pertinent association between the content of the exhibition and its location.

The research has been led by Dr Corinna Wagner and Dr Joanne Parker, both Senior Lecturers at the University of Exeter, who provide the essays in this volume. Without their dedication and enthusiasm, and that of their colleagues at the university, this book and the exhibition would not have been possible. To place the South West contribution into a national context, RAMM has benefitted from the generosity of lenders prepared to let much treasured works travel to Exeter; while, on a more local level, loans have been released by Devon churches and libraries. My sincere thanks are extended to all those institutions that have kindly agreed to lend works for the exhibition.

Particular thanks are due to our principal funders in this enterprise. Without Arts and Humanities Research Council (AHRC) funding, RAMM and the University of Exeter could not have staged an exhibition and book of such ambition and scope. RAMM is a service of Exeter City Council and gratefully acknowledges the support of ECC and Arts Council England as part of its Major Partner Museum Scheme.

IMAGINING THE MIDDLE AGES

JOANNE PARKER

'You get medieval immediately on these people and you come down much harder'.[1]

FROM THE GOTHIC TO THE MEDIEVAL

When Mayor Boris Johnson told the London Assembly recently that the capital's police needed to 'get medieval' to prevent a replay of the 2011 Tottenham riots, what 'medieval' measures might he have been imagining? The Anglo-Saxon *scramasax* (a single-bladed knife), used in battle in the sixth and seventh centuries? The mythical 'blood eagle' rite (the cutting out of a victim's lungs and ribcage) once believed to have been indulged in by the Vikings of the ninth and tenth centuries? Or the ordeal by fire or water resorted to in Henry II's twelfth-century courts?[2] 'Getting medieval', today's slang dictionaries tell us, now means 'to treat with extreme savagery'.[3] The phrase was first used in Quentin Tarantino's 1994 ultra-violent film *Pulp Fiction*, and has since been used to describe American military action in Kosovo on the one hand, and the experimental electronic sound of 1970s 'Krautrock' band Faust on the other.[4]

We don't just 'get medieval' today. We also use the term 'medieval' broadly and readily to allude to a widely differing array of historical periods, peoples, and cultures, spanning the millennium from the fifth to the fifteenth century. Even a new off-road car can be 'medieval' according to the *New York Times*.[5] The word 'medieval' is, however, of relatively recent coinage. Its recorded use goes back only as far as 1817, to the antiquary Thomas Dudley Fosbroke, who in the preface to the second edition of his book *British Monachism: Or, Manners and Customs of the Monks and Nuns of England* inserted what must then have been an impressively new-fangled-sounding term, promising that his study would 'illustrate mediæval customs' and 'mediæval principles'.[6]

Around the time that Fosbroke was writing, other spans and shifts of history were also being identified and named as distinct periods: it was just eleven years later, in 1828, that 'the Renaissance' was first identified as a distinct historical moment which, with the spread of humanism across Europe, the rediscovery of classical culture, and the beginnings of exploration to the New World, had brought to an end the 'medieval' period.[7] Fosbroke's own neologism came from the Latin 'medium aevum', meaning literally 'middle age'. The concept of a 'middle age' separating the classical age of antiquity (before the fall of the Western Roman Empire, or the conversion of the emperor Constantine to Christianity) from the modern age (after the fall of Constantinople, or the start of the Renaissance) itself only originated in the latter half of the sixteenth century.[8] And in England, there was no consensus about what it should be called until the seventeenth century. The poet John Donne and the historian Henry Spelman began using 'middle ages' and 'middle age' from about 1611.[9] Before that, history had been divided more simply into the ancient world and the modern.

The intervening period between the ancient and the modern ages was not only known as 'the middle ages' in the seventeenth century. After the Reformation, Protestant scholars looking back to those centuries of Roman Catholic culture began increasingly to consider them a period of spiritual and intellectual darkness. This view was popularised by writers like John Milton and (in the next century) by the poet Oliver Goldsmith and the historian and philosopher David Hume, who spoke of the Middle Ages as a time when 'the light of ancient science and history, had very nearly suffered a total extinction'.[10] It was from this association that the name 'the Dark Ages' — still sometimes used today — first arose. During the seventeenth and eighteenth centuries, it was used as a derogatory synonym for 'Middle Ages' to describe the entire period between Roman times and the Renaissance.[11] Hume, however, had argued that the Norman Conquest had marked the first step towards the light of civilisation, and later writers echoed this sentiment. William Godwin (the husband of Mary Wollstonecraft and father of Mary Shelley) argued in his 1803 *Life of Geoffrey Chaucer* that:

> *The muddy effervescence which was stirred up in Europe by the continual influx of the barbarians, subsided in a considerable degree in the eleventh century. William the Norman may be considered as having introduced politeness and learning to this island.*[12]

Gradually, by the second half of the nineteenth century, 'the dark ages' came to be identified not as the entire Middle Ages, but more specifically as its early period — up to either the Norman Conquest in 1066, or the first Crusade in 1095. 'The Middle Ages' was then reserved for the period from the late eleventh century until the Renaissance.[13]

Dim views of what we now call the medieval period — and even dimmer views of their earliest centuries — also gave birth in the seventeenth century to the use of the term 'Gothic' for the cultures of the Middle Ages. The capricious term 'Gothic' can today allude to many different things — from novels to footwear.[14] For the Roman authors who first used the term 'Goth' in the fourth and fifth centuries AD, however, it meant quite specifically the various Germanic tribes who had invaded both the Eastern and Western Roman empires.[15] The first use of the word in English was by the Venerable Bede in his eighth-century *Ecclesiastical History*, in which he simply echoed the use of ancient historians.[16] But by the seventeenth century, the meaning of 'Gothic' had grown in English so that it was now also used to describe the culture and language of any Germanic tribe, including the Angles, Saxons and Jutes who had migrated to Britain in the fifth and sixth centuries. And in the eighteenth century, this sense of 'Gothic' widened again, so that the term effectively meant 'an alternative to the classical' and could now indicate peoples, objects, or social practices from the whole medieval period — thus the Anglo-Saxon parliament could be described as 'Gothic', but so could the jousting practised in Norman England.[17]

Because the original 'Gothic' tribes had sacked Rome — the emblem of classical culture and authority, variously identified with either the aristocratic and monarchical establishment or the Roman Catholic Church — 'Gothic' was rarely a politically neutral term when it was used to describe Britain's Middle Ages in the seventeenth and eighteenth centuries. For Protestant and Parliamentarian Whigs, the 'Gothic' carried positive connotations of liberty and rebellion against tyranny. So by the 1740s, it had become mainstream thinking to claim: 'It is to the Gothick Constitution that we owe our Parliaments, which are the Guardians of our Rights and Liberties'.[18] And by the 1760s, the English law could be likened to a sturdy 'Gothic castle', requiring only slight modernization.[19] Yet at the same time strong pejorative associations of the Goths and the Gothic remained, particularly among Tories and those who tended towards neo-classicist taste. Jonathan Swift, for instance, contrasted the elegant 'example of the Greeks and Romans' in literature with a 'Gothick Strain', which displayed 'a natural Tendency towards relapsing into Barbarity'.[20] Accordingly, during the eighteenth century, 'Gothic' also assumed a broad, ahistorical meaning as a synonym for 'barbarous, rude, uncouth, unpolished, or savage'. So duelling could be considered a 'Gothic crime', an individual's temper could be described as 'fierce and Gothick', or a late dinner could be eaten at a 'Gothic hour'.[21]

After Fosbroke had coined the adjective 'medieval' in 1817, however, so many subsequent writers adopted the word that by the mid-nineteenth century the meaning of 'Gothic' had retrenched so that in the main it was only used to describe a medieval typeface, and the style of architecture that had been common in Western Europe between around 1200 and 1540 — and also modern imitations of it.[22] Adopting the new word 'medieval' for all other aspects of the Middle Ages allowed writers thereafter to celebrate the post-classical past without the danger of invoking any of the old negative associations of benighted barbarians at the gates of Rome. Indeed, avoiding those meanings could perhaps have been one of the main motivations for Fosbroke's creation of the new word. At the time at which he wrote, the dominant British attitude to the post-classical period was shifting. For the remainder of the nineteenth century, it would no longer be particular groups of constitutional monarchists or anti-Catholic thinkers who celebrated the 'Gothic' past rather than denigrating it. Instead, the 'medieval' period would be drawn on and celebrated by thinkers of almost every political, aesthetic, and religious persuasion. The widespread phenomenon that we now know as Victorian 'medievalism' had begun.

THE VICTORIANS AND THE PAST

The Victorian interest in the medieval period was just one aspect of a pervasive nineteenth-century fascination with history. In 1901, looking back across the nineteenth century in a speech given at the British Museum, the historian Frederic Harrison asserted, 'if ours was the age of progress, it was also the age of history'.[23] The Victorian year abounded in anniversaries to mark momentous historical events – from the Battle of Marston Moor, to the coronation of Queen Elizabeth, to the execution of Charles I.[24] And Victorian bookshelves heaved under the weight of three-volume historical novels on subjects ranging from the ancient Greeks to the relatively recent events of the eighteenth century.[25]

In part, the Victorian obsession with history was the result of generalised anxiety about what the future might hold in store. This concern had begun in the eighteenth century, following the discovery of the remains of the devastated Roman cities of Herculaneum and Pompeii, and the publication of Edward Gibbon's popular *History of the Decline and Fall of the Roman Empire* (1776-88). Then in the early nineteenth century, the geologist Charles Lyell had published his widely-read study *Principles of Geology*, in which he stated that the earth had been shaped by a series of natural catastrophes. By the mid-century, sufficient dinosaur bones and fossils had been discovered for palaeontologists to begin publishing theories about sudden extinction. And in 1859, Charles Darwin published *On the Origin of Species*, with its theories about natural selection which were quickly applied to the rise and fall of nations. These developments together encouraged anxieties about mass extermination among many thinkers of the period. The art critic and author

John Ruskin complained that he could hear the haunting sound of geologists' hammers at the end of every verse of the Bible.[26] And uncertainty about the future led to a natural turning away from future destinies, and towards interest, instead, in the past.[27]

That interest in the past was also fuelled by the increasing speed of social, political and cultural change in the eighteenth and nineteenth centuries – whether that meant revolutions across Europe, the introduction of mechanised agriculture and railways in Britain, or shifting roles in the family.[28] The sense that Britain's population was somehow becoming dislocated from previous generations led to increased enthusiasm for collecting and preserving as much history as possible. This endeavour took many different forms. One was the protection and preservation of ancient buildings (which although it had been a pursuit of antiquaries since the seventeenth century, first became a coordinated campaign in the eighteenth century, with the foundation of the Society of Antiquaries). Another form was the collecting of folk traditions and songs, in response to the gradual mechanisation of farming, and the disappearance of peasant farmers.[29] In 1765 Thomas Percy published the first serious collection of early ballads, *Reliques of Ancient English Poetry*. In 1774 the first volume of Thomas Warton's *History of English Poetry* appeared – a study of literature from between the eleventh and the sixteenth century. And in the nineteenth century, one of the foremost of these preservers of ancient tales and traditions was the Devon author, clergyman, and general polymath Sabine Baring-Gould whose published collections included early tales of werewolves from across Europe, myths from the Middle Ages, and traditional songs and ballads from the south west of England.[30]

A third response to the pervasive sense of dislocation from the past was the publishing of histories. From the middle of the eighteenth century, history publishing in Britain boomed. One motivation for writing histories in this period was the desire to teach by past example – authors often focussed in particular on historical periods of social turbulence as a means of obliquely discussing current problems, and offering reassurance and inspiration for the present.[31] So the siege of Troy, the European Reformation, and the fall of the Roman Empire were all popular subjects. In particular, however, a veritable rash of histories of England and Britain appeared at this time – one of the most notable and enduring early examples being David Hume's multi-volume *History of England*, published between 1754 and 1762. These works were motivated above all by national pride in Britain's place in the world economy – by the desire to trace the cultural

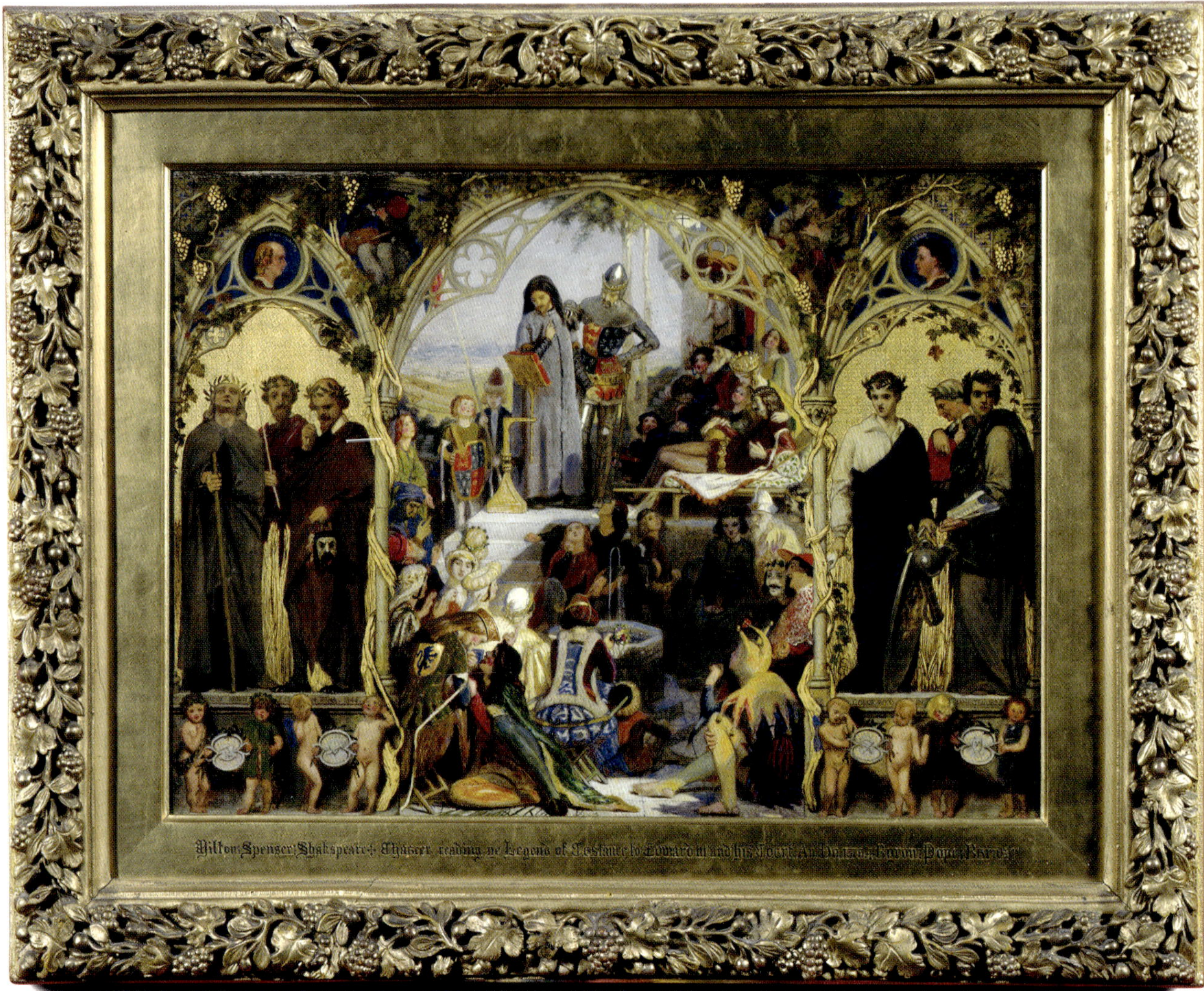

Fig. 1 / Cat. 2

The Seeds and Fruits of English Poetry
Ford Madox Brown

1853 / oil on canvas / celebrating the work of Geoffrey Chaucer, the central
panel of the painting shows the poet reading at the court of Edward III
© Ashmolean Museum, University of Oxford

roots of the nation's current achievements and (even more importantly) to demonstrate that Britain had a heritage that was every bit as impressive as the classical legacy of modern Greece and Italy.[32]

With increasing numbers of British histories being published from the mid-eighteenth century onwards, the British taste for history really became widespread. This was particularly the case once improved printing technology had allowed the histories to be cheaply illustrated, allowing the past to be 'seen' for the first time by the general public.[33] The past also became far more vibrant and accessible from the early nineteenth century, as public art galleries opened for the first time.[34] In 1824 the National Gallery opened in London, followed by the opening of the Scottish Academy of Art in 1827. As public institutions, the galleries demanded works of national interest and so led to a new vogue for producing paintings not of private estates or families, but of historical scenes. Admittedly, many of the earliest historical paintings were far from historically accurate. Anglo-Saxons in togas and Roman sandals were all too common. However, for many members of the public the large and colourful historical paintings that could now be viewed in galleries breathed an entirely new life into distant centuries.[35]

THE VICTORIANS AND THE MEDIEVAL

Of all the subjects that were depicted by the new school of history painters, figures and scenes from the medieval period gradually became the most popular and numerous. By the 1840s, when a series of competitions was held to find artworks for the newly rebuilt Houses of Parliament, artists were given a free rein to choose any theme 'from British history, or from the works of Spenser, Shakespeare, or Milton', but over a third (in total around eighty) chose medieval subjects, including Canute the Viking king, Alfred the Great, the poet Chaucer, Edward I, and St Augustine.[36]

The most obvious reason why the medieval became the period of British history most commonly celebrated in the nineteenth century as equal in interest (if not superior) to the classical past was simply that it was the earliest British era to be fully documented. So historians could scrutinise Anglo-Saxon chronicles for evidence that Britain's parliament, its legal system, and its Anglican church had a heritage of a thousand years, or they could look to Old Norse sagas to claim that the country's navy had roots stretching back across a millennium, or they could celebrate the fourteenth-century *Vision of Piers Plowman* or *The Canterbury Tales* as the seeds of modern English Literature (rather than, say, Homer's *Odyssey*).

Several other important factors also contributed to the appeal of the medieval, however. The omnipresence of the Roman Catholic Church in those pre-Reformation centuries meant that they were often looked back upon as a golden age of faith, by religious writers like the Roman Catholic architect Augustus Pugin (responsible for the interiors of the Palace of Westminster) who were concerned that the values of capitalism were gradually replacing those of Christianity.[37] And in the increasingly industrialised nineteenth century, with its landscape of polluted rivers, busy railway lines, and factory chimneys belching out smoke, the pastoralism of the Middle Ages was understandably alluring.[38] This can be seen particularly in the fashion that developed for Robin Hood novels, plays and children's stories, with their leafy Greenwood settings. In his 1843 Robin Hood novel, *Forest Days*, for instance, the popular author G.P.R. James looked back to the thirteenth century, lamenting:

I cannot help grieving when I look back to a time when wide forests waved their green boughs over many of the richest manufacturing districts of Great Britain, and the lair of the fawn and the burrow of the coney were found, where now appear the fabric [factory] and the mill.[39]

The Victorian perception that the 'Gothic' church architecture of the thirteenth and fourteenth centuries had an inherently organic form, echoing the arching shapes of broadleaf trees, added to the view of the medieval as a time when man had existed in a now-forgotten harmony with nature.[40] Chief among the proponents of this particular idea was John Ruskin, whose 1846 study *Modern Painters* looked back to the years before the Renaissance as a time when artists had been closer to the natural world and therefore capable of creating truer art.[41] Ruskin also believed that the roughness and irregularity of 'Gothic' buildings was an index of the medieval craftsman's 'liberty' and 'freedom of thought'.[42] This contrasted with the precision of mass-produced modern goods which were created at the cost of the modern workman's imagination and humanity. Indeed, he argued, in his 1851 work *The Stones of Venice*, there was far more freedom in medieval England, 'than there is while the animation of her multitudes is sent like fuel to feed factory smoke, and the strength of them is given daily to be wasted into the fineness of a web, or racked into the exactness of a line'.[43]

The growth of industrialism in the nineteenth century did not only lead to the loss of craftsmanship – it also resulted in numerous social problems. For much of the century, British government was based on strongly utilitarian principles, which were concerned primarily with encouraging capitalism and promoting national prosperity, rather than prioritising the living and working conditions of the individual worker. This resulted in shoddily-built housing, unregulated working hours, pollution, dangerous machinery in factories, and poor healthcare. These problems led to widespread fears about social disintegration – and those anxieties were another reason why Victorian thinkers became interested in the medieval period. A key figure among them was the Scottish essayist, philosopher and historian Thomas Carlyle. In his 1843 novel, *Past and Present*, Carlyle contrasted the welfare of the modern factory worker with the conditions that had been enjoyed by serfs in the twelfth century:

Gurth born thrall of Cedric the Saxon has been greatly pitied by Dryasdust and others. Gurth with the brass collar round his neck, tending Cedric's pigs in the glades of the wood, is not what I call

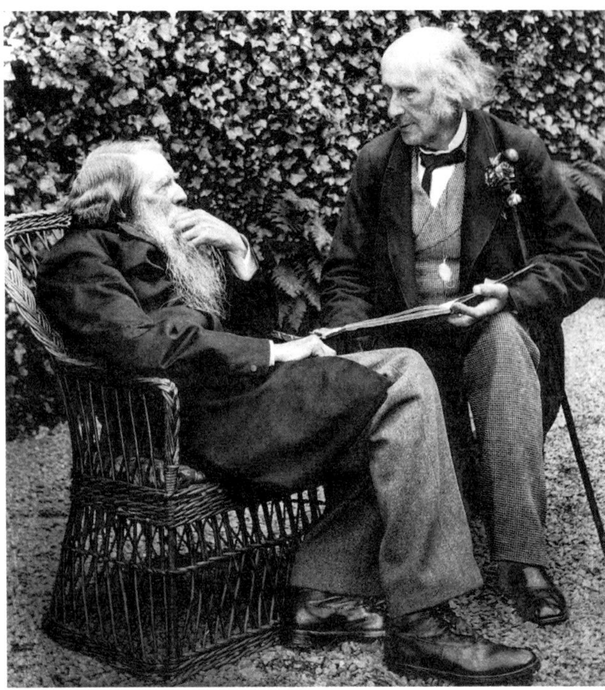

Fig. 2

Professor Ruskin and Sir Henry Acland Bart

Photograph by Miss Sarah Angelina Acland at Brantwood, 1 August 1893
© National Portrait Gallery, London

an exemplar of human felicity: but Gurth, with the sky above him, with the free air and tinted boscage [mass of shrubs] and umbrage [shadow of trees] round him, and in him at least the certainty of supper and social lodging when he came home,—Gurth to me seems happy, in comparison with many a Lancashire and Buckinghamshire man of these days not born thrall of anybody![44]

The association of the medieval period with access to nature and plenty of food in this extract is typical of writings from the 1840s (a decade known as 'the hungry forties' – when both of those things were in short supply in many areas), as is the use of archaic-sounding language to introduce a wistful, backward-looking tone.

What Carlyle was primarily wistful about was the feudalism of the twelfth century – the hierarchical social system in which the church and aristocracy had been responsible for the welfare of the poor. In his eyes, it had been a system founded on the admirable values of loyalty, duty, and adherence to tradition. And he believed that the key to a better future was a system of neo-feudalism, in which modern captains of industry would assume the responsibilities of medieval lords, and relations between them and their workers would be based on mutual reciprocity, rather than on the simple exchange of money. Carlyle's ideas influenced later writers like Charles Kingsley (author of *The Water Babies*) and the Conservative Prime Minister Benjamin Disraeli, and they also fed into the Young England movement – a group of far-right-wing aristocrats who attempted to translate the ideals of neo-feudalism into practical politics in the 1840s – largely as a reaction to the French revolutions of 1789 and 1830.[45]

Like Carlyle, the Young Englanders believed that a responsible aristocracy was the only key to avoiding revolution in Britain, but unlike him, they looked to the existing, hereditary gentry to fulfil that role, rather than to the nouveau-riche industrialists. One of the most interesting features of nineteenth-century 'medievalism' is that it was a movement that incorporated all parts of the political spectrum. Both arch-conservatives like Disraeli and political radicals looked back to the medieval period – sometimes even to the same centuries, specific events, or particular figures. They simply re-interpreted conveniently sketchy early accounts to support their own political standpoint.

Radical use of the Middle Ages began long before the nineteenth century. In the mid-seventeenth century, rebels like the 'Digger' Gerrard Winstanley who were campaigning for the redistribution of enclosed land and the reform of government became interested in the idea that the Saxons had been early democrats, who had shared their own values.[47] Drawing on accounts of the Saxon 'witenagemot' or meeting of elders, they concluded that the Normans, on their arrival in England, had replaced democratic institutions with feudalism, native Christianity with Roman Catholicism, and trial by jury with trial-by-ordeal. The descendants of these Norman usurpers, so their argument went, now constituted the gentry (Winstanley called Charles I himself a 'Norman oppresour').[47] And they continued their oppression of the Saxons in the person of the lower classes – so drastic voting and property reform could be justified on the grounds that it represented merely the restitution of ancient, lost rights.[48]

Winstanley's belief system – known as 'the Norman Yoke' – was revived in the late eighteenth and early nineteenth century by radicals such as Thomas Paine and Major John Cartwright who were calling for constitutional reform.[49] It was drawn upon again in the 1840s by Whigs campaigning for the abolition of the House of Lords, who argued that whereas the House of Commons was of 'honest' Saxon descent, the forbears of the Lords had been Norman usurpers who should now relinquish their ill-gotten privileges.[50] And as late as 1885 an article published in the *Contemporary Review* attempted to calculate the sum owed by the Norman aristocracy to the Saxon middle classes for the land they had wrongfully held since 1066 – including compound interest.[51]

The desire to define identities – not just class identities, but also national ones – was another crucial motivation for the nineteenth-century obsession with the medieval period. Victorian society was fanatical about taxonomising – organising into categories – and that interest extended to pinning themselves down as a nation. Who were the English? (or the British for that matter?) Where did they come from? Who were they related to? This curiosity manifested itself in attempts to identify the seeds of a distinct 'national character' in figures from early British history. So medieval figures like King Arthur and Edward I were celebrated as quintessentially English or British figures, while Alfred the Great was claimed to be the prototype of 'the qualities which we cherish in our national character'.[52] This interest in national character was particularly keen in the early years of the century, when the 1801 Act of Union with Ireland, which created the United Kingdom, was still a relatively recent event. And it also gained impetus from the desire to disassociate the British from the French, during the wars that followed the 1789 French Revolution.

Anxiety to distinguish the British from the French was one element which fed into the nineteenth-centu-ry revival of interest in the Anglo-Saxons, in particular. In the second half of the nineteenth century, it was not only political radicals who looked back with interest to the centuries before the Norman Conquest. In 1861, the linguistic researcher Max Müller gave a series of lectures at the Royal Institution in London, in which he demonstrated that the English language was essentially 'Teutonic' like modern German. His findings led to increased interest in the centuries before the Norman Conquest and it was soon being argued that England's culture and institutions were also Germanic and that there had been a racial continuity from the Anglo-Saxons to the English-speaking nations of the nineteenth century – upon which the Normans had had little effect.[53] As this belief spread, the Anglo-Saxons began to be thought of as 'the English', and the term 'Old English' (which we continue to use today) was coined to describe their language, while on the other hand in both Britain and America, English speakers began to refer to themselves as part of 'the Anglo-Saxon race'.[54]

THE MONARCHY AND THE MEDIEVAL

Another reason why the Anglo-Saxons, in particular, attracted interest in Victorian Britain was the presence on the throne of a monarch from a Germanic family. From the coronation of George I in 1714, royalist writers had tried to counter discontent about a foreign royal family by encouraging interest in the Anglo-Saxon rulers of history, and by promoting the notion that the Hanoverians were similarly 'Teutonic'.[55] In 1740, for instance, the anthem 'Rule, Britannia' was penned as part of a play about the Saxon King Alfred which was commissioned by Frederick, the son of George II (and father of George III). It was performed on 1 August, to commemorate the date on which Queen Anne had died, and the Hanoverians had first succeeded to the British throne.[56] This vein of propaganda continued through the eighteenth and early nineteenth centuries and intensified during Victoria's reign, when concerns about the queen's Germanic ancestry were compounded by anxieties about her gender.

Victoria's marriage in 1840 to a German – Albert – also led to fears that he might exercise undue, foreign influence over affairs of state.[57] One of the first concerted attempts to quell these rumblings of discontent was an appeal to the popularity of the Middle Ages. On 12 May 1842 Victoria held a costumed ball at Buckingham Palace. The theme was the fourteenth-century reign of Edward III, founder of the Order of the Garter and as such often viewed as the father of medieval chivalry.

Fig. 3 / Cat. 3

Queen Victoria and Prince Albert at the Bal Costumé of 12 May 1842
Sir Edwin Landseer

1842–46 / oil on canvas
Royal Collection Trust © Her Majesty Queen Elizabeth II 2014

Albert dressed for the occasion as Edward, his clothes modelled on those of a tomb effigy in Westminster Abbey. Victoria was Edward's queen Philippa of Hainault – famous for safeguarding the kingdom in his absence, and for obtaining mercy from her husband for the burghers of Calais. Her costume was based on the crowns, gowns and even shoes illustrated in medieval manuscripts and was carefully designed under the supervision of James Planche, an author on historical costume. All other members of the royal household were also required to dress in fourteenth-century costume; for the 2,000 guests, fancy dress was optional.[58]

The ball, then, went to considerable lengths to present Albert to the public as the epitome of English chivalric virtues, while Victoria was depicted as a queen renowned for strength and justice. The event was commemorated by the commissioning of a portrait of the royal couple in their remarkable costumes. Painted by Edwin Landseer, the work was careful to position Victoria centrally, with Albert to her right and a step lower (though none-the-less heroic and knightly-looking) suggesting that he was her strength and support but by no means her rival for power.[59] It was hung in the ballroom where the ball itself had taken place – a relatively public location where its symbolism could continue to reassure viewers about Albert's chivalric role and assert Victoria's links with the medieval past.[60]

Landseer's painting was not Queen Victoria's only use of art to position herself and her role in relation to the medieval period. In 1867, she commissioned another, rather different medievalist image of herself and Albert. William Theed's statue *The Parting* presents the royal couple as a ninth-century queen and warrior king, bidding farewell to each other on the seashore. It is different from the Landseer painting in several important respects. Firstly, it was created six years after Albert's death in 1861, and consequently all suspicions about the Prince Consort's influence over the queen were by then redundant. This emerges in the composition of the pair – Victoria looks up to Albert and leans on him; he gazes ahead. It was also created at a time when Victoria was one of the few monarchs left in Europe, and was gradually becoming less interventionist in British politics – instead evolving into a symbolic figurehead, the 'mother of the nation' – which is again reflected by the emphasis on her domestic role rath-

er than her position as monarch.[61] Finally, by the time of the Theed statue, Victoria had become almost exclusively associated not with the Middle Ages of Edward III, but with the earlier, pre-Norman centuries of Britain's past. The long-standing general association of the Hanoverians with the Saxons had developed into the more specific claim that Victoria represented the rightful return of the usurped Anglo-Saxon line to the English throne – that she symbolized the reversal of the Conquest.[62] By the time of the queen's Golden and Diamond jubilees in 1887 and 1897, it was being widely claimed that she was the direct descendant of King Alfred, that she had 'in her veins the blood of Cerdic of Wessex', and that she was 'the most perfect representative of Teutonic royalty'.[63]

The jubilee celebrations themselves were also influenced by the popular taste for the medieval. For the first three quarters of the nineteenth century, commentators noted that Britain had 'few if any public pageants' and 'no real taste for ceremonial'.[64] The coronations of Victoria and of William IV and George IV before her were unimpressive occasions – unrehearsed, often bungled, and with little sense of stateliness.[65] From the 1870s, though, splendid rituals became central to the image of the British monarchy as the institution developed into an emblem of continuity, stability and community in the face of accelerated social change.[66] Much of that pageantry drew on popular images of the medieval period. At the Golden Jubilee, the Queen wore the Order of the Garter, the clergy and choir dressed in rich vestments, and London's streets were awash with red and gold.[67] Around the country, bonfires were lit and whole oxen were roasted in the streets – particularly in manufacturing towns and cities such as Birmingham, Burnley and Northampton, where the celebrations were an assertion of links back to a pre-industrial golden age.[68] And as part of the Diamond Jubilee celebrations, ten years later, while Victoria took part in a long progress through the city of London, in Coventry the first Lady Godiva pageant to be staged for many years took place, directly associating Victoria with that eleventh-century legendary defender of the people who had ridden naked through the city's streets to relieve its people from onerous taxes.[69]

The medieval-inspired rituals that added such drama to Victoria's jubilees were drawn on even more liberally for the coronation of her son Edward VII (commentators

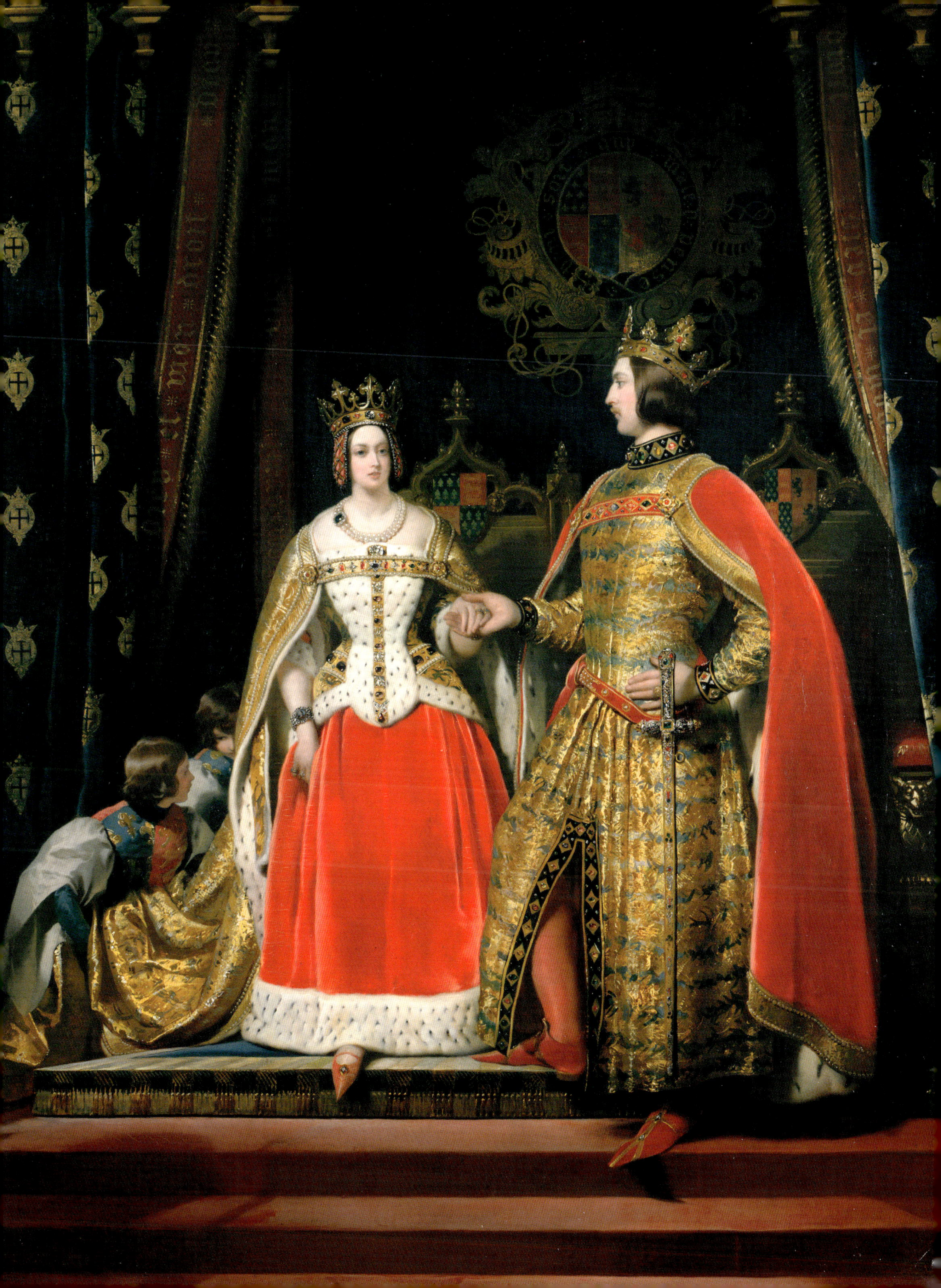

described the event as combining 'the archaic traditions of the Middle Ages' with 'modern splendour') and they continue to colour royal ceremonies today.[70] Edward himself was also, like his mother, associated with the Saxons. And in 1863, when he married the Danish Princess Alexandra, the British public was reminded that as well as having Saxon heritage, the country also had a 'Viking' history. The poet laureate Alfred, Lord Tennyson proclaimed at the coronation: 'Saxon and Norman and Dane are we,/ But all of us Danes in our welcome of thee'.[71] And in a later play dedicated to her (in which King Alfred's son marries the daughter of the Viking king Guthrum) Alexandra was celebrated as the 'daughter of vanished Vikings and mother of English kings to be'.[72]

SIR WALTER SCOTT AND MEDIEVALIST LITERATURE

The celebration of early-medieval Scandinavian sea-adventurers was another aspect of the nineteenth-century fascination with the medieval. Old Norse poetry had been first popularised in Britain in the late eighteenth century through the translations of the ballad-collector and antiquarian Thomas Percy. In his 1763 *Five Pieces of Runic Poetry* and his 1770 *Northern Antiquities*, Percy had introduced the British public for the first time to runic letters, the otherworld Valhalla, the god Odin, and heroes who died laughing. He had also launched the enduring stereotype of the bloodthirsty Norse warrior, drinking from the skulls of his enemies – the result of an unfortunate mistranslation of 'drinking horn'.[73] The early medieval world of the Old North was further popularised in the late eighteenth century through Thomas Gray's two short poems 'The Fatal Sisters' (about the Valkyries who choose the slain in Old Norse mythology) and 'The Descent of Odin'. Both were re-writings (rather than straight translations) of Old Norse works, and with their eerie 'Gothic' atmosphere proved hugely appealing to the general public.

The actual word 'Viking', however, was not used in England until 1807 (just ten years before 'medieval' was coined), and it was not until 1822 that English authors began to turn to the world of the Vikings as a subject for original literature.[74] That year saw the publication of Sir Walter Scott's novel *The Pirate*, set in the Shetland Isles – the first new English literary work to draw on Viking lore and legend. In the following decades, this work helped to encourage the publication of several English translations of Norse sagas, and by the end of the nineteenth century it had also inspired literally dozens of British novels

featuring horn-helmeted Viking heroes bellowing from their longships.[75] The fascination was to endure through the Viking films, festivals, merchandise, and comics of the twentieth century: from the 1928 Technicolor talkie *The Viking*, to Terry Jones's 1989 fantasy film *Erik the Viking* and the horned drinking helmets sold by lager-company Carlsberg in the same decade, to the 2008 X-box game *Viking: Battle for Asgard*.

The medievalist novels and poetry of Sir Walter Scott have often been credited with having initiated not just Britain's love-affair with horn-helmeted raiders, but also the entire medieval revival that occurred in nineteenth-century literature. The great medievalising church reformer Cardinal Newman, for instance, claimed in his 1864 autobiography, *Apologia Pro Vita Sua*, that it had been Scott who had first 'turned men's minds in the direction of the middle ages'.[76] This is not entirely true. To some extent, 'medievalism' in literature – the imitation or celebration of medieval culture and society – began even as the medieval period itself was drawing to a close.[77] Geoffrey Chaucer's *Canterbury Tales* was studied and edited as an historical curiosity before the end of the fifteenth century.[78] Edmund Spenser's *Faerie Queene*, written between 1590 and 1596, was composed using words and phrases of Middle English that were deliberately designed to bring to mind older romances (later readers such as Walter Scott accepted these elements of the Renaissance text as genuinely 'medieval', rather than as self-conscious medievalism).[79] Shakespeare famously wrote plays about the fifteenth-century Wars of the Roses just over a century after their conclusion, to legitimate the rule of the Tudors. And in the wake of the English Reformation, Anglican theologians and scholars like the sixteenth-century Archbishop of Canterbury Matthew Parker not only collected and printed Anglo-Saxon histories and saints lives, but also 'improved' them as part of a campaign to demonstrate that there had long been a native English church that had worked independently from Rome.[80]

Taking Parker's work of 'enlargement' a step further, several eighteenth-century authors forged texts that purported to be genuinely medieval works. James Macpherson's collections of poetry published in the 1760s may have been loosely based on some old sources, but claimed to be the translated works of a third-century Scots bard, Ossian.[81] In the same decade, Thomas Chatterton produced pseudo-medieval poetry, which he claimed was written by an imaginary fifteenth-century monk, Thomas Rowley.[82] And in 1764, Horace Walpole's novel *The Castle of Otranto* was published, claiming to be the translation of a tale written sometime 'between 1095, the era of the First

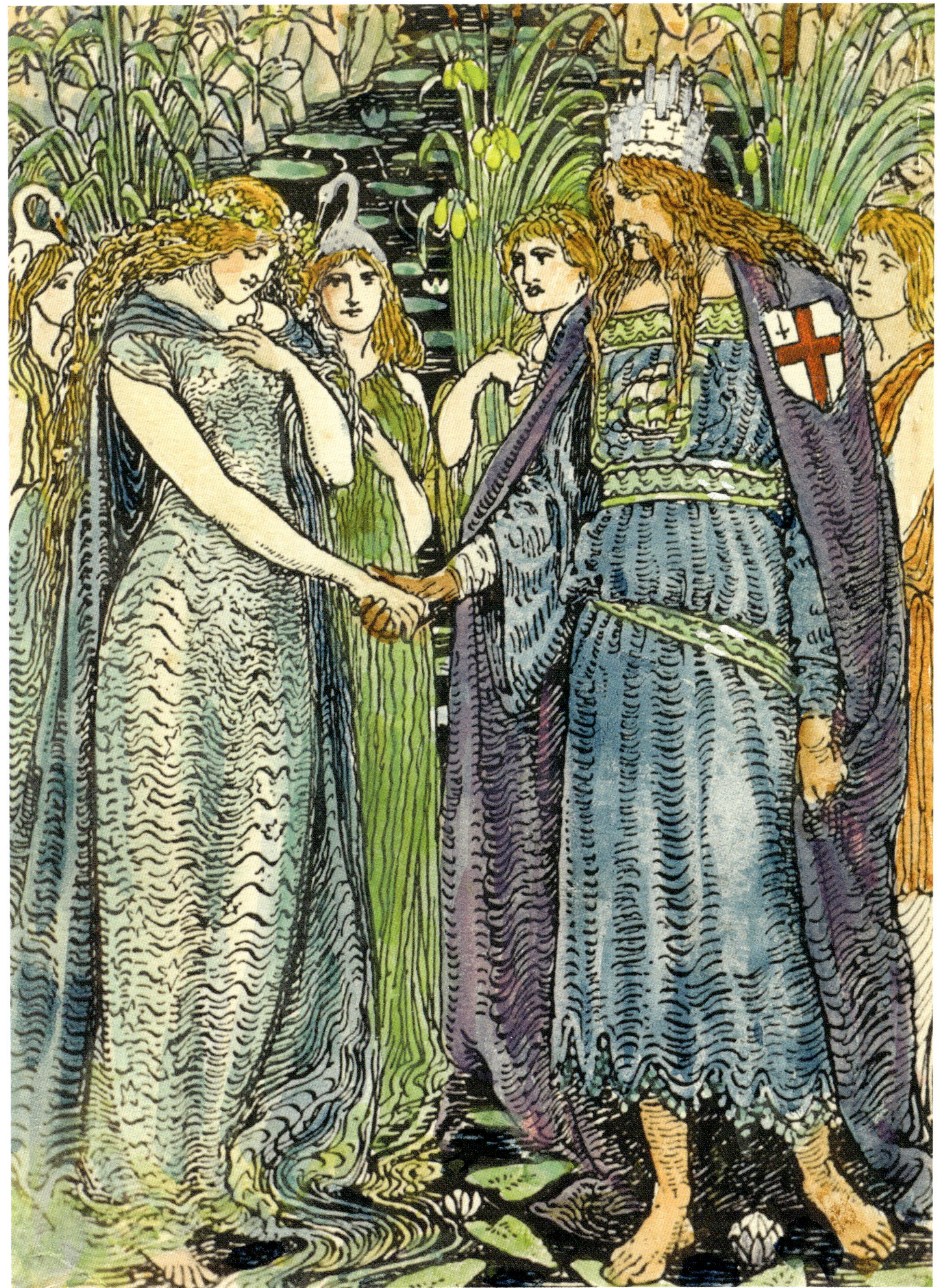

Fig. 4 / Cat. 44

Illustration from 'Faerie Queene'

Walter Crane

1897 / line prints, hand-coloured by the artist / from Edmund Spenser's *Faerie Queene*
© Royal Albert Memorial Museum & Art Gallery, Exeter City Council

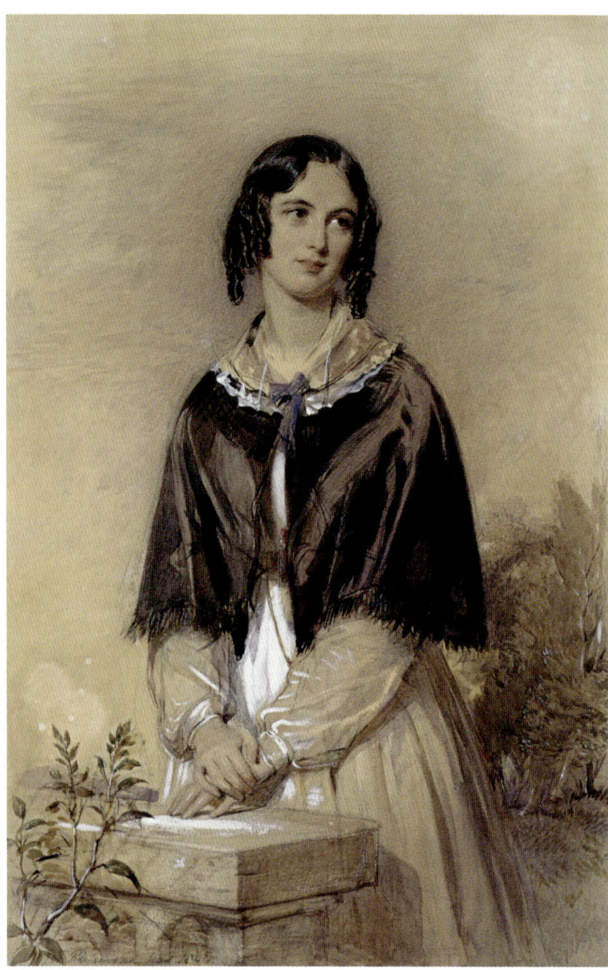

Fig. 5
Charlotte Mary Yonge
George Richmond

1844 / watercolour and chalk
© National Portrait Gallery, London

Crusade, and 1243, the date of the last'.[83] The popularity of the text induced Walpole to later confess to having composed it himself – as an attempt to blend two kinds of romance, the ancient and the modern.[84] And its popularity also spawned a shower of imitations – now collectively classified as 'Gothic novels'. While Gothic novels sometimes used explicitly medieval settings, however, they more often simply featured monks, abbeys, castles and feudal lords reminiscent of the medieval period as a way of creating 'atmosphere' while being set at periods closer to the present. And although a few more carefully historicised medieval novels (such as those of Anne Fuller) were published before 1800, it was not until after the hugely successful 1819 publication of *Ivanhoe*, the first of Scott's eight medieval novels, that medievalist works of literature really became a widespread literary phenomenon.[85]

Scott's impact was partly due to timing – his medieval novels appeared within decades of the shock of the French Revolution. Prior to that, it had widely been held that history revealed the gradual improvement of humanity, but the violence and turmoil of events in 1789 cast doubt on this self-confidence, increasing the appeal of the medieval past.[86] Scott was also so influential because while his novels mixed together fact and fantasy about the medieval period, many of his first readers read them as straight histories.[87] His works influenced the direction of later nineteenth-century medievalist literature (and indeed the Victorian medieval revival more generally) in several important ways. The notion of the Middle Ages as a time of plenty, contrasting with the starvation of the present, may be traced back to his work. Great, lavish feasts occur in almost all of his medieval novels.[88] And his depiction of nobles hosting regular festivities and feasting should also be seen as among the earliest nineteenth-century recognitions of the importance of ceremony to the maintenance of power – a realisation that would eventually lead to the revival of royal ritual at Victoria's jubilees.[89]

Although they were communal, social rank is always strictly observed at Scott's feasts, with nobles at the head of the table, and this is linked to another of the writer's influences – on the idealisation of medieval feudalism. For Scott, the feudal system represented an ideal state of interdependence and mutual loyalty in which different ranks had lived in close harmony.[90] He looked back wistfully to days when 'knight, and page, and household squire [...] crowded round the ample fire'.[91] Although his novels may present tensions between master and serf, or Saxon and Norman, they always work towards the restoration of harmony, as old feudal ties pull characters back together in times of crisis – Scott's Saxon serf Gurth may leave when his master is unjust, but he returns to his rescue as soon as Cedric is in danger.[92] There was a conservative political message in this idealisation. Scott's son-in-law and biographer John Gibson Lockhart wrote that Sir Walter Scott's 'services, direct and indirect, towards repressing the revolutionary propensities of his age were vast'.[93] His rose-tinted view of feudal relations certainly fed directly into the later neo-feudalism of Thomas Carlyle, the architect Augustus Pugin, and the practical politics of Benjamin Disraeli and the Young England movement. (Indeed, Carlyle explicitly echoed Scott in his celebration of the contentment of the medieval serf in *Past and Present*, deliberately using the names 'Gurth' and 'Cedric' from *Ivanhoe*.)

Scott's praise for medieval chivalric ideals was also influential. As recent commentators have noted, for the medieval knight, chivalric protectiveness was 'accorded usually to women, always of the upper class'; serfs and villeins were 'ignored or despised'.[94] In Scott's refiguring of chivalry, though, it meant protection to the weak more broadly, including the poor and the labouring classes. Indeed, he defined chivalry for the *Encyclopaedia Britannica* as 'the use of individual freedom [...] to defend the social order'.[95] It was this version of chivalry that Victorian gentlemen began to aspire to. It saw its most common expression in the dramatic late-Victorian growth in freemasonry, and in the founding of other chivalric fellowships and brotherhoods with social agendas.[96] But its most dramatic manifestation was the lavish 1839 Eglinton Tournament, a medieval re-enactment held at Eglinton Castle in Ayrshire in which 40 modern 'knights' tilted in front of a crowd estimated at around 100,000.[97]

It was also in Scott's novels that medieval craftsmanship was first praised as superior to the products of the industrialised modern world. His 1828 novel *The Fair Maid of Perth* stresses the pride that medieval artisans took in their work – an emphasis that would later be central to the idealisation of the medieval period seen in the writings of John Ruskin and the designer and author William Morris.[98] In the mass of medieval novels published after Scott, likewise, the quality of hand-made goods in the Middle Ages was typically emphasized. In Charlotte Yonge's 1865 children's novel *The Prince and the Page*, for instance, characters wear 'homespun' clothing and possess jewellery and weapons of 'exquisite workmanship'.[99]

Charlotte Yonge is perhaps the Victorian novelist in whose work the influence of Scott can be seen most clearly. Like him she wrote 'apocryphal histories' – stories like Scott's Robin Hood tale *Ivanhoe* that were based on legends, or written between the lines of historical records. In

The Prince and the Page, for instance, she retold and elaborated the legend that the thirteenth-century rebel lord Henry de Montfort had lived on after the Battle of Evesham as the Blind Beggar of Bethnal Green. Again like Scott, feasting is a common trope of Yonge's medievalist novels. And like him she was a keen believer in feudalism and in chivalric ideals – as a member of the Oxford Movement (the nineteenth-century Anglican campaign to revive the spirit, ritual, and political power of the medieval English church) she believed that the clergy and aristocracy should take responsibility for the welfare of the lower orders of society.[100]

Like Scott, Yonge did not only write about the medieval period. Just as some of Scott's Waverley novels were set in the sixteenth, the seventeenth and the eighteenth centuries, so she also wrote Tudor novels, works based on eighteenth-century history, and contemporary stories. What is interesting, however, is the way in which the medievalism of both writers bled into their other works. Scott's novels set in the seventeenth and eighteenth centuries so convincingly transferred medieval social practices to that period that he convinced most early readers that feudalism had survived in the Scottish Highlands until the 1745 rebellion as 'a time-capsule, a semi-feudal enclave surviving within modern Europe'.[101] Similarly, although Yonge's 1853 novel *The Heir of Redclyffe* has a contemporary setting, it is saturated with medievalism. Not only does its hero live in a Gothic building, he also realises that he should live like a feudal lord, taking responsibility for the tenants of his estate. And inspired by reading the story of a tenth-century hero's spiritual quest, he too learns to act chivalrously – finally dying as a result of selflessly nursing his diseased rival.[102] The book, which is virtually forgotten today, was one of the most popular novels of the nineteenth century. By 1878 it was in its 23rd edition. It was read seven times by the daughter of the Prime Minister Herbert Asquith (making her cry every time). And it was influential on works of explicit medievalism. Among its admirers were the poet Alfred Lord Tennyson, William Morris, and the Pre-Raphaelite artists Edward Burne-Jones and Dante Gabriel Rossetti who adopted its hero as one of their ideals.[103]

While Yonge's medievalism followed very much in the armour-clad footsteps of Scott's, however, as a whole the nineteenth-century medieval revival in literature was varied and diverse. It produced works in all genres – not just novels but also poetry, plays, children's stories, and even ballets and pantomimes.[104] In some cases, works were influenced by medieval literary texts and traditions, echoing their forms and styles. John Ruskin's long-serving assistant, the author, artist and antiquary W.G.

Fig. 6 / Cat. 5
Edward III Conferring the Order of the Garter on Edward the Black Prince
Charles West Cope

c.1847 / oil on canvas
© Sheffield Galleries and Museums Trust, UK / Photo © Museums Sheffield / Bridgeman Images

Collingwood, spent the 1890s writing 'Norse sagas' set in the Lake District. The poet Algernon Charles Swinburne imitated the *aubades* (morning love songs) and *rondels* (repeating songs) of fourteenth-century Troubadour poets.[105] And Alfred Tennyson drew on the alliterative style of Old English poetry (most notably in his poetic translation of the tenth-century poem 'The Battle of Brunanburh') and also the later medieval dream-vision form (in his 'Dream of Fair Women' – a poem based on Chaucer's late-fourteenth-century *Legend of Good Women*).[106]

The most prolific imitator of medieval literary forms, however, was William Morris. Morris's most ambitious medievalist output was his 1868 narrative poem *The Earthly Paradise* (one of the longest poetic works in the English language) which echoes the form of Chaucer's *Canterbury Tales* with a group of travelling Norsemen (fleeing the Black Death) who exchange stories with the inhabitants of a Greek island. After the publication of this gargantuan work, however, he also produced the verse masque, *Love is Enough* (based on a story in the medieval Welsh collection of stories, the *Mabinogion*) which was modelled on medieval morality plays and imitated Middle English alliteration. And besides this he wrote Arthurian poetry, created translations of Old Norse sagas, and composed prose romances modelled on late-medieval tales of heroic quests – his most famous being *The Well at the World's End*, and *The Wood Beyond the World*, both of which were influential upon the later work of C.S. Lewis and J.R.R. Tolkien.

Only a minority of medievalist authors had Morris's genius for recreating centuries-old literary forms. Far more nineteenth-century medievalism took the form of modern literature which was simply based on events or figures from the medieval past. Certain characters and periods attracted particular attention. Edward the Black Prince, the thirteenth-century hero of the great English victories over the French at Crécy and Poitiers was a popular subject for novelists (and artists) – especially at times of conflict with France.[107] The Norman Conquest of 1066 was frequently drawn on as a source for novels and plays – particularly when fears of imminent French invasion were circulating, when it could be used as a means of investigating those.[108] And King Alfred's temporary defeat by invading Danes in the ninth century (not to mention his legendary burning of the cakes) was phenomenally popular as a subject for novelists, poets, and playwrights, as well as sculptors and painters.[109] In all, over a hundred works about that particular Saxon monarch were produced between 1800 and 1901 – the year in which this enthusiasm culminated in a national anniversary to mark what was believed (wrongly) to be the thousandth anniversary of his death.

ARCHITECTURE AND MEDIEVALIST LITERATURE IN THE SOUTH WEST

Nineteenth-century medievalist literature was also often inspired by architecture – both by the remains of medieval edifices and by newly-built neo-Gothic buildings. Close relationships between literary and architectural expressions of medievalism began in the eighteenth century. Horace Walpole wrote his 1764 *Castle of Otranto* whilst living in what he called his 'little Gothic castle' – a Thameside Georgian villa which he spent almost 30 years adorning with pinnacles, battlements and a round tower to turn it into into a monastic Gothic mansion. Walter Scott's novels paid for and were later inspired by Abbotsford – the turreted manor house he had built on the banks of the Tweed in 1824, partly constructed using materials salvaged from medieval ruins. And later in the nineteenth century, Charlotte Yonge's medievalism was inspired by visits to Tyntesfield, the splendid neo-Gothic, north Somerset home of her cousin Blanche Gibbs.[110] The Tyntesfield that Yonge visited, with its spires, pinnacles, and vaulted ceilings, had been created from a simple Regency house in 1843 for Blanche's husband, the guano-importer and enthusiast for Gothic architecture William Gibbs.[111] After one of her regular stays there, Yonge wrote to her sister to enthuse how: 'That beautiful house was like a church in spirit. I used to think so when going up and down the great stairs'.[112] With this heightened atmosphere, and with its impressive library and position close to the Bristol Channel, Tyntesfield is likely to have been the model for Redclyffe, the ancestral estate inherited by the chivalrous hero of Yonge's *Heir of Redclyffe*.

Yonge was also inspired by visits to genuinely medieval buildings – particularly cathedrals and abbeys, of which she visited many, including Winchester, Lichfield, Westminster, Salisbury, Exeter and Glastonbury Abbey.[113]

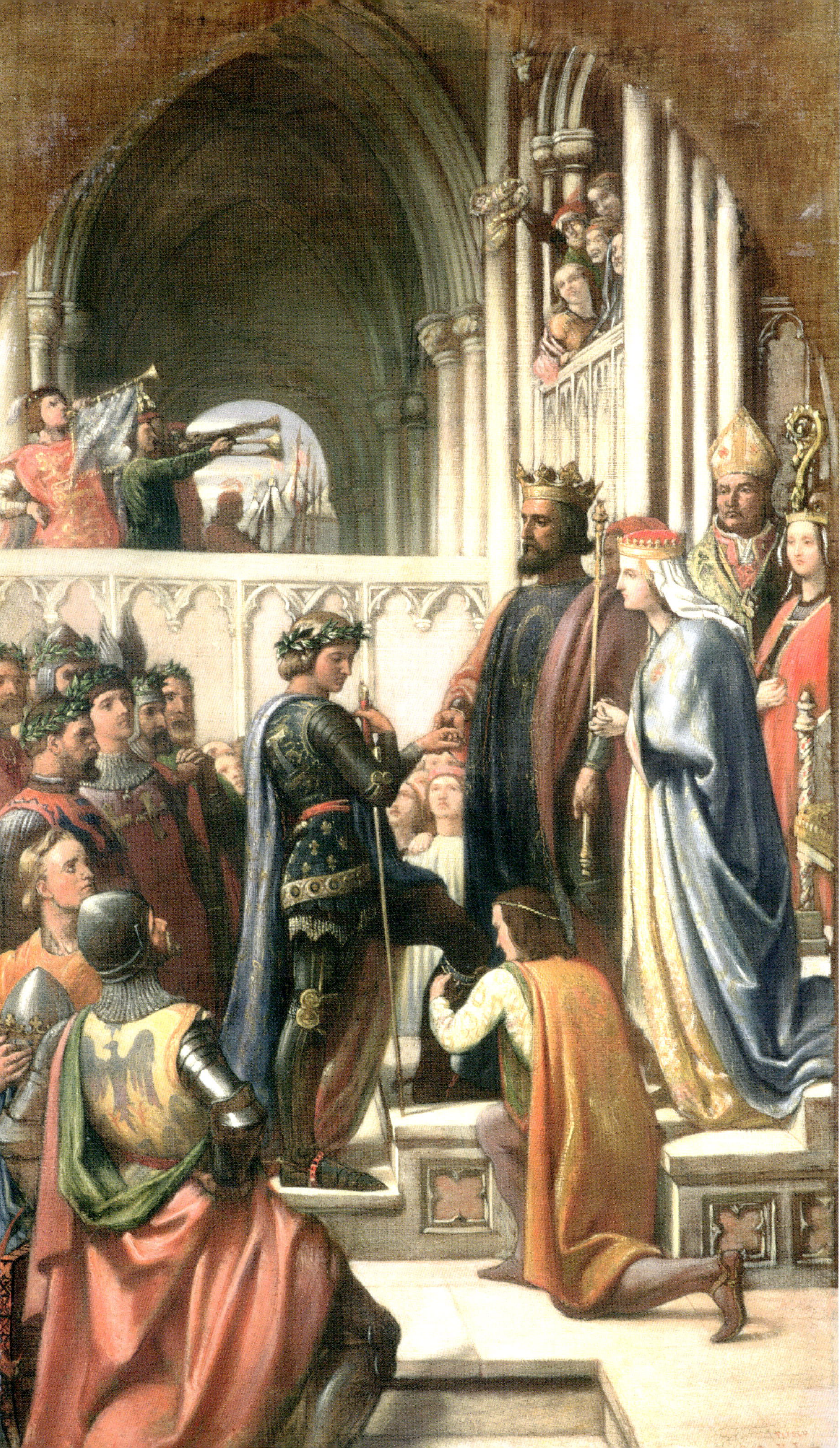

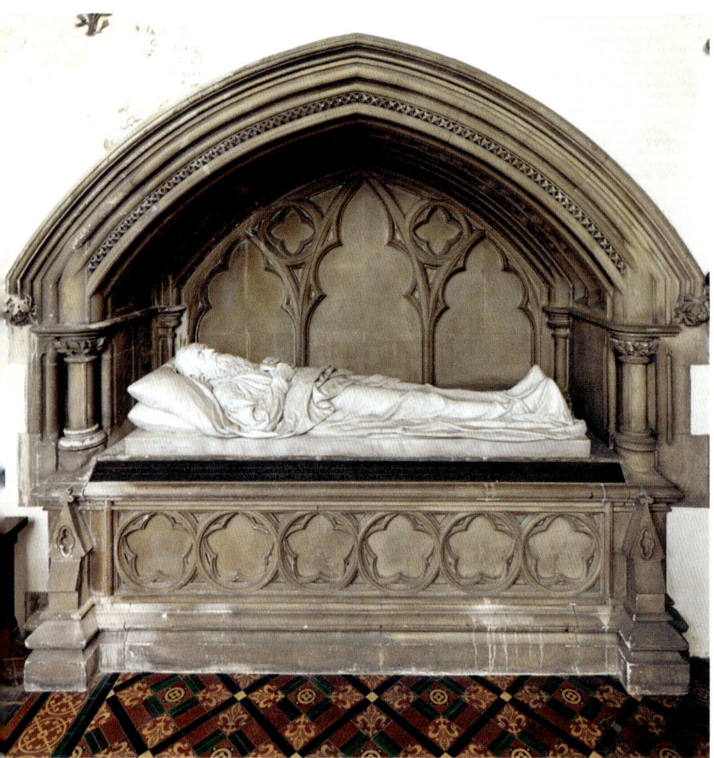

Fig. 7
William Gibbs memorial
H.H. Armstead (sculptor)
1882 / marble / in St Michael and All Angels, Exeter
© Royal Albert Memorial Museum & Art Gallery, Exeter City Council

Such visits often fed directly into her work. In 1845, she composed 'Lines on a monument at Lichfield', a short poem which later became the epigraph to the novel *The Daisy Chain*. And the Crusader novel *The Prince and the Page* contains a vivid passage in which the author imagines how Westminster Abbey must have looked when new-built.[114] Yonge was enthusiastic about the restoration of such buildings – on hearing of a plan to repair Carlisle Cathedral she wrote to friends 'I hope there is some truth in it, for I was much dismayed at its naveless condition when I saw it'.[115] This attitude is at one with her adamant belief that medieval ideals could once again act as patterns for living in the modern day. For some nineteenth-century authors, however, medieval buildings served rather as a reminder of an ideal past that was now beyond reach.

Thomas Hardy's novel *The Bluest Eye* was inspired by the author's visit to Cornwall in 1870 to oversee the restoration of the fourteenth-century church of St Juliot near Boscastle. It features the medievally named heroine Elfrida Swanpool, the descendant of a once noble family, whom Hardy restores through marriage to her lost social position in a move that would surely have appealed to Sir Walter Scott and the members of Young England. However, while the novel is awash with nostalgic references to old families and dying traditions, in contrast to Yonge it is also deeply sceptical of any attempt to return to the Middle Ages. Its preface explains that it was written 'at a time when the craze for indiscriminate church-restoration had just reached the remotest nooks of western England' – a situation which it bewails, protesting that 'to restore the grey carcases of a mediaevalism whose spirit had fled, seemed a not less incongruous act than to set about renovating the adjoining crags themselves'.[116] Indeed, in the story itself when a young architect arrives in Cornwall to restore the local medieval church this ultimately leads to tragedy. And the book also features a 'Mr Knight' who proves far from chivalrous, and a heroine who is mocked for attempting to write 'a Romance of the Middle Ages' – a period about which she knows nothing.

Both Hardy and Yonge's interest in the South West's architecture was that of visitors to the area. For nineteenth-century authors who lived in the region, however, writing about medieval edifices could be a way of expressing regional pride and asserting the importance of the area's heritage. This was undoubtedly the case for the Dartmoor author Eliza Bray whose historical novel *Henry de Pomeroy: Or, The Eve of St John* was published in 1841. The book is set in the twelfth century, at Pomeroy Castle near Totnes – a building actually not built until the late fifteenth century, but which was believed in Bray's day to be of Norman origin.[117] It also incorporates chapters about 'the monks of Tavistock Abbey, in the days of their power and pride'.[118] This element of the text was included, she said, in response to a request by a friend 'of considerable literary taste', while she wrote the novel as a whole after being repeatedly urged to do so 'by more than one literary friend, natives of the west'.[119] These claims may well have been genuine – Bray was a frequent correspondent with the poet laureate Robert Southey and was a cousin of the Pre-Raphaelite poet Christina Rossetti, so was well connected in literary circles. Certainly the novel seems to have had the clear aim of putting Dartmoor on the medievalist's map in the same way as Sherwood Forest and Scott's Highlands and so must have delighted any medieval enthusiasts with ties to the area.

The work shows considerable influence from Scott. It is set, like *Ivanhoe*, during the absence of King Richard on crusade. It draws on legend – not Robin Hood stories, but melodramatic tales about Henry de Pomeroy's suicidal horseback leap from his castle walls, and his death by blood-letting at St Michael's Mount in Cornwall. It stresses the quality of medieval craftsmanship and the plentifulnesss of food. And as Scott famously did in *Ivanhoe*, it imagines that the aftermath of the Norman Conquest continued to rumble on into the late twelfth century. Bray's Devonshire Saxons are still 'smarting under the yoke' by the time of her tale, while her Norman Abbot of Tavistock shares 'to the fullest extent in the pride and spirit of oppression' of the Norman conquerors of 1066.[120]

Forgetting the fact that Berry Pomeroy Castle wasn't even a twinkle in its builder's eye in the 1190s, Bray's novel goes to great lengths to achieve historical accuracy. Her abbot wears a 'scapular' (an upper garment worn beneath his tunic) and a 'girdle'. Her heroine dresses in a 'kirtle' (gown), and 'volupure' (veil).[121] And her Saxon swineherd is named Caedmon after a famous seventh-century one from Whitby Abbey. The text contrasts markedly with an earlier novel about the same building – Edward Montague's 1806 book *The Castle of Berry Pomeroy*, a melodramatic tale of attempted fratricide, rash murders, ghostly apparitions, and pirates. The pairing of this book with Bray's Berry Pomeroy novel neatly epitomises the way in which Victorian medievalism developed out of the traditions of the Gothic – adding additional layers of sociological and linguistic historical detail, and gradually moving away from the association of the Middle Ages with the sinister and cruel.

As part of her research for the novel, Bray visited Berry Pomeroy Castle. The building had started to receive visits from curious sightseers in the late eighteenth century, when nearby Torquay had first been developed into a holiday resort. This was at a time when the develop-

ment of Romanticism, in the literature of writers like William Wordsworth and in the art of painters like J.M.W. Turner had made visits to 'picturesque' ruins a vogue. Edward Montague's novel no doubt helped encourage this fashion in the case of Berry Pomeroy. It promised gullible readers that the stones of the castle were somehow 'yet blood-stained', that 'flitting shades [ghosts] nightly hover over their sad remains', and that 'often do [...] wailing shrieks vex the nocturnal breeze'.[122] Turner's atmospheric painting of Berry Pomeroy, exhibited in 1812 as part of a series on castles in the South West, also doubtless contributed to sightseeing at the site. When Bray visited Berry Pomeroy in 1838, however, the ruins were still far from developed as a tourist destination. She collected the key from 'a little girl who lived nearby', but had trouble finding the entrance because it was 'so overgrown with ivy, that, on a first approach, it is no easy matter to make out what it is'. Bray concluded that the castle 'would be a most interesting ruin, if it were not so encumbered with brambles and trees, as in many places you can see nothing else'.[123]

Tourism to Berry Pomeroy Castle did gradually become a little more organised. Some time after Eliza Bray's visit, the offices of the local newspaper – the *Totnes Times and Western Guardian* – published a short pamphlet to guide the increasing numbers of visitors around it.[124] Tourism to medieval castles and abbeys increased dramatically from the 1840s onwards, as the spread of the railways across Britain made travel quicker and cheaper, allowing the middle classes to visit such remains.[125] This sightseeing was another important facet of the Victorian medieval revival, and several sites in the South West attracted interest as part of it – among them the cathedrals at Exeter, Salisbury and Wells. The most popular sites in the south west of England for Victorian tourists seeking to commune with the medieval, however, were almost certainly Tintagel Castle and Glastonbury Abbey – buildings said to be, respectively, the birthplace and burial site of the legendary King Arthur.

THE VICTORIAN REDISCOVERY OF KING ARTHUR

If Arthur ever existed, it was probably not as a king but as a sixth-century 'dux bellorum' – a battle commander leading troops against invading Anglo-Saxons.[126] This is how he appears in the earliest references to him – which were written more than two centuries after he is supposed to have lived, and are frustratingly scant.[127] When nineteenth-century visitors made their way to Tintagel

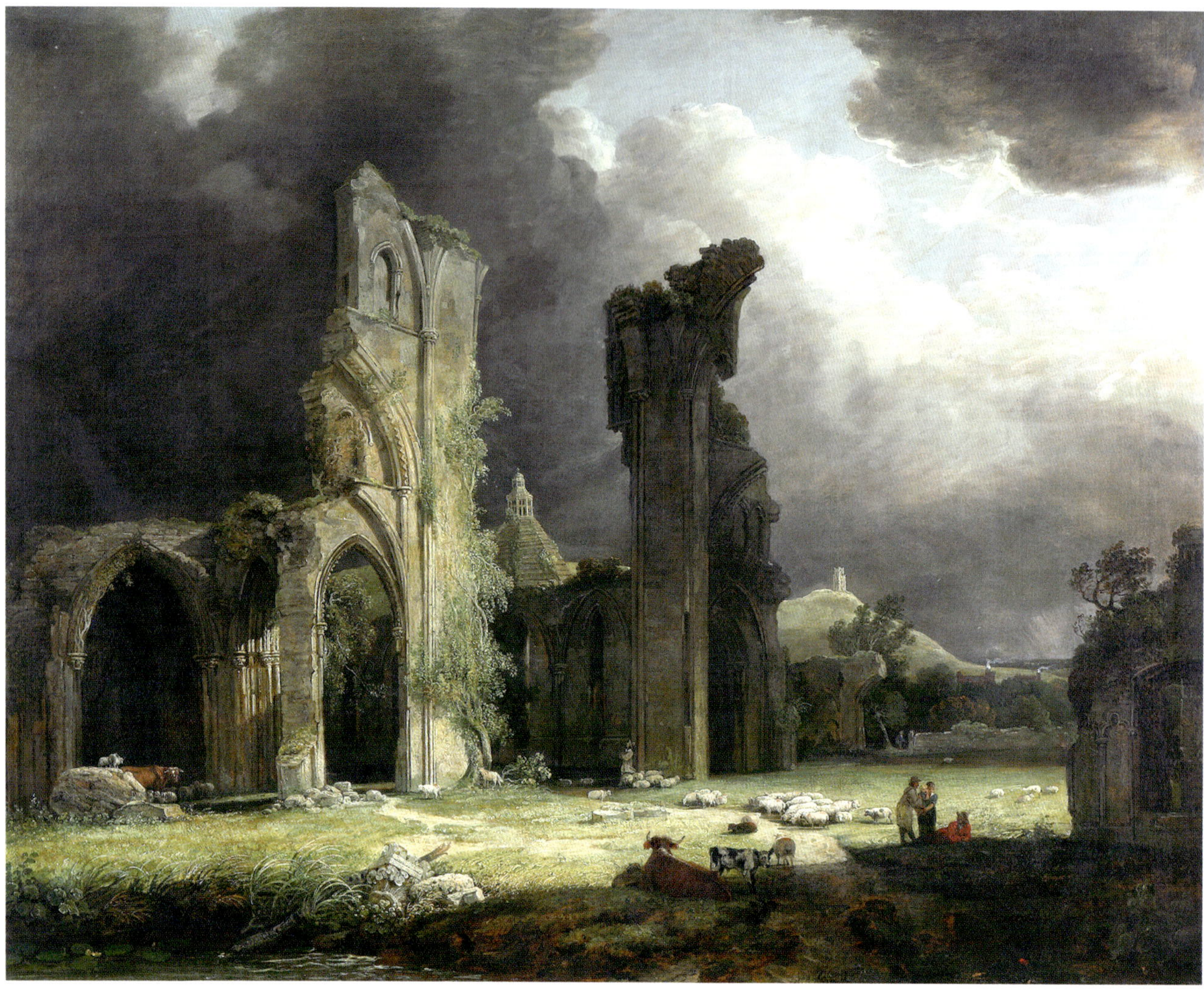

Fig. 8 / Cat. 1
The Ruins of Glastonbury Abbey
George Arnald

c.1810 / oil on canvas
© The Museum of Somerset

and Glastonbury, however, the Arthur whose birthplace they were seeking was not the British soldier mentioned in these early historical records but rather the grand, legendary king who first appeared as a fully-formed hero in the climactic chapters of the twelfth-century *History of the Kings of Britain* written by the Welsh cleric and scholar Geoffrey of Monmouth. This was a work that combined historical elements with romance, propaganda, and myth, and was condemned even at the time for being more fiction than fact.[128]

Geoffrey of Monmouth introduced many of the key elements of King Arthur's story with which we are familiar today – his birth at Tintagel, the wizard Merlin, his marriage to Guanhamara (the fore-runner of Guinevere) and a magical sword called Caliburn (that was to evolve into Excalibur).[129] The legendary Arthur's story was embellished by later medieval writers – not just in England but across Europe. It was particularly prevalent in France, where the most popular versions of the tale were the twelfth-century verse romances written by Chrétien de

Troyes – which were the first Arthurian texts to name Camelot as the site of Arthur's court. These poems provided one of the sources for a 21-book English version of the Arthurian story, *Le Morte d'Arthur* [*Death of Arthur*] by Sir Thomas Malory, which drew together many earlier, individual tales into a long narrative that begins with the founding of Arthur's kingdom and the institution of the Round Table, covers the various adventures of individual knights and their quest for the Holy Grail, and ends with the death of King Arthur and the fall of his kingdom.

Malory's account was written in 1469, during England's Wars of the Roses (and when the author himself was a prisoner) – a time when political upheaval meant that there was a strong revival of interest in older chivalric values and in Britain's past.[130] It was this book which was largely to prove the catalyst for the rediscovery of Arthur four hundred years later, when the English once again looked back to history in the midst of social change. Between the publication of Malory's text and the late eighteenth century, however, there was very little interest in King Arthur. The poets John Milton and John Dryden both considered writing an Arthurian epic – but rejected the idea.[131] And *Le Morte d'Arthur* itself was out of print for almost two hundred years – 'virtuallly unknown and more or less unattainable'.[132]

From the late eighteenth century, though, King Arthur began to find his way back into print. Among the first places that he appeared were Thomas Percy's and Thomas Warton's respective studies of early English literature – Percy's 1765 *Reliques of Ancient English Poetry*, for instance, contained six Arthurian ballads. Read in this new context, Arthurian works began to be viewed not as bad history, but rather as fascinating historical artefacts. Following Arthur's revaluation by antiquaries, new Arthurian literature began to appear once again. Some of the earliest examples were written in the south west of England, where Arthurian place-names had been a constant reminder of Arthur even during his years of literary neglect, and where writers were able to 'claim' the king as part of their home region's heritage.[133] In 1789, the East Devon clergyman Richard Hole completed his long poem *Arthur, or the Northern Enchantment* – an account of the medieval king that deviates quite dramatically from all medieval versions of the story (in it a set of weird sisters from the North try to bring about Arthur's downfall through a series of tricks, deceits, and shipwrecks – but the story ends happily, with Arthur marrying Merlin's daughter Imogen).[134] Similarly, in 1819, the Dartmouth-born poet and editor of the *Royal Cornwall Gazette*, George Woodley, produced an epic poem *Cornu-*

bia [*Cornwall*] containing a long and bizarre section on Arthur in which the king's son Mordred is presented as the true hero, while Arthur himself is a weak and unscrupulous figure who is deservingly trounced at the Battle of Camlan.[135]

Odd works like *Cornubia* continued to appear while Malory's *Le Morte d'Arthur* was still generally unknown. In 1816, though, the first cheaply available, modernised edition of the text was published – followed by at least nine other editions before 1900.[136] This established the broad shape of the Arthurian legend for subsequent re-writers – and opened the doors to a new era of interest in the king. By the 1830s, the legends of King Arthur were widely known in Britain, and a flood of new Arthurian literature began to appear.[137] Literally scores of Arthurian texts appeared between 1830 and 1900. They included long works such as Edward Bulwer-Lytton's 12-book epic poem *King Arthur* (1848) and Joseph Shorthouse's 1886 novel *Sir Percival*, as well as many shorter poems like Andrew Lang's poem 'Sir Launcelot', published in 1863. Children's stories on the subject of Arthur also appeared, as did Arthurian dramas. One of the most remarkable of these was Joseph Comyns Carr's 1895 play *King Arthur*, which was produced by Henry Irving, and had music composed by Arthur Sullivan and sets and costumes designed by the artist Edward Burne-Jones. Phenomenally popular, it ran for more than 100 performances and also toured North America.[138]

Comyns Carr's *King Arthur* was based on Malory's *Morte d'Arthur*, but also on a more recent Arthurian work – Alfred, Lord Tennyson's *Idylls of the King*. The publication of this vast cycle of 12 poems – which was written over the course of 55 years – was in itself an important catalyst to the Victorian interest in King Arthur. (Tourists in search of Arthurian sites in Cornwall in the nineteenth century, for instance, often recorded that they took with them two books – *Le Morte d'Arthur* and *Idylls of the King*.)[139] Tennyson began work on his first two Arthurian poems, 'The Epic: Morte d'Arthur' and 'Sir Launcelot and Queen Guinevere: A Fragment' in the early 1830s. The latter, which would eventually form part of the last book of *Idylls of the King*, was written shortly after the death of his close friend Arthur Hallam and has often been read biographically. More importantly, however, it also spoke to the wider anxieties and concerns of early-nineteenth-century Britain.

The novelist Charles Kingsley once explained the remarkable popularity of Tennyson's Arthurian works by remarking that the poet had 'discovered the great historic secret of finding the Present in the Past' – of focussing on contemporary issues through the lens of historical legend. In the case of 'The Epic: Morte d'Arthur', its depiction of Arthur's removal to the sacred island-valley of Avilion which is 'Deep-meadowed, happy, fair with orchard lawns' appealed to nostalgia for a lost and idealised pastoral England, while the poem's promise that Arthur would one day return to the world of men intervened in nineteenth-century debates about immortality.[140] Indeed, the poem proved so popular for these reasons that it instigated a particular fascination with King Arthur's death in the 1840s, which saw various other works investigating the subject – from Robert Buchanan's poem 'Arthur's Weird' (1840), to William Bell Scott's painting *Arthur Carried to the Land of Enchantment* (1847), to Dinah Marie Mulock's story *Avillion: or, The Happy Isles* (1853).[141]

The later poems that made up *Idylls of the King* also spoke to nineteenth-century concerns. In 'The Coming of Arthur' (written after Tennyson's visit to Tintagel in 1848), Tennyson presented the king as a model for modern leaders, in line with the argument made by Thomas Carlyle in his influential 1840 study *On Heroes, Hero-Worship and the Heroic in History* that the 'ablest man' should always be king.[142] 'The Holy Grail' (about the quest of Arthur's knights for the chalice used to catch the blood of Christ during the Crucifixion) related to Victorian anxieties about the contemporary loss of faith, and the question of whether spiritual retreat from the world and its social problems could ever be morally justified.[143] And the two poems about the knight Geraint and his wife Enid have been described as a 'primer for modern gentlemen' – dealing as they do with the question of how a husband should reconcile his role within the home with his social responsibilities out of it.[144]

'Geraint and Enid' was one of six poems, out of the twelve that were eventually collected together as *Idylls of the King*, to have a woman's name in its title. Tennyson placed women at the centre of his Arthurian world, reflecting a distinctly nineteenth-century view that as the guardians of the home and the educators of children, women were central to social order, morality, and national stability.[145] On the one hand, he depicted ideally virtuous and loyal women such as Enid and Elaine of Astolat – whose passivity was often emphasised compared to that of their medieval models.[146] On the other hand, his poems about Guinevere's adulterous relationship with Lancelot, Vivien's seduction of Merlin, and Ettare's infidelity with Gawain depict uncontrolled female sexuality as lying at the root of social disintegration – it is ultimately the acts of these three women that lead to the death of the ideal Arthur and the downfall of his chivalrous order of knights. Indeed, as recent commentators have pointed out, Tennyson deliberately revised Malory's version of the story so that Arthur and Lancelot's share of the blame was effectively removed.[147]

Tennyson was not the only nineteenth-century author to be fascinated by the figure of Guinevere and the other women who played a part in the Arthurian legends. However, later writers were often less moralising and more sympathetic to the legend's female figures, particularly in the wake of the 1857 Divorce Act, which enabled couples (though principally men) to obtain a divorce through civil proceedings.[148] William Morris's 1858 poem 'The Defence of Guenevere', for instance, is an investigation of the queen's character that relates events from her perspective (and mostly in her own voice) and can be read as a radical justification of chivalric over marital love.[149] Indeed, in the poem Morris draws on the medieval tradition of using colour symbolically and associates Guenevere with blue – the colour of purity (and of the Virgin Mary).[150] Later works by the poets Algernon Charles Swinburne, George Simcox, and Edmund Gosse likewise explored sympathetically the figure of Guinevere, and other Arthurian adulteresses such as Isolde/Iseult, the Irish princess who fell in love with Sir Tristram.[151] Such works were sometimes a riposte to Tennyson's work and in other instances a direct response to Malory – but in some cases they were responses not to literary medievalism at all, but to works of art.

THE PRE-RAPHAELITES AND THE MEDIEVAL

When he wrote his 'Defence of Guenevere', William Morris had been planning to write an entire cycle of poems on the subject of King Arthur.[152] However, he completed just three other Arthurian works – *Sir Galahad: A Christmas Mystery*, *The Chapel in Lyoness* and *King Arthur's Tomb*. The last of these was a response to a watercolour painting, *Arthur's Tomb*, which Morris had bought from the artist Dante Gabriel Rossetti – and which in its turn had been inspired by the conclusion of Malory's *Le Morte d'Arthur*.[153]

Rossetti, along with the painters Holman Hunt and John Everett Millais, was one of the founding members of the Pre-Raphaelite brotherhood. Founded in 1848, the group (as its name suggests) aimed to revive the style of the medieval Italian and Flemish art that had preceded the formulaic and neo-classical Renaissance style that the sixteenth-century painter Raphael had switched to during the course of his career – and which had dominated British art ever since. Soon after its inception, the writer William Michael Rossetti, and the artists Thomas

Woolner, James Collinson, and F.G. Stephens also joined the group, and it exhibited its first paintings produced in accordance with Pre-Raphaelite principles in 1849. The brotherhood dissolved officially in 1853. However, many of its members continued to work in the Pre-Raphaelite mode in the later 1850s and 1860s, as did other artists who became part of their circle, including Morris and Edward Burne-Jones, who became friends of Rossetti in 1856.[154] And the influence of the Pre-Raphaelites continued to be felt in the last decades of the nineteenth century in the work of the painter John William Waterhouse.[155]

The artwork produced by the Pre-Raphaelites and their followers had two main characteristics. On the one hand, it aimed at painstaking naturalism, rejecting the formulaic style of the Renaissance which attempted to aesthetically surpass the natural world – and in which conventions dictated the ratio of light to shadow, the positioning of ideally beautiful figures, and so on. In contrast to this, the Pre-Raphaelites used real models, complete with all their idiosyncrasies and physical imperfections, and often painted real settings filled with natural light.[156] On the other hand, however, the group not only painted many medieval subjects – drawn from both history and literature – they also aimed to revive the medieval relationship between fine art and Christianity, so that their paintings were imbued with spiritual meaning and often had a moral or didactic purpose. As part of this, colours and objects were often used symbolically, as they had been in the medieval period (dogs to symbolise fidelity, oranges to represent love, for instance), and medieval numerology was also drawn on, so that, for example, angels, stars and anything heavenly tend to appear in threes in Pre-Raphaelite painting, just as they did in medieval manuscripts.[157]

There are numerous references in the letters of the Pre-Raphaelites and their circle to visits that they made to the British Museum or the Bodleian Library to study illuminated medieval manuscripts.[158] These seem to have provided inspiration in a generalised way – Ruskin, for instance, was one of the first commentators to note that Rossetti's use of colour was 'based on the former art of illumination'.[159] And illuminated manuscripts themselves often appear as objects within Pre-Raphaelite paintings – in, for instance, Rossetti's 1856 painting of a medieval illuminator, *Fra Pace*. But the miniatures painstakingly painted around the margins of medieval texts also served, more specifically, as a source-book for details of costume, fabrics, and furniture in Pre-Raphaelite works.[160]

The Pre-Raphaelite use of such medieval source material was, however, typical of the vast majority of nineteenth-century medievalism. Artists tended to pick

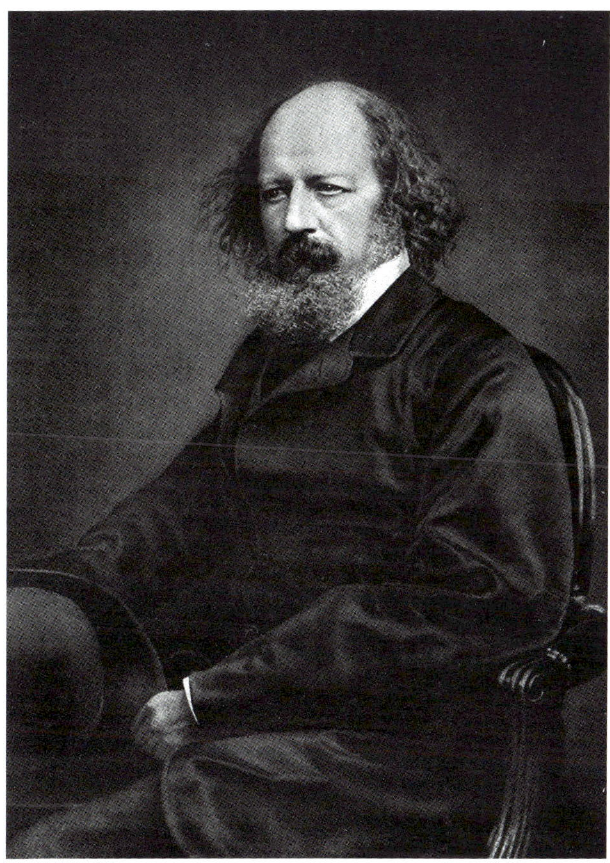

Fig. 9 / Cat. 88
Alfred Lord Tennyson
Elliot & Fry (photograph)
McClure, Macdonald & Co. (engraving)

c.1880 / engraving on paper
© Royal Albert Memorial Museum & Art Gallery, Exeter City Council

and choose among materials to fit their own aesthetic ends. Rossetti, in particular, had 'no patience with literal copying' in his work.[161] In his watercolour *The Tune of the Seven Towers*, for instance (a mysterious medieval scene with no clear source or meaning) the characters are dressed in a hodgepodge of styles from the late fourteenth and fifteenth centuries, while in another watercolour *The Blue Closet* the musical instrument that the four women play is a curious hybrid, combining keyboard, plucked strings and bells.[162] Pre-Raphaelite art is also characteristic of Victorian medievalism more widely in that its use of the medieval past reveals much about the values of nineteenth-century society. Knights rescuing ladies, or preparing for tournament while women passively watch and await their return, were particularly favoured subjects – exemplifying the Victorian middle-class belief that men and women should inhabit 'separate spheres': man out in society, woman in the home.[163] As John Ruskin famously put it, in his 1865 *Sesame and Lilies*, 'The man's power is active, progressive, defensive. He is eminently the doer, the creator, the discoverer, the defender. But the woman's power is [...] not for battle [...] Her great function is praise.'[164]

While Pre-Raphaelite artists often depicted ideally submissive and objectified medieval women, however, many were also captivated by female characters who transgressed social codes. Morris's sympathy for Guenevere extended into his art – one of his few oil paintings was an 1858 painting of the queen.[165] And Edward Burne-Jones was fascinated by the figure of Nimue or 'Vivien', the enchantress who seduces Merlin in Malory's *Morte d'Arthur*, spending five years painting the scene in oils.[166] It was partly this fascination that drew them, like Tennyson, to the Arthurian legend. Burne-Jones and Morris both encountered the Arthurian legend initially through the early works of Tennyson that preceded his full-length *Idylls of the King* – though they soon switched their attention to the less censorious version of the legend written by Malory. Burne-Jones recalled that one of his first memories of Morris was of the latter reading aloud Tennyson's 1832 poem 'The Lady of Shalott', when the pair were still students at Oxford.[167]

'The Lady of Shalott' is based ultimately on the story of Elaine of Astolat in Malory's *Morte d'Arthur*, though Tennyson's source was a fifteenth-century Italian version of the tale, which he read before having encountered Malory.[168] Tennyson's lady, who risks a curse by looking out of her tower at the wider world, and ends by floating downriver to Camelot – a beautiful corpse for Arthur's knights to marvel at – can be read as one of the transgressive women, discontent with the domestic sphere, that ap-

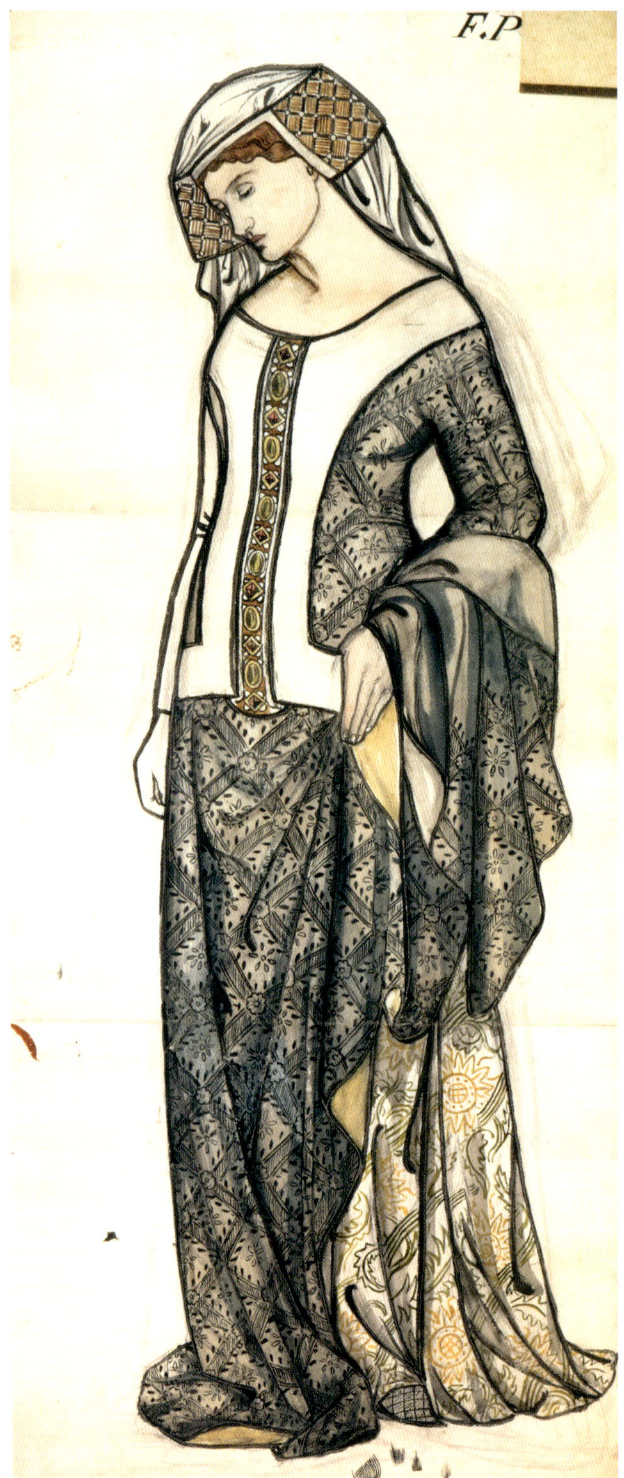

Fig. 10 / Cat. 81
Figure of Guinevere
William Morris
c.1858 / watercolour and graphite on paper
© Tate, London 2014

pear in so much Pre-Raphaelite art. As Lancelot's hopeless admirer, she could also, however, be depicted as an ideally (if tragically) devoted lover by an artistic movement that tended (like Swinburne) to value chivalric above married love. And she could also be seen as a type of the artist – her escape from the tower representing both the delights and the dangers of artistic engagement with the real world – since while in her tower she weaves tapestries.[169]

It was perhaps the mysterious ambiguity of the Lady of Shalott/Elaine that, above all, made her an attractive subject for Pre-Raphaelite artists. More than 26 pictures illustrating the story were exhibited between 1862 and 1913, provoking one reviewer to protest:

> We are well-nigh satiated with 'Elaine' and her surroundings upon canvas, and can most sincerely hope that this young lady will be allowed at least one season's respite, for she has been sadly tortured lately by artistic devotees.[170]

Just as the nineteenth-century Oxford Movement looked back to the Middle Ages as a time of heightened spirituality, Pre-Raphaelitism was attracted to the medieval as a period of history that was both mysterious and mystical. Consequently, one of the most favoured Arthurian episodes among artists was the quest for the Grail. In 1857, Rossetti painted *The Damsel of the Sanct Grael*, returning to the subject in 1864 with *How Sir Galahad, Sir Bors and Sir Perceval were fed with the Sanc Grael*, and in 1886, Burne-Jones completed four stained-glass panels depicting *The Quest for the Sangreal*. Burne-Jones was particularly drawn to the legend of the Grail, and returned to it again four years later – this time, interestingly, making the costumes of figures less carefully historicised than in his earlier work, suggesting a deliberate attempt to make the legend ahistorical and timeless.[171]

Burne-Jones's 1890 Grail images were produced for a joint-project with William Morris, to create a series of six huge tapestries depicting the quest, and modelled on the style of early Flemish tapestries. They had been commissioned by William Knox D'Arcy, an Australian mining engineer, to hang in the dining room of Stanmore Hall in Middlesex. Morris's interest in home furnishings had begun shortly after his marriage to Jane Burden in 1859, when he had found it impossible to find medieval-style furniture and fabrics for his own home, the Red House, which had been built for the couple at Bexleyheath in Kent. The Morrises began to produce things themselves and with help from their circle of friends – hangings which William designed and Jane embroidered, and furniture which was designed by the architect Philip Webb

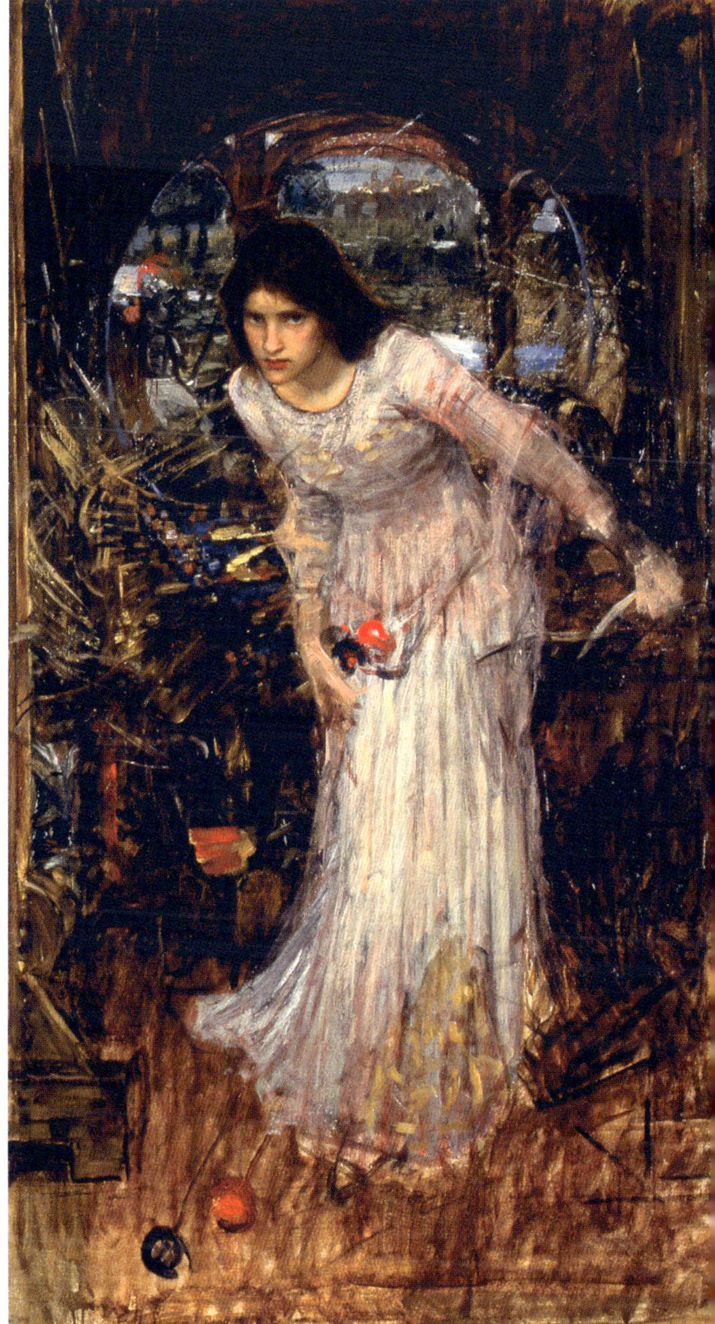

Fig. 11 / Cat. 80
The Lady of Shalott
John William Waterhouse

1894 / oil on canvas
© Falmouth Art Gallery

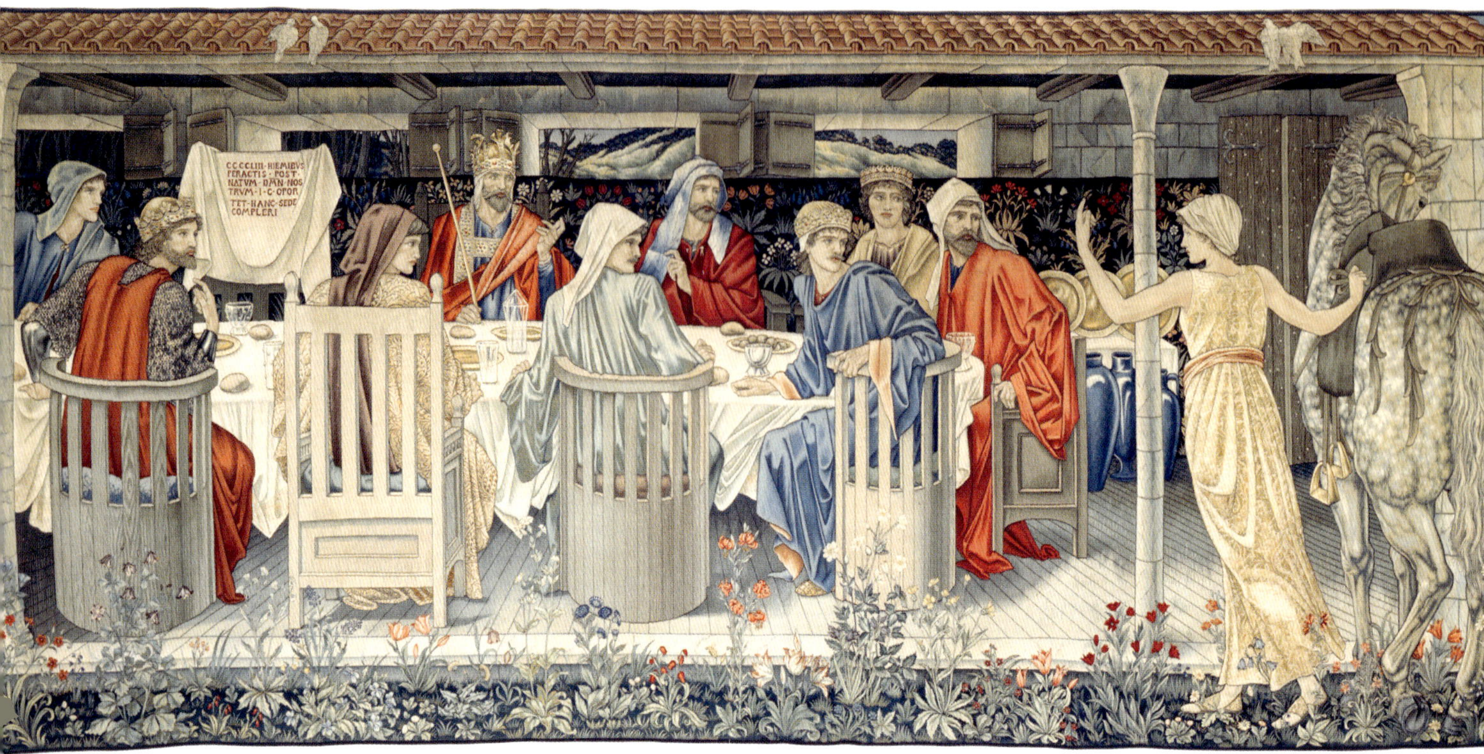

Fig. 12 / Cat. 89

Holy Grail tapestry 'Knights of the Round Table Summoned to the Quest by the Strange Damsel'
Edward Coley Burne-Jones, William Morris, John Henry Dearle (designers) / Morris & Co. (weaver)
1898–99 / wool, silk, mohair and camel hair weft on cotton warp
© Birmingham Museums Trust

and then painted by Morris, Burne-Jones, or Rossetti. From this private enterprise developed the company Morris, Marshall, Faulkner and Co., founded in 1861 and known affectionately as 'The Firm' (and later simply as Morris and Co., after Morris had bought out his partners in 1875).[172]

The Firm was in part a practical expression of Morris's belief that modern industrialism had taken away the joy, pride and freedom of the workplace – and that a far superior form of industry had existed in the fourteenth century. So its workers were carefully trained to be craftsmen – Morris declared that they were 'both in nature and training, artists, not merely animated machines', and a system of profit-sharing was also introduced.[173] As with so many nineteenth-century attempts to put medieval principles into practice, however, the reality often fell short of the ideal. While Morris paid standard wages, he charged premium prices for his goods. And the young boys who produced tapestries for The Firm, for instance, were given little freedom in the copying of designs – although they were allowed some choice in terms of colours.[174]

As well as furniture and tapestries, The Firm produced stained glass panels, taking much of its inspiration from the thirteenth- and fourteenth-century stained glass found in Oxford colleges.[175] One of its largest early commissions was Arthurian – a series of 13 panels illustrating the story of Tristram and Isolde, which was made in 1862

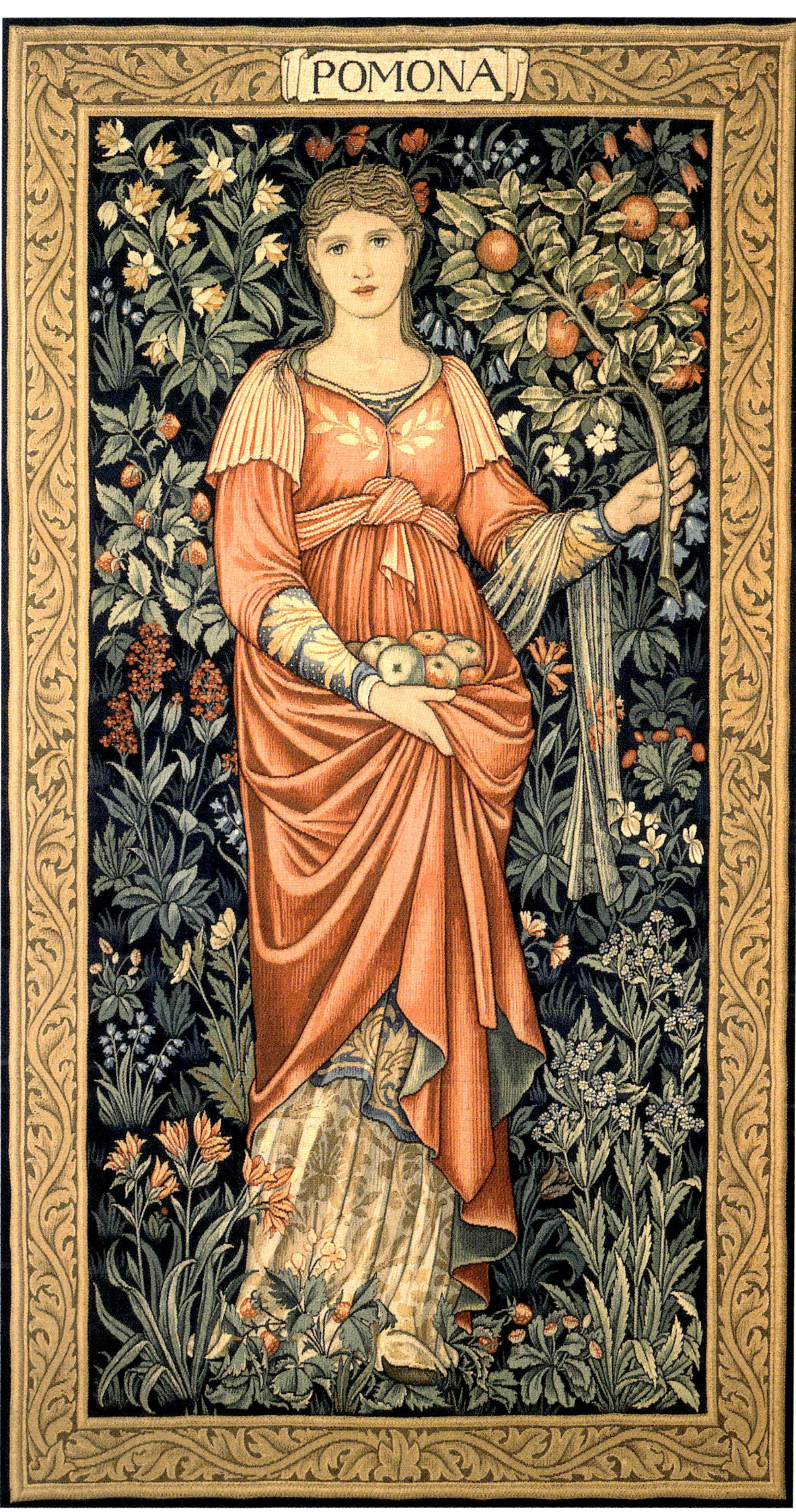

Fig. 13 / Cat. 18
Tapestry panel 'Pomona'
Edward Coley Burne-Jones
and Morris & Co

c.1900 / wool and silk on cotton warp
© Victoria and Albert Museum,
London

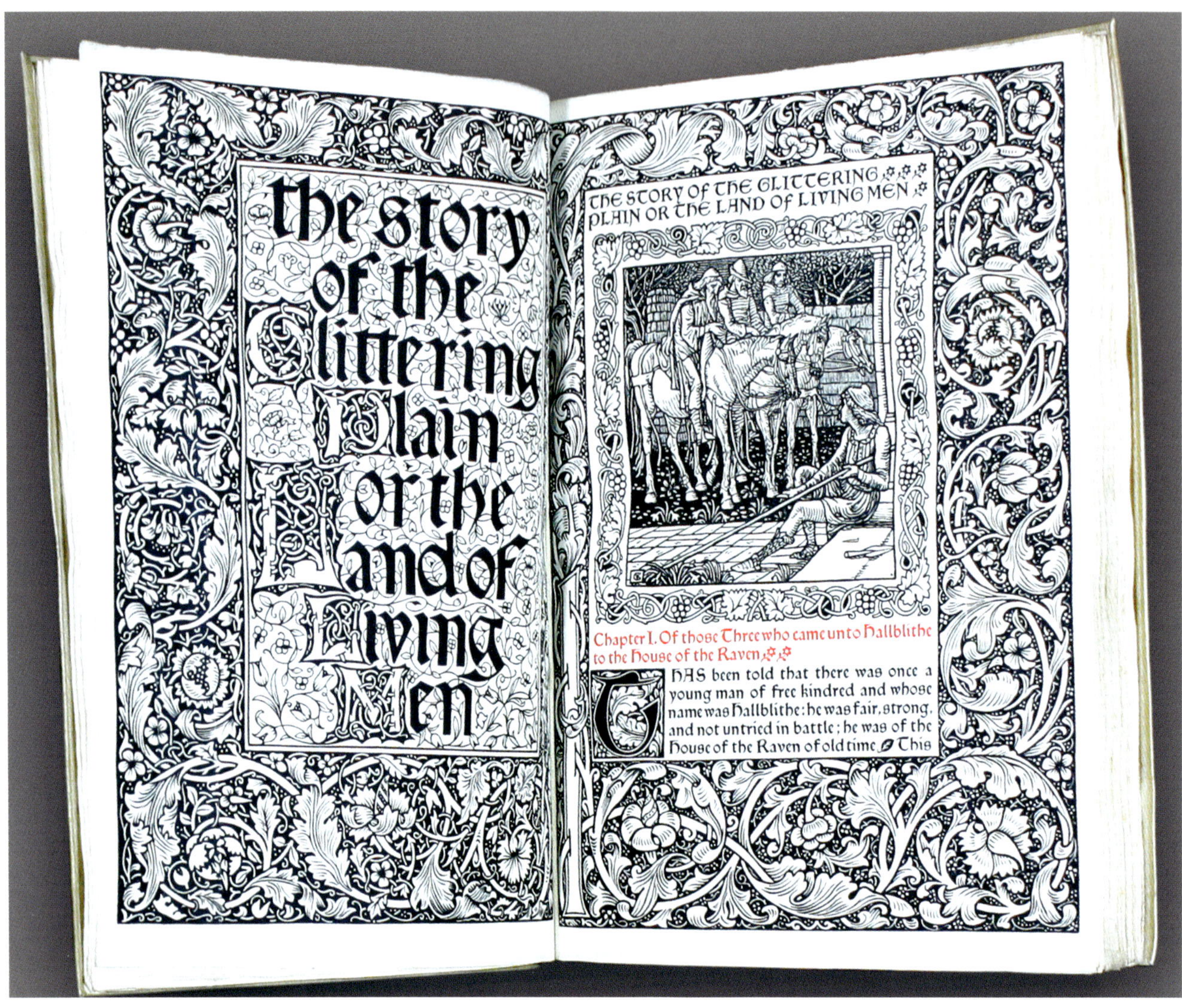

Fig. 14 / Cat. 43
*'The story of the Glittering Plain
or the Land Of Living Men'*
Walter Crane

1894 / published by the Kelmscott Press
© The Wilson: Cheltenham Art Gallery & Museum

for the home of the Bradford merchant Walter Dunlop
and based on designs by Burne-Jones.[176] Burne-Jones
and Morris also collaborated on projects for the Kelmscott Press, the printing works which Morris founded in
1891. Like Morris and Co., the press's aim was a return to
basics – it hand-printed texts in small quantities, on hand-
made paper, aiming to create books which, like the early
printed works of the fifteenth century, would have 'a definite claim to beauty'. While Burne-Jones illustrated the
works, Morris designed decorative initials, borders and
title pages for them, and also created two new 'Gothic'
typefaces.[177] The press printed Morris's own medievalist
works, but also translations of medieval histories, medieval poetry, and early English romances.[178] Its crowning
achievement, though, was the *Kelmscott Chaucer*: an exquisite edition of Chaucer's work with 87 illustrations,
which took four years to complete. Finally printed shortly before Morris's death, Burne-Jones called it 'a pocket
cathedral'.[179]

THE LEGACY OF VICTORIAN MEDIEVALISM

Just 425 copies of the Kelmscott Press Chaucer were print-ed, costing £20 each.[180] And only three sets of the huge Grail tapestries were ever made.[181] It is one of the greatest ironies of the nineteenth-century medieval revival that the desire to revive medieval craftsmanship should have led Morris, a socialist, to end his career by creating objects to satisfy what he termed 'the swinish luxury of the rich'.[182] However, while just a tiny minority of Victorian families possessed such prestige objects, many affluent homes in nineteenth-century Britain were decorated with fabrics (and, later, with the still cheaper wallpapers) based on me-dieval designs that were sold by Morris and Co. These objects are a reminder that the nineteenth-century med-ieval revival was not a phenomenon that was restricted to a scholarly or aristocratic elite – it permeated many lev-els of society and there was evidence of it in every town and city. One of the more mundane expressions of the nineteenth century's fascination with the medieval was the fashion for Christian names from the Middle Ages. Nineteenth-century British schools were filled with chil-dren named Emma, Ethel, Bertha, Alfred, Harold, or Arthur – as the names of some of the best-remembered writers from the period still attest.[183]

The large, bushy beards that we associate with many of the nineteenth-century's writers and thinkers (Alfred Tennyson, Charles Dickens, Charles Darwin) were also products of the widespread enthusiasm for the medieval period. The hirsuteness that we now think of as typically Victorian wasn't fashionable at all until the 1850s. In 1833, a writer for *Blackwoods* magazine could lament the lack of beards since medieval times. And when they began to reappear, it was as part of a conscious effort to make British men appear more Anglo-Saxon.[184] 'Looking med-dieval' was taken to extremes by the 40 jousting nobles who wore full armour at the 1839 Eglinton Tournament. However, more British men took part in the briefly pop-ular fashion of getting married in chain-mail, even more participated in the century's many medieval-themed pag-eants and fancy-dress parties, and after the publication of *Ivanhoe* until the end of the nineteenth century, the arch-ery that Robin Hood had excelled at became a popular pastime for both men and women.[185]

The heraldry that was so important in the medieval period as a means of identification and a way of mark-ing allegiance to particular lords, factions or beliefs also enjoyed a revival of interest in the nineteenth century. Long-forgotten family coats of arms began to be carved into the walls of many family homes or depicted in stained-glass panels.[186] And everything from furniture

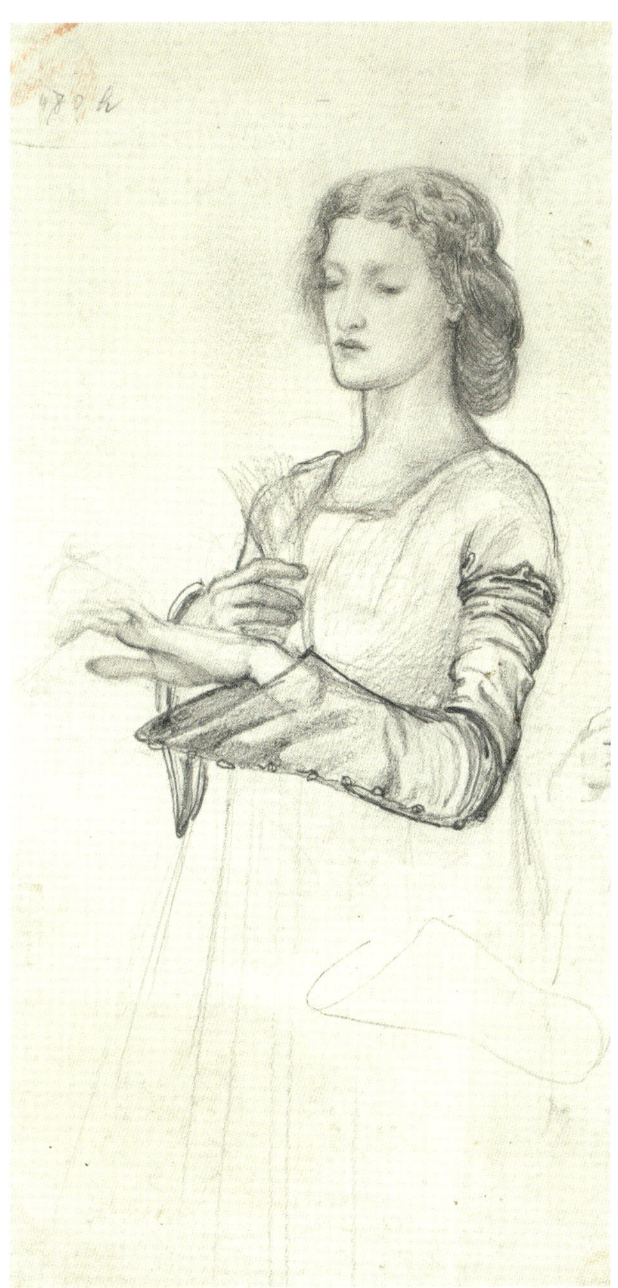

Fig. 15 / Cat. 82
Study of Iseult for 'The Marriage of Sir Tristram'
Edward Coley Burne-Jones

c.1862 / graphite on paper / verso: *Figure of Sir Tristram*
© Tate, London 2014

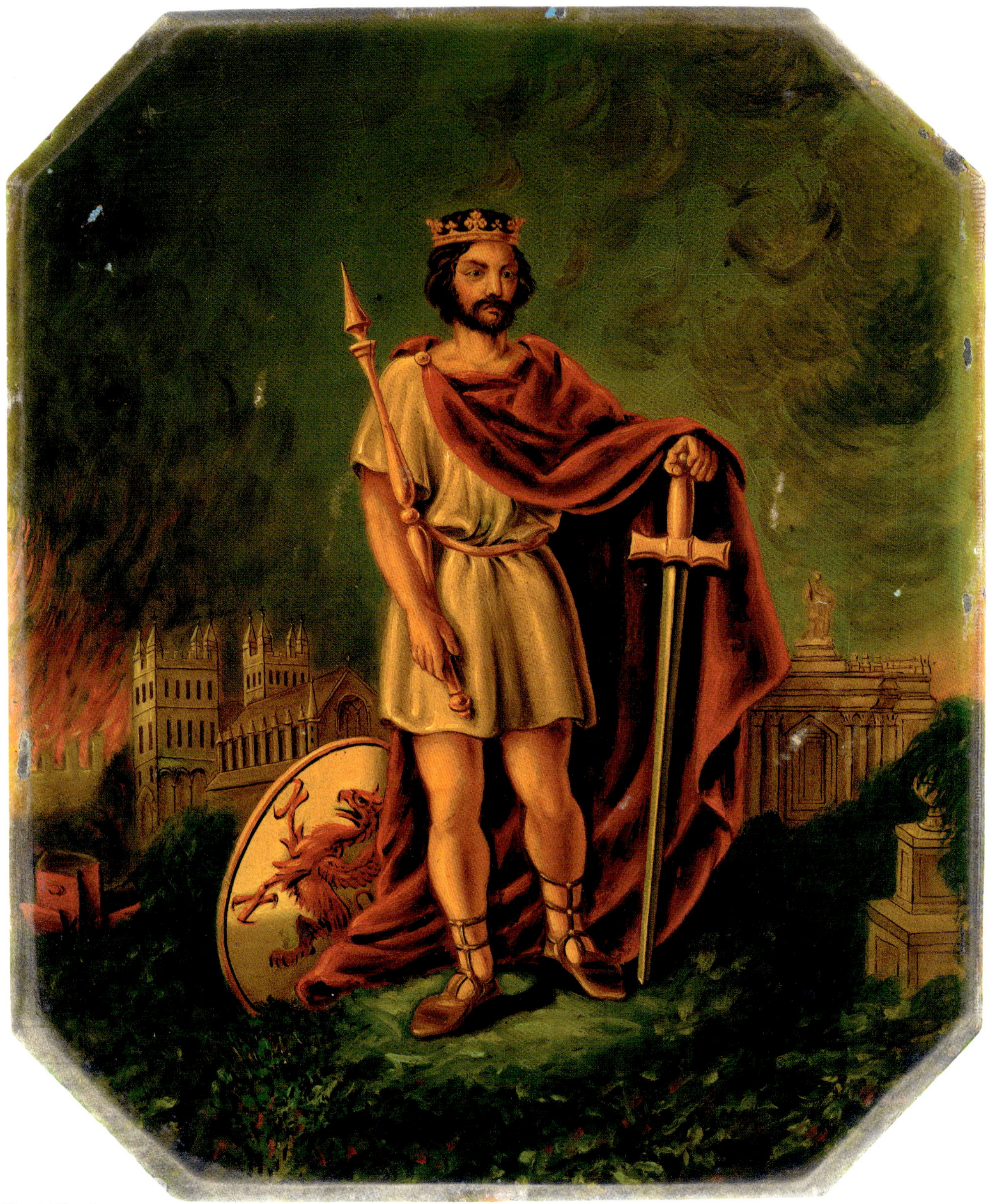

Fig. 16 / Cat. 69

Plaque of Alfred the Great

c.1840 / oil on copper panel / produced for the West of England Fire and Life Insurance Company
© Royal Albert Memorial Museum & Art Gallery, Exeter City Council

to buttons bearing family crests were produced for those keen to make a claim to gentility. In 1845, buttons bearing heraldic crests were even being exported to Australia so that British settlers in the new towns established there could assert an ancient lineage going back to the medieval period.[187]

It was not just families who drew on medieval insignia — just as the nineteenth-century monarchy began to incorporate medievalism into their rituals as a way of asserting authority and an ancient heritage, so too did local authorities. Around the country, the nineteenth-century saw the commissioning of medieval-inspired civic regalia for local authorities. Oxford's lord mayor's chain — inscribed with the city's Anglo-Saxon name 'Oxenford' — was made in 1884.[188] Sheffield's mayor's chain was created in 1856 (the money for it having been raised by public subscription after the city's mayor had been denied a seat of honour at the 1855 Paris Exhibition because he had no badge of office). It was adorned with the figure of the hammer-wielding Norse god Thor, as a link to the city's industrial heritage but also as an assertion that there was evidence for Viking settlement in the area.[189]

Institutions, professions, companies, and charitable organisations around the country also drew on images of the Middle Ages as a way of adding prestige and legitimacy to their activities. Rampant lions, fleurs-de-lys, medieval kings and queens, and Gothic typescript appeared on seals, emblems and badges. In Tiverton, a castle, Saxon church, and Gothic-style script appeared on the medal issued by the Science, Art and Technical School, while in Exeter the Middle School for Girls awarded medals featuring the city's three-towered castle, which were made in the distinctively medieval 'vesica' [almond] shape that had been commonly used for ecclesiastical seals in the Middle Ages. Exeter had been the site of many attempted Danish invasions in the ninth century, and this heritage was drawn on by the West of England Fire Insurance company, which from 1801 until 1894 used the image of the Saxon king Alfred (who had defended the city) as a symbol of protective power on the 'fire-marks' attached to any buildings that they had insured. And between 1815 and 1831 Alfred's portrait (surround by axes, swords, and the raven banner that he had reputedly captured from the Danes) also appeared on the front cover of Exeter's local newspaper, *The Alfred, West of England Journal and General Advertiser.*[190]

In many ways in our daily lives we are still surrounded by the legacy of Victorian medievalism. The lord mayors of Exeter, Sheffield, and Oxford still wear their Victorian medieval-inspired chains of office — at least for civic ceremonies. Many of our universities, libraries,

churches and town halls contain nineteenth-century stained glass that was commissioned as part of the medieval revival. William Morris's medieval-inspired designs can still be bought from Morris and Co. as wallpaper and upholstery fabric and can be found adorning wrapping paper, bags, and tablecloths. And reproductions of Pre-Raphaelite paintings of medieval subjects (above all, perhaps, *The Lady of Shalott*) can be cheaply bought as posters, place-mats and aprons.

The nineteenth-century obsession with the Anglo-Saxons came to an end in the early twentieth century after the first and second World Wars, as commentators observed disturbing connections and continuities between the 'Teutonism' of the nineteenth century and the active fascism of the twentieth century.[191] Thereafter there were few writers in Britain keen to assert a Germanic heritage for the country. But England's Anglo-Saxon heritage has seen a resurgence of interest amid recent discussions about the possible break-up of the United Kingdom, and the search for English, rather than British, cultural icons. A string of popular television programmes about Anglo-Saxon history has been screened, the historical novelist Bernard Cornwell has produced a series of five novels about that darling of the Victorians, King Alfred, and there has been extensive media coverage of a search for that Saxon monarch's remains in Winchester.

Above all, perhaps, the Victorian rediscovery of King Arthur still endures today. Since the 1940s more than fifty films, animations, and television series have been made, based on the legend of Arthur. And from T.H. White's 1958 fantasy *The Once and Future King* to Marion Zimmer Bradley's 1983 feminist adaptation *The Mists of Avalon*, to Mari Mancusi's 2014 young adult novel *The Camelot Code*, there have been scores of Arthurian novels published, many of them echoing themes and concerns (like Morris and Tennyson's focus on Arthurian women) that were developed in the nineteenth century. We also, more generally, still cherish today the Scott-derived image of the Middle Ages as a time of feasting and plenty — medieval feasts are regularly staged as tourist attractions around the country. And the Victorian association of the medieval with the spiritual or mystical fed into late twentieth-century phenomena ranging from self-help CDs of Gregorian chanting to *Dungeons and Dragons* role-playing games.

The nineteenth-century fascination with the medieval was not restricted to Britain. There were parallel movements in France, Spain, and Germany, and nostalgia for the British medieval past also spread to America and Australia where it has continued to the present day.[192] In Australia today, as in Britain, there is a wealth of Gothic revival architecture and a flourishing fashion for medieval re-enactment, while New York State still has towns named Alfred and Ossian, and Manhattan has an annual medieval festival.[193] Indeed, the most recent widely-popular expression of medievalism has travelled to Britain from America. George R.R. Martin's series of novels *A Song of Ice and Fire* first appeared in 1996 with the publication of *A Game of Thrones*. Since then, a further four novels have appeared, and a hugely popular and award-winning television adaptation (named after the first book in the series) has been produced, which has attracted audiences of over 18 million.[194]

A Game of Thrones is in many ways clearly the progeny of Victorian medievalism. Feasting and great battles are as much at its heart as in many novels from the nineteenth century. Its manipulative queen who instigates civil war is a reminder of the faithless women in Tennyson's *Idylls of the King*, with which it also shares an interest in succession and bastardy. And it has the same 'pick-and-mix' quality as many nineteenth-century medievalist texts – while the main storyline is a fantastical reflection of the fifteenth-century Wars of the Roses, it also has Viking-like characters, a great, guarded wall across the north of its fictional kingdom which resembles the Romano-British Hadrian's Wall, and an orientalist subplot. However, the character of George R.R. Martin's medieval fantasy world is far removed from the simple and idealised societies based on mutual loyalty that appear in the works of Victorian authors like William Morris and Charlotte Yonge. And although it shares Tennyson's vision of a chivalric society falling apart through the actions of women, the levels of violence (in particular sexual violence), faithlessness and suffering in *A Song of Ice and Fire* are far removed from the chivalry of Tennyson's Camelot. The closest it comes to expressions of the nineteenth-century medieval revival is probably the work of Swinburne who was almost alone in the Victoran period in depicting the medieval world as 'disharmonious and corrupt, populated with men and women who are fickle in their emotional attachments, capricious in their loyalties, and misguided in their adherence to Christianity'.[195] However, even in Swinburne's poetry, there is nostalgia for the chivalric values of the medieval period and the Arthurian lovers in his poems, though adulterous, are still heroic figures who remain true to themselves.[196]

The violence in George R.R. Martin's novels – particularly in the television adaptations – is often lamented in the media, but its readers and viewers continue to increase in number. Thinking of this as twenty-first-century medievalism, it is interesting to consider how the phenomenon is likely to be looked back upon in a hundred years' time. Since the end of the medieval period, each age has found in the figures, the literature, or the historical events of the Middle Ages the means of expressing something of its own ideals and anxieties. This essay has considered what Victorian medievalism can tell us about the concerns of nineteenth-century Britain, in particular. But if we can gain important insights from interpreting the cultural movements of our great-grandparents' society, then it is perhaps still more important for us to ask the same questions about our own. The phenomenal success of *A Song of Ice and Fire* with its particular vision of the medieval period as a time of betrayal, faithlessness, and violence must surely lead us to think seriously about the values, the myths and the beliefs of the early twenty-first century. If we no longer dream of the Middle Ages as a perpetual pastoral summer of fulfilling industry, heroic achievement, spirituality, and loyalty, then perhaps it is indeed true, as the characters in *A Game of Thrones* frequently assert, that 'Winter is coming'.

1. Boris Johnson, quoted in the *Telegraph*, 29 January 2014, www.telegraph.co.uk.

2. On the truth of the 'blood eagle' rite see Roberta Frank, 'Viking atrocity and Skaldic Verse: The Rite of the Blood-Eagle', *The English Historical Review* (1984), www.oxfordjournals.org.

3. According to slang lexicographer Jonathan Green, author of *Green's Dictionary of Slang* (London: Chambers, 2010).

4. *Oxford English Dictionary*, www.oed.com.

5. Phil Patton, 'If Medieval Suits the Mood' [review of the Hummer H1 Alpha], the *New York Times*, 25 September 2005, www.nytimes.com.

6. *Oxford English Dictionary*.

7. *Oxford English Dictionary*

8. The idea may have emerged a little earlier than this in the European countries that are south of the Alps. On this see E.G. Stanley, 'The Early Middle Ages = The Dark Ages = The Heroic Age of England and in English', in Marie-Francoise Alamichel and Derek Brewer, *The Middle Ages after the Middle Ages*, pp. 43-77, p. 44.

9. See Stanley, p. 45.

10. David Hume, *The History of England* (London: A. Millar, 1762), vol. 2, p. 441.

11. Stanley, p. 53.

12. W. Godwin, *Life of Geoffrey Chaucer, the Early English Poet* (London: Richard Phillips, 1803), p. 13.

13. Stanley, p. 65.

14. For a full account of this see Nick Groom, *The Gothic: A Very Short Introduction* (Oxford University Press, 2012).

15. See Groom, pp. 3-11.

16. *Oxford English Dictionary*.

17. *Oxford English Dictionary*.

18. Andrew MacDowall, Lord Bankton, *An Essay upon Feudal Holdings, Superiorities, and Hereditary Jurisdictions, in Scotland* (London: R. Lee, 1747), p. 28.

19. William Blackstone, *Commentaries on the Laws of England* (1765-9), vol. 3, p. 268.

20. Jonathan Swift, spoof letter to *The Tatler*, no. 230, 26 September 1710, p. 193.

21. *Oxford English Dictionary*

22. See Nick Groom, *The Gothic: A Very Short Introduction* (Oxford University Press, 2012), pp. 54-86 for a full account of this.

23. Alfred Bowker, *The King Alfred Millenary: A Record of the National Commemoration* (London: Macmillan, 1902), p. 39.

24. In 1897, every single edition of the *Cornhill Magazine* carried an 'anniversary study' of a significant event, and in 1858, Thomas Gill's volume *The Anniversaries* (London: n.pub., 1858) was published, containing commemorative poems to be read on each day of the year.

25. See, for instance, the historical novels of Eva March Tappan and Eliza Kerr.

26. John Ruskin, 'Letter to Henry Ackland', in E.T. Cook and A. Wedderburn, eds, *The Works of Ruskin*, 39 vols (London: George Allen, 1909), vol. 36, p. 115.

27. See Robin Gilmour, *The Victorian Period: The Intellectual and Cultural Context of English Literature, 1830-1890* (New York: Longman, 1993), p. 25.

28. See Rosemary Mitchell, *Picturing the Past: English History in Text and Image 1830-1870* (Oxford: Clarendon, 2000), p. 2.

29. See Mitchell, p. 2.

30. Sabine Baring-Gould, *The Book of Werewolves* (London: Smith Elder, 1865); *Curious Myths of the Middle Ages* (London: Rivingtons, 1868); *Songs and Ballads of the West* (London: Methuen, 1891).

31. See Gilmour, p. 31

32. See Charles Dellheim, *The Face of the Past: The Preservation of the Medieval Inheritance in Victorian England* (Cambridge University Press, 1982), p. 28.

33. One of the first illustrated histories was the sixth edition of Lockman's *History of England*. Published in 1747, it was squarely aimed at the bottom end of the market, but was illustrated by a set of thirty drawings. Robert Bowyer's *Complete History of England* was perhaps the most ambitious of eighteenth-century projects to illustrate English history. Advertised as 'the most superb publication, without exception, in Europe' it contained enough illustrations to entirely fill one of its six volumes. For more on this subject see Roy Strong, *And When Did You Last See your Father: The Victorian Painter and British History* (London: Thames and Hudson, 1978), p. 20.

34. For a full account of this development, see Simon Keynes, 'The Cult of King Alfred the Great', *Anglo-Saxon England*, 28 (2000), pp. 296-303.

35. See Mitchell, p. 2.

36. See Frederick Knight Hunt, *The Book of Art: Cartoons, Frescoes, Sculptures and Decorative Art, as Applied to the New Houses of Parliament and to Buildings in General* (London: [n.pub.], 1846).

37. This subject will be dealt with in full in the next essay.

38. See Dellheim, p. 37.

39. G.P.R. James, *Forest Days* (London: Saunders and Otley, 1843), pp. 1-2.

40. See Kevin L. Morris, *The Image of the Middle Ages in Romantic and Victorian Literature* (London: Croom Helm, 1984), p. 36; Dellheim, The Face of the Past, p. 44; Alice Chandler, *A Dream of Order: The Medieval Ideal in Nineteenth-Century English Literature* (Lincoln: University of Nebraska Press, 1970), p. 9.

41. See Jennifer Harris, 'William Morris and the Middle Ages', in Joanna Banham and Jennifer Harris, *William Morris and the Middle Ages* (Manchester University Press, 1984), p. 6.

42. John Ruskin, *The Stones of Venice*, in *The Works of John Ruskin* (1902-12), vol. 10, p. 194.

43. John Ruskin, *The Stones of Venice*, p. 193.

44. Thomas Carlyle, *Past and Present*, in *Thomas Carlyle's Works* (London: Chapman and Hall, n.d.), vol. 3, p. 182.

45. For more on this see William Stafford, '"This Once Happy Country": Nostalgia for Pre-Modern Society', in Christopher Shaw and Malcolm Chase, *The Imagined Past: History and Nostalgia* (Manchester University Press, 1989), p. 34.

46. See Gerrard Winstanley, *The Law of Freedom and Other Writings* (Cambridge University Press, 1983), p. 280-99.

47. Winstanley, p. 86.

48. Clare Simmons, *Reversing the Conquest: History and Myth in Nineteenth-Century British Literature* (New Brunswick: Rutgers University Press, 1990), pp. 32, 16.

49. Simmons, *Reversing the Conquest*, pp. 3, 34, 141.

50. See for instance Anon, 'The Anglo-Normans' *The North British Review*, 6 (1847), pp. 431-472, p. 468.

51. Arthur Arnold, 'The Indebtedness of the Landed Gentry', *The Contemporary Review*, 47 (1885), pp. 225-232.

52. *The Times* (Sep. 21, 1901), p. 10.

53. See, for instance, Edward A. Freeman, *Old English History* [2nd edn] (London: Macmillan, 1871), p. xiii.

54. On this subject see Simmons, *Reversing the Conquest*, pp. 182-184; Clare Simmons 'Iron-worded Proof: Victorian Identity and the Old English Language', *Studies in Medievalism*, 4 (1992), pp. 202-214. p. 210.

55. For an overview of this see W.S. Lilly, 'British Monarchy and Modern Democracy' *Nineteenth Century*, 41 (1897), pp. 853-864, p. 860. For an early example of pro-Hanoverian rhetoric see for instance the dedication to George I in Elizabeth Elstob, *The Rudiments of Grammar for the English-Saxon Tongue* (London: William Bowyer, 1715).

56. The play was *Alfred: A Masque*, by David Mallet and James Thomson, and was commissioned by Frederick, the son of George II and father of George III.

57. On the initial suspicion surrounding Albert, see Frank H. Hill, 'The Future of the English Monarchy', *The Contemporary Review*, 57 (1890), pp. 187-205.

58. For more on this event see Ian Hunter, 'Ludicrous or Lucid? Medieval Costumes and Royal Politics in Mid-Nineteenth Century Britain', *MLA Volume of Interdisciplinary Essays*, I (2013), 75-84, pp. 75-78.

59. See Hunter, p. 78.

60. Hunter, p. 77.

61. Nikolaus Pevsner, *The Buildings of England: Berkshire* (Harmondsworth: Penguin, 1966), pp. 283-4. See also Hunter, pp. 79-83.

62. On this subject see Simmons, *Reversing the Conquest*, p. 175. Victoria is defended in these terms in W.S. Lilly, 'British Monarchy and Modern Democracy', *Nineteenth Century*, 41 (1897), pp. 853-864.

63. See, for instance, Lilly, p. 859. In 1899, the Bishop of London declared that 'the blood of Alfred still ran in the veins of her Most Gracious Majesty Queen Victoria' (see Bowker, *The King Alfred Millenary*, p. 13).

64. According to articles published in *The Illustrated London News* in 1852 and 1858, quoted in David Cannadine, 'The Context, Performance and Meaning of Ritual: The British Monarchy and the "Invention of Tradition"', in Eric Hobsbawm and Terence Ranger, *The Invention of Tradition* (Cambridge University Press, 1983), p. 117.

65. See Cannadine, p. 118 for a full description of these events.

66. See Cannadine, pp. 120-122.

67. See the official website of the British Monarchy, www.royal.gov.uk and press reports from 22nd June 1887. For instance, Anon, 'The Jubilee Celebration', *Western Times*, 22 June 1887, p. 2.

68. This was reported proudly in the local press

– for instance in the *Birmingham Daily Post*, 23 June 1887, p. 5. For more on this see Anthony Taylor, *Down with the Crown: British Anti-Monarchism and Debates about Royalty since 1790* (London: Reaktion, 1999), p. 130.

69. See Taylor, p. 130.

70. On this see Cannadine, p. 125.

71. Alfred Austin, *England's Darling* [5th edn] (London: Macmillan, 1896), p. v.

72. Austin, *England's Darling*, p. v.

73. For more on Percy see Nick Groom, *The Making of Percy's Reliques* (Oxford: Clarendon, 1999), pp. 84-86.

74. Andrew Wawn, *The Vikings and the Victorians* (Cambridge: D.S. Brewer, 2000), pp. 21, 24, 3.

75. Wawn, p. 3-4.

76. John Newman, *Apologia Pro Vita Sua* (London: Longman, 1890 [1864]), p. 51. For more on Newman and the medievalist Oxford Movement see the following chapter.

77. See David Matthews, *The Invention of Middle English: An Anthology of Primary Sources* (Turnhout, Belgium: Brepols, 2000) p. 8.

78. See Matthews, p. 9.

79. See Michael Alexander, *Medievalism: The Middle Ages in Modern England* (New Haven: Yale University Press, 2007), p. 14.

80. See Alfred P. Smyth, *King Alfred the Great* (Oxford: Oxford University Press, 1995), pp. 86-88; Matthews, p. 8.

81. On this see Dafydd Moore, *Enlightenment and Romance in James Macpherson's 'The Poems of Ossian': Myth, Genre and Cultural Change* (Farnham: Ashgate, 2003).

82. On this see Nick Groom, *The Forger's Shadow: How Forgery Changed the Shape of Literature* (London: Picador, 2002), pp. 140-216.

83. See Horace Walpole, *The Castle of Otranto: A Gothic Story*, ed. Nick Groom (Oxford University Press, 2014), p. v.

84. Groom (ed.), *The Castle of Otranto*, pp. xxxiv-xxxv.

85. Scott's other medieval novels were: *Count Robert* (1831), *The Betrothed* (1825), *The Talisman* (1825), *The Fair Maid of Perth* (1828), *Castle Dangerous* (1831), *Quentin Durward* (1823), and *Anne of Geierstein* (1829). Two further novels, *The Abbot* (1820) and *The Monastery* (1820), are also often classed among his medieval novels, though they are actually set in the sixteenth century.

86. Alexander, p. xxiv.

87. Chandler, p. 315.

88. See Chandler, p 331.

89. See Chandler, p. 331.

90. See Stafford, p. 40.

91. Walter Scott, 'The Lay of the Last Minstrel', in *Poetical Works*, vi (Edinburgh: Blackwoods, 1833), pp. 49-50. For more on this see Chandler, p. 332.

92. See Alexander, p. 30.

93. John Gibson Lockhart, *Memoirs of the Life of Sir Walter Scott* (Paris: Baudry, 1838), vol. 4, p. 339.

94. Stafford, p. 44.

95. Quoted in Chandler, p. 326.

96. See Andrew Prescott, 'Brother Irving: Sir Henry Irving and Freemasonry', *First Knight: Journal of the Irving Society* (n.d.), www.theirvingsociety.org.uk.

97. On this see Ian Anstruther, *The Knight and the Umbrella: An Account of the Eglinton Tournament 1839* (Gloucester: Sutton, 1986).

98. See Chandler, p. 328.

99. Charlotte Yonge, *The Prince and the Page: A Story of the Last Crusade* (London: Macmillan, 1893 [1865]), p. 2.

100. See, for instance, Yonge, *The Prince and the Page*, p. 40, in which the mutual loyalty of the characters of the title is described at length.

101. Stafford, p. 40.

102. Guy Mannering reads *Sintram and His Companions* (1814), a medievalist work by the German Romantic author Baron Friedrich de la Motte Fouqué.

103. See Alethea Hayter *Charlotte Yonge* (Plymouth: Northcote House, 1996), p. 2. Also see the *ODNB* and records on the Open University's *UK Reading Experience Database*, www.open.ac.uk.

104. See, for instance, M. Lonsdale, *Sketch of Alfred the Great: Or, The Danish Invasion: A Grand Historical Ballet* (London, 1865) and Tom Matthews, *Harlequin Alfred the Great! Or, the Magic Banjo and the Mystic Raven* (London, 1850).

105. Antony H. Harrison, *Swinburne's Medievalism* (Baton Rouge: Louisiana University Press, 1988), p. 4.

106. See Joanne Parker, 'Brunanburh and the Victorian Imagination', in Michael Livingston, *The Battle of Brunanburh: A Casebook* (Exeter: University of Exeter Press, 2011), pp. 385-409.

107. See Barbara Gribling, *Nationalising the Hero: The Image of Edward the Black Prince 1780-1903* (unpublished PhD thesis, University of York, 2009).

108. See Simmons, *Reversing the Conquest*.

109. See Joanne Parker, *England's Darling: The Victorian Cult of Alfred the Great* (Manchester University Press, 2014 [2009]).

110. In *The Prince and the Page*, Yonge imagines how Westminster Abbey must have looked when newly made.

111. James Miller, *Fertile Fortune: The Story of Tyntsfield* (London: The National Trust, 2003), p. 98.

112. Charlotte Yonge, letter to Mary Yonge, 17 August 1876, www.yongeletters.com

113. Christabel Coleridge, *Charlotte Mary Yonge: Her Life and Letters* (London: Macmillan, 1903), p. 100.

114. See Coleridge, p. 40; *The Prince and the Page*, p. 1.

115. See Coleridge, p. 97.

116. Thomas Hardy, *A Pair of Blue Eyes* (Oxford University Press, 1985 [1873]), p. vii.

117. Charles Kightly, English Heritage, www.english-heritage.org.uk.

118. Eliza Bray, *Henry de Pomeroy: Or, The Eve of St John* (London: Longman, 1845), p. 8.

119. Bray, p.8.

120. Bray, p. 35.

121. Bray, pp. 38, 25.

122. Edward Montague, *The Castle of Berry Pomeroy* (London: Valancourt, 2014), p. 9.

123. Bray, pp. 5, 3.

124. T.C. Mortimer, *Berry Pomeroy Castle: An Historical and Descriptive Sketch* (Totnes: Totnes Times and Western Guardian, n.d.).

125. On historical tourism see Dellheim, *The Face of the Past*, p. 39.

126. The earliest references to Arthur can be found in the *Historia Brittonum* which was completed in the year 829 or 830. For more on this see Ronald Hutton, *Witches, Druids and King Arthur* (London: Hambledon, 2003), p. 39.

127. Hutton, *Witches, Druids and King Arthur*, pp. 40-42.

128. See Inga Bryden, *Reinventing King Arthur: The Arthurian Legends in Victorian Culture* (Aldershot: Ashgate, 2005), pp. 10-11; Geoffrey Ashe, *The Traveller's Guide to Arthurian Britain* (Glastonbury: Gothic Image, 1997), p. 5.

129. See Bryden, p. 11; Ashe, *The Traveller's Guide*, pp. 2, 4.

130. See Bryden, p. 14.

131. Bryden, p. 16.

132. James P. Carley (ed.), *Arthurian Poets: Matthew Arnold and William Morris* (Woodbridge: Boydell, 1990), p. 1; Alexander, p. 34.

133. Cornwall alone has more than 30 Arthurian place-names. See Geoffrey Ashe, *A Guidebook to Arthurian Britain* (Wellingborough: Aquarian, 1983), p. 223

134. On this work see Dafydd Moore, 'Ossianism and the Arthurian Revival: The Case of Richard Hole's *Arthur; or the Northern Enchantment* (1789)', in Joanne Parker, *The Harp and the Constitution: Myths of Celtic and Gothic Origin* (Leiden: Brill, forthcoming).

135. Robert Gossedge, 'Peacock's Misfortunes of Elphin and the Romantic Arthur', in *Arthurian Literature* xxiii (2006), p. 161.

136. Carley, p. 1.

137. Roger Simpson, *Camelot Regained: The Arthurian Revival and Tennyson, 1800-1849* (Cambridge: Brewer, 1990), p. 221.

138. *O.D.N.B.*

139. The novelist Dinah Marie Craik and her two nieces, for instance, took Malory's and Tennyson's texts with them on a trip to Cornwall, consequently seeing 'an Arthurian influence everywhere'. See Bryden, p. 128.

140. See Bryden, p. 120.

141. See Bryden, pp. 119-120, 128.

142. See Thomas Carlyle, *On Heroes, Hero Worship and the Heroic in History* (London: Chapman and Hall, 1840), p. 182.

143. See Bryden, p. 49.

144. Linda K. Hughes, '"All that Makes a Man": Tennyson's *Idylls of the King* as a Primer for Modern Gentlemen', *Arthurian Interpretations*, vol. 1, no. 1 (1986), pp. 54-63.

145. See Ingrid Ranum, 'Domestic Development in Tennyson's *Geraint and Enid* and *The Marriage of Geraint*', *Victorian Poetry*, 47:1 (2009), pp. 242-257.

146. See Maureen Fries, 'What Tennyson Really Did to Malory's Women', *Quondam et Futurus*, vol. 1, no. 1 (1991), pp. 44-55, pp. 50-51.

147. See Fries, pp. 52-53.

148. C. Poulson, *The Quest for the Grail: Arthurian Legend in British Art 1840-1920* (Manchester University Press, 1999), pp. 215-217.

149. See Bryden, p. 100.

150. Carley, p. 11.

151. Bryden, pp. 110-116. See also Baswell and Sharpe, *The Passing of Arthur: New Essays in Arthurian Tradition* (London: Garland, 1988), p. 251.

152. According to his daughter May Morris. See Banham and Harris, p. 179.

153. See Carley, p. 13.

154. Banham and Harris, p. 92.

155. See Aubrey Noakes, *Waterhouse: John William Waterhouse* (London: Chaucer, 2004).

156. See Elizabeth Prettejohn, *The Art of the Pre-Raphaelites* (London: Tate, 2007).

157. See Alastair Grieve, 'The Pre-Raphaelite Brotherhood and the Anglican High Church', *Burlington Magazine*, 111 (1969), pp. 294-5; Banham and Harris, p 116.

158. Julian Treuherz, 'The Pre-Raphaelites and Medieval Illuminated Manuscripts', in Leslie Parris (ed), *Pre-Raphaelite Papers* (London: Tate, 1984), p. 153.

159. Treuherz, p. 153.

160. Treuherz, pp. 155, 165.

161. Banham and Harris, p. 100.

162. www.liverpoolmuseums.org.uk.

163. Banham and Harris, pp. 107-108.

164. John Ruskin, 'Of Queens' Gardens', in *Sesame and Lilies*, 1865.

165. It should be noted, however, that there is disagreement as to whether the figure is Guenevere or Iseult. See Banham and Harris, p. 115.

166. Burne-Jones created the large oil painting *The Beguiling of Merlin* between 1872 and 1877.

167. J. W. Mackail, *The Life of William Morris* (London: Longmans, 1907), vol. 1, p. 38.

168. See L.S. Potwin, 'The Source of Tennyson's "Lady of Shalott"', *Modern Language Notes*, vol. 17, no. 8 (1902), p. 237.

169. This reading of Tennyson's poem is often favoured by modern critics, since at the time of writing it, Tennyson's medievalism had attracted criticism for its failure to engage with the real world.

170. Anon, *Art Journal* (1861), p. 195.

171. Banham and Harris, p. 188.

172. Banham and Harris, pp. 188, 113, 114.

173. Linda Parry, *William Morris Textiles* (London: V&A, 2013), p. 116.

174. Larry Shiner, *The Invention of Art: A Cultural History* (University of Chicago Press, 2001), p. 239.

175. Banham and Harris, p. 95.

176. Banham and Harris, p. 181.

177. Morris designed three typefaces in all for the Kelmscott Press – a Gothicised Roman typeface, followed by two Gothic typefaces. www.bl.uk.

178. www.bl.uk.

179. www.bl.uk.

180. A further 13 copies printed on vellum were priced at £126. www.bl.uk.

181. Banham and Harris, pp. 210; 189.

182. Gillian Naylor, *William Morris by Himself: Designs and Writings* (London: MacDonald, 1990), p. 108

183. www.1901census.com

184. See O.W.T. Heighway, 'A Few Words Upon Beards', *Tait's Edinburgh Magazine*, 19 (1852), p. 164.

185. On Victorian medieval-themed fancy dress see Stephanie L. Barczewski, *Myth and National Identity: The Legends of King Arthur and Robin Hood* (Oxford University Press, 2000), pp. 54-55

186. On this see Alexander, p. 109.

187. See 'Livery Buttons Leading Families of New South Wales', *Medievalism in Australian Cultural Memory*, http://ausmed.arts.uwa.edu.au/items/show/247.

188. www.oxfordhistory.org.uk.

189. www.sheffield.gov.uk.

190. On *The Alfred* see Gosta Langenfelt, *The Historical Origin of the Eight Hours Day* (Westport: Greenwood, 1974), pp. 119-122.

191. See Joanne Parker, *England's Darling: The Victorian Cult of Alfred the Great* (Manchester University Press, 2014 [2009]), pp. 299-303.

192. On medievalism in Europe see *Studies in Medievalism* v (1994), edited by Leslie J. Workman, and *Studies in Medievalism* viii (1997), edited by Leslie J. Workman and Katherine Verduin.

193. On Australian medievalism see the *Medievalism in Australian Cultural Memory* project, http://ausmed.arts.uwa.edu.au.

194. Daniel Fienberg, ' "Game of Thrones" has become more popular than 'The Sopranos', *HitFix*, 5 June 2014, www.hitfix.com.

195. Harrison, p. 4.

196. Harrison, p. 40. On Swinburne's medievalism see also Bryden, pp. 111-112.

VICTORIAN RESURRECTIONS
Gothic and the Challenges of Modernity

CORINNA WAGNER

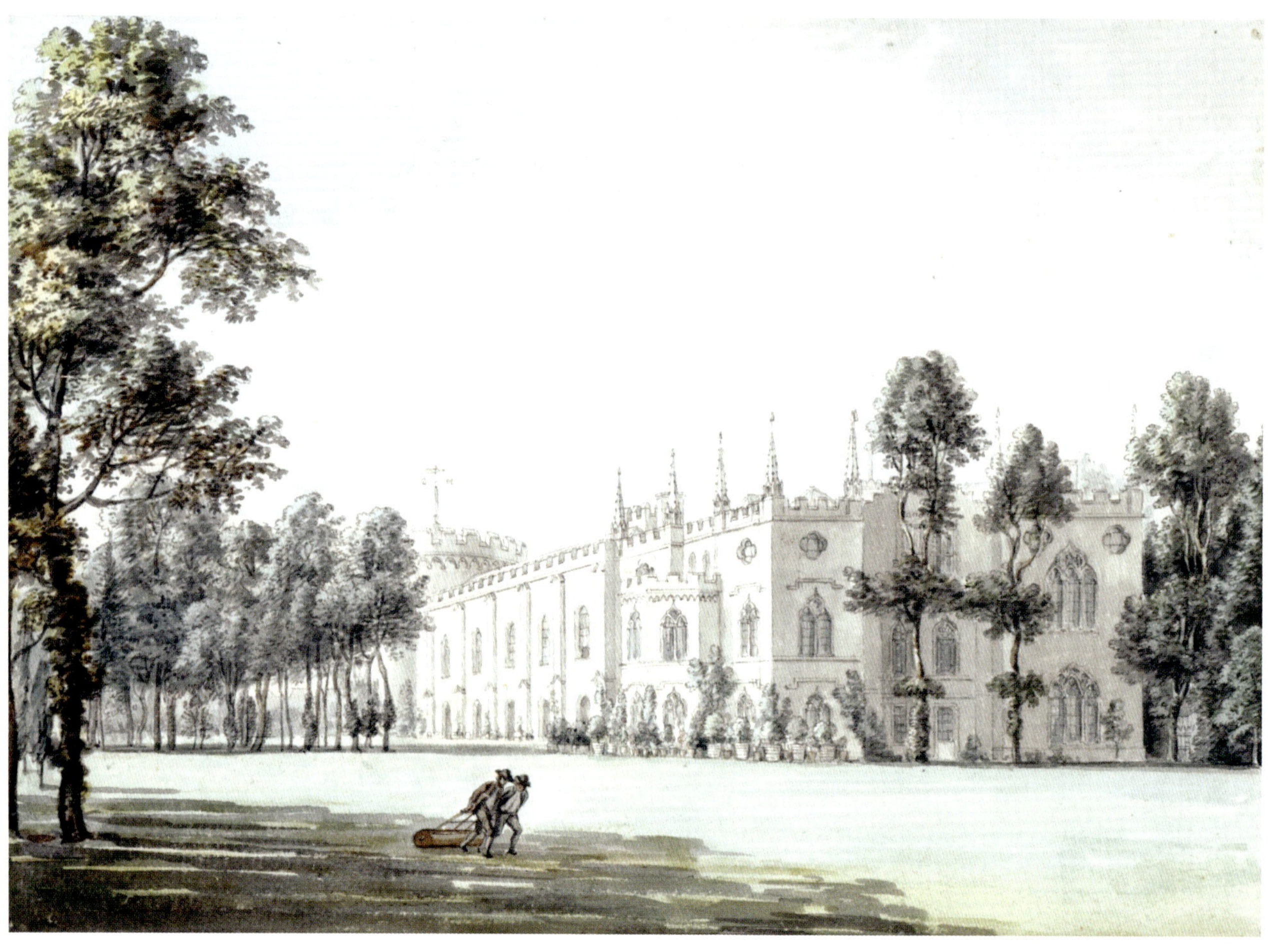

Fig. 17
East Front of Strawberry Hill
Paul Sandby

1769 / watercolour
© The Lewis Walpole Library, Yale University

In 1932, the British war artist, surrealist painter and photographer Paul Nash struggled to reconcile Britain's significant history with the pull of the avant-garde. Like other artists in his circle, he asked: was it possible to 'go modern' and still 'be British'? Unquestionably, this is a question of its time, a product of a decade best characterized by the American poet Ezra Pound's injunction to 'Make it new!' And yet Nash expresses a question that had been articulated in the two previous centuries – a question that preoccupied the minds of Europeans, Britons and Americans who looked to the past for guidance as they grappled with the challenges of modernity.

In the nineteenth century in particular, nations aimed to answer the urgent question 'where are we going?' by considering 'where have we been?' As we have seen in the previous essay, the Victorians were especially fascinated by their medieval past. They fashioned an often nostalgic, idealised vision of the Middle Ages, as a means of criticising the effects of rapid industrialisation, urbanisation, commercialisation and colonisation. Whether their version of history was historically accurate or inaccurate matters little; what is much more significant is that they created truly *modern* forms of creative expression out of their imaginative engagement with the past. These forms came to be described as Gothic.

Perhaps even more difficult to pin down than medievalism, Gothic is a word that may conjure up strong images – castles, cathedrals, catacombs, black cats and blood-sucking counts – but it is almost impossible to delimit. In the words of art critic and thinker John Ruskin, it is as difficult to describe the 'Gothicness' of buildings as to describe 'the Nature of Redness, without any actually red thing to point to, but only orange and purple things', for the 'character' of Gothic 'is made up of many mingled ideas'.[1] Ruskin refers specifically to architecture here, but over the past three centuries, the term Gothic has also been applied to a whole range of creative expression in the fields of art, literature, film, music and fashion; moreover, it has been deployed in political and philosophical debate. In this exploration of some of the important branches of Victorian Gothic, indeterminacy, ambiguity and flexibility are consistent themes, as is its sustained engagement with the past.

Indeed, that architects, artists and writers often spoke about resurrecting the spirit of Gothic – a deeply ambiguous phrase – is telling. Many Gothic revivalists sought to resuscitate religious feeling, reignite an extinguished spirit of community, rekindle a sense of national unity, or restore a sense of beauty to their world. Other 'Goths' had no interest in waxing nostalgic about the past; instead these novelists, poets and painters resurrected a darker side of human history, which was marked by destructive human desires, familial conflicts, secret crimes and other nasty deeds. Often, they did so to challenge the modern emphasis on rationality, economy and progress, which had resulted in the mechanisation of society. Whatever the diverse motives of writers and artists, the Gothic was – and still is – very often about *resurrections*. Just what kind of things were resurrected is the focus of this essay.

A TALE OF TWO RIVALS
Walpole, Beckford and the Origins of Modern Gothic

Gothic literature, art and architecture share an emphasis on the visual. As Martin Myrone has recently pointed out, 'the characteristic ornamental and spatial features' of Gothic buildings pervades the Gothic sister arts, so that 'towering spaces and pointed arches' invariably come to mind when reading novels like *The Monk* or *Dracula*.[2] Indeed, an emphasis on visuality connects all Gothic forms. They have an ekphrastic relationship; that is, one art form represents another, as in the way Gothic horror film uses cathedrals and castles to create atmosphere. In addition, all of these forms engage with each other intertextually; in other words, Gothic poems or paintings take shape through reference to earlier texts and images. The vampire in popular culture, even those found in Stephanie Meyer's recent *Twilight* saga, have roots (whether their creators like it or not) in Bram Stoker's *Dracula*, which in turn has roots in John Polidori's 1819 short story *The Vampyre*, which in turn has connections to Lord Byron's poetry.

The intertextual and visual aspects of Gothic are best illustrated by the endeavours of one of its earliest proponents, the eighteenth-century antiquarian, aesthete and man of letters, Horace Walpole. During the various building stages of his fantastically neo-Gothic villa Strawberry Hill at Twickenham (1749–76), Walpole wrote the first modern Gothic novel, *The Castle of Otranto* (1764). In the ten years before the novel was published, he added battlements, cloisters, Gothic galleries and libraries, and even a 'Holbein Chamber'. He filled the interior with collected objects, arranging them idiosyncratically for the greatest visual impact. The Gothic novelist William Beckford followed in Walpole's footsteps by combining writing with building, but he intended his extravagant showplace, Fonthill, to far surpass what he described as his predecessor's 'miserable child's box – a species of Gothic mousetrap – a reflection of Walpole's littleness.'[3] Also a collector, Beckford had two 100-foot long galleries to house his huge art collection. In a case of life imitating art,

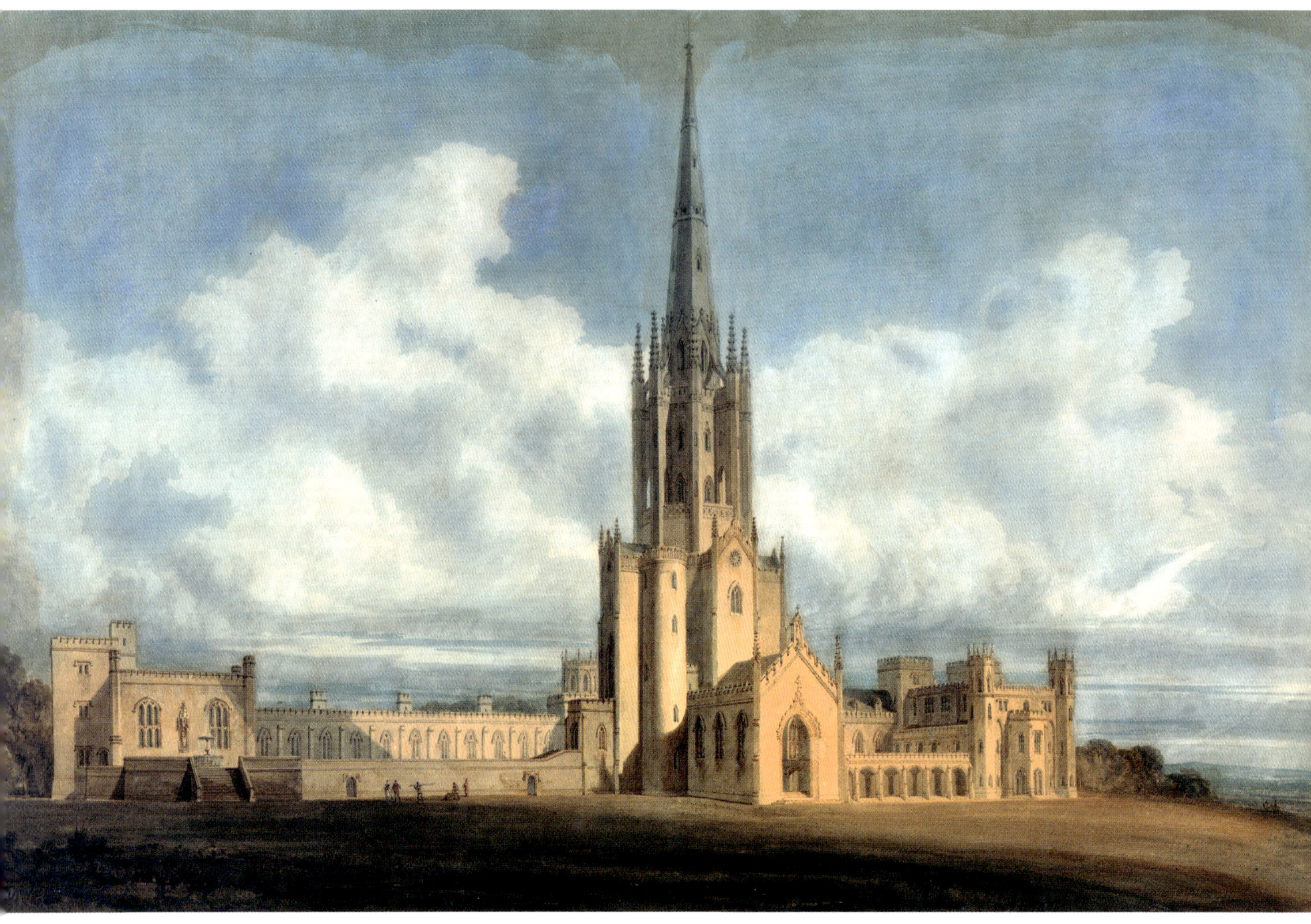

Fig. 18
Projected Design for Fonthill Abbey, Wiltshire
James Wyatt
1798 / watercolour
© Yale Centre for British Art. Paul Mellon Collection

he built a tower resembling the one in his Gothic novel *Vathek*, which was intended to 'penetrate the secrets of heaven'. To do so, he commissioned the noted architect, James Wyatt (also infamous for his careless 'restoration' of Gothic piles), to create an ambitious soaring octagonal steeple that rivalled the cathedrals at Salisbury and York in scale.

Both Walpole and Beckford developed an inventory of spatial *tropes* that have since become recognisable hallmarks of Gothic fiction, from subterranean tunnels to labyrinthine passageways to echoing vaults. These spaces stood in symbolically for a range of social issues and political problems. So, in the courtyard, gallery and underground tunnels of the eponymous castle of Otranto, there occur appalling incidents of incest, death, divorce, murder and mistaken identity — all of which originate in the abusive exercise of patriarchal power. Beckford's *Vathek* engages intertextually with Walpole's novel, and has some of the same themes and *tropes*: abuse of power, lust, ambition, and suppressive familial obligations; however, Vathek is also strongly influenced by decadence, Orientalism and Islamic mythology. As literary critic Nicole Reynolds notes, these Gothic narratives are linked with 'the fate of a house: real and imagined, architectural and ancestral.'[4] By the end of both novels, castles and lives lay in ruins, a material marker of deeply entrenched social problems. In such a way, literature is bound up with architecture ideologically, imaginatively, and materially. Interestingly, as in art, so too in life: in 1823, Beckford sold Fonthill to an unsuspecting owner; within a couple of years, the tower had collapsed. Beckford's blind desire for Fonthill to be constructed as quickly and as extravagantly as possible, and for its spire to reach unsustainable heights, had resulted in its destruction. Less than twenty years later, two successive owners of Walpole's Strawberry Hill stripped it bare and sold off its contents in less than a month, leaving it in ruin.

A TALE OF TWO REVIVALS
Neo-Classicism and the Neo-Gothic

If Gothic is about resurrections, it is also about reactions. Gothic revival came into being in the 1740s, but really took hold in the 1830s and flourished throughout the nineteenth century. As is often the way with cultural movements, it gained its momentum in opposition to something else. Gothic revival defined itself against the earlier classical revival, which looked to the world of the ancient Greeks and Romans for inspiration. In previous decades, the classical revival had itself emerged in opposition to the highly ornamented Baroque and Rococo styles of architecture. Arguably, the centre of the Gothic revival was Britain, where revivalists set about understanding the structures, forms and design elements of the cathedrals, monasteries and palaces of twelfth- to sixteenth-century Europe. These forms were resurrected in newly built ecclesiastical, civic and domestic buildings, which had flying buttresses, pointed arches, jutting towers and spires, steeply sloping roofs, decorative tracery, chimeras and gargoyles.

As soon as we begin to define these styles, exceptions inevitably spring to mind; some buildings, for instance, incorporate both Gothic and classical designs. Yet, if we compare Henry Boneval Latrobe's 1807 designs for the United States White House with the British Houses of Parliament, the exterior of which was designed by Charles Barry in 1836, we can identify distinct aesthetic and philosophical differences (see overleaf). Latrobe's neo-classical building is perfectly symmetrical; if we were to bisect the building we would have equal numbers of windows, columns, and every other feature on each side. Although the Palace of Westminster has a regular structure, reflective of Barry's interest in classical symmetry, its vertical accents (Victoria Tower, Big Ben and the central fleche or spire) make it asymmetrical. Moreover, the details are clearly Gothic: the steep gables, the rows of pointed arcades (series of arches), the highly decorated spandrelles (spaces between the arches), the towers and soaring, open, skeleton-like spires.

In keeping with neo-classical aims, the White House design is serenely composed and reaches after ideal beauty through symmetry and order. As with every aesthetic mode, the classic revival reflected the values of its age; in the picture of the White House, we should be able to intuit an Enlightenment emphasis on rationality, analysis and progress, and detect the political values associated with the civic humanism of the Roman republic. We will see more about the specific political and social values associated with the Gothic in further sections, but from the picture of Westminster we can identify an asymmetry that expresses changefulness, individuality, and liberation from order. The irregular forms and vertical lines reach towards sublimity instead of perfection, and are thus meant to inspire imagination and elicit strong emotion. Horace Walpole thought it

> *difficult for the noblest Grecian temple to convey half so many impressions to the mind, as a cathedral does of the best Gothic taste … One must have taste to be sensible of the beauties of Grecian architecture; one only wants passions to feel Gothic.*[5]

Almost a century later, similar sentiments underpinned John Ruskin's doctrine of the Gothic, as outlined most comprehensively in *The Seven Lamps of Architecture* (1849) and in his essay on the 'Nature of Gothic' from his collection *Stones of Venice* (1851–53). Proclaiming his partiality, Ruskin observed that the Greek craftsman may have been content to calmly carve his 'triglyph' furrows (the regular, vertical channels on top of classical columns), but the Gothic artist's restlessness was reflected in complex and often distorted detail:

> *It is that strange* disquietude *of the Gothic spirit that is its greatness; that restlessness of the dreaming mind, that wanders hither and thither among the niches, and flickers feverishly around the pinnacles, and frets and fades in labyrinthine knots and shadows along wall and roof, and yet is not satisfied, nor shall be satisfied.*[6]

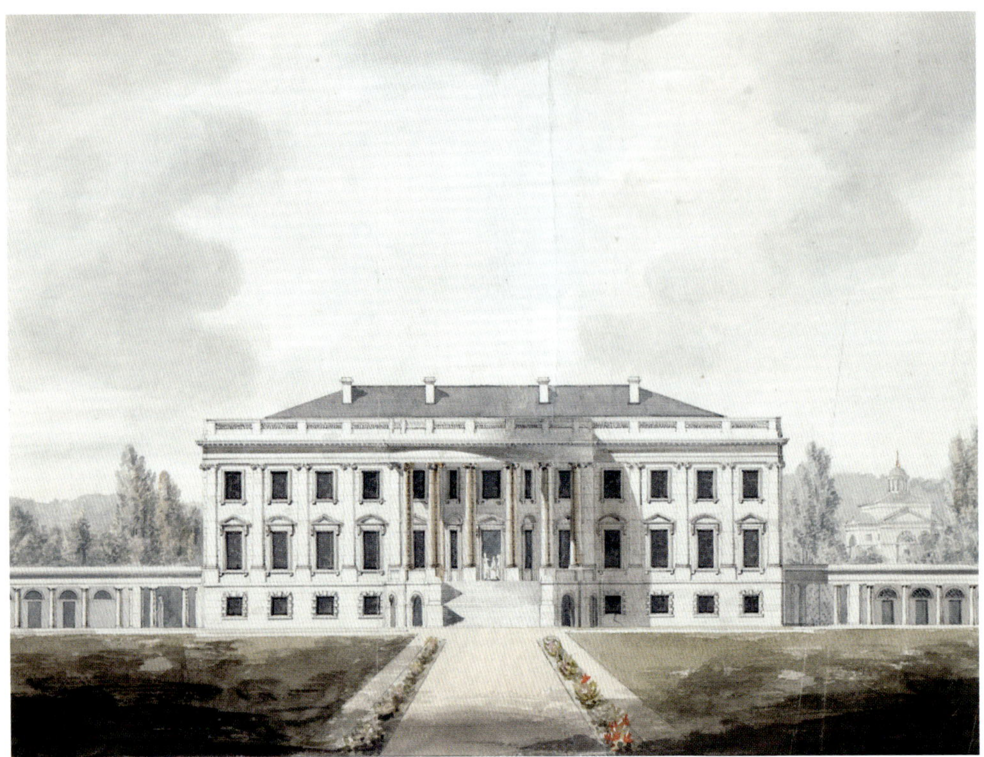

Fig. 19
Study of the White House south façade
Benjamin Henry Latrobe

1817 / watercolour
© Library of Congress, LC-DIG-ppmsca-09502

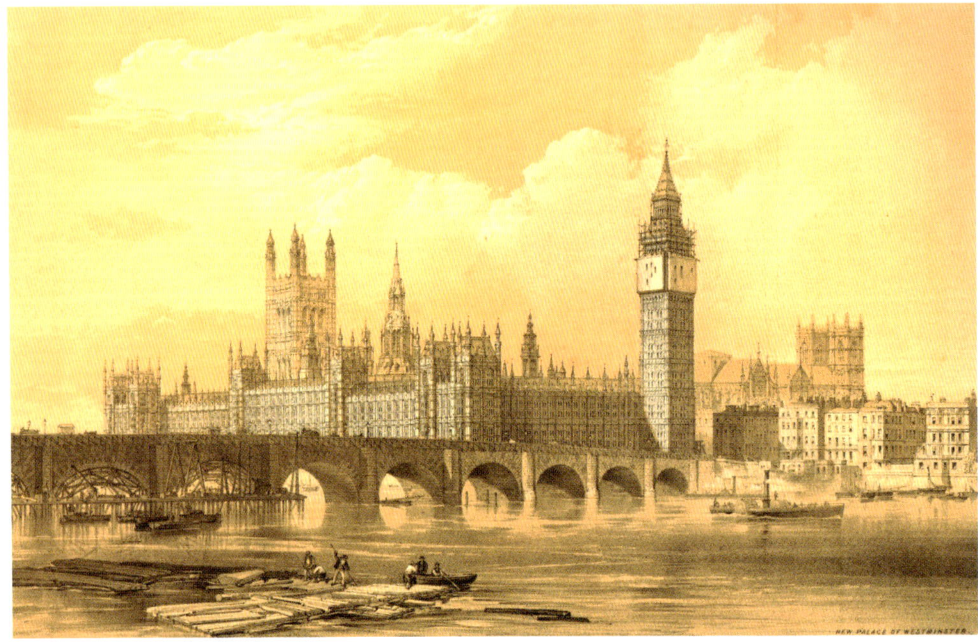

Fig. 20
New Palace of Westminster

1858 / lithograph
© The Trustees of the British Museum

Ruskin's sketches of Venetian buildings (see pp. 46–7), intended to inspire a resurrection of Gothic in England, mirrors in visual terms the literary qualities of this passage. The obscure, unfinished or heavily shadowed areas of his notebook sketches only heighten the sense of mystery and dream. His language – full of niches, feverish flickers, pinnacles, labyrinthine knots and shadows – sounds straight out of poetry by Robert Browning or Charles Baudelaire. Ruskin's description of space reflects states of mind, hidden histories, human feelings, and the wanderings of imaginations and dreams.

Binary opposites can share more than we might expect (or that their respective advocates would be willing to admit!). If Gothic was, amongst other things, a manifestation of a struggle to reconcile modernity and the past, so too was neo-classicism. Both engaged with a widening world, in which goods, knowledge, and styles circulated via exploration and trade routes, as is illustrated by the American emigrant Thomas Cole's 1840 painting, *The Architect's Dream* (see p. 48). In this painting, the Romanesque arch creates a *trompe l'oeil* effect, and the curtains are drawn back, so that we might view this fantastical catalogue – this grand sweep – of architectural history.

In a description reminiscent of the Romantic poet S.T. Coleridge's preface to 'Kubla Khan' – in which he claimed to have dreamed the poem after falling asleep reading a Renaissance travelogue – the American poet William Cullen Bryant described Cole's painting as:

> *an assemblage of structures, Egyptian, Grecian, Gothic, Moorish, such as might present itself to the imagination of one who had fallen asleep after reading a work on the different styles of architecture.*[7]

Cole's 'assemblage' originated in the Grand Tour of Europe, a rite of passage for wealthy young men in search of culture, experience and art treasures. On his two trips (1829–32 and 1841–42) Cole made many architectural sketches, which formed an archive of his contact with the European masters. In the foreground of *The Architects Dream*, a poet/artist/architect reclines on a column, likely modelled on the second-century Roman Column of Trajan. The capitals at the famous Monreale cathedral in Sicily informs the Romanesque arch that frames the image; likewise, we can trace the row of Roman arches to Cole's sketchbook. The colonnaded Greek temple, bathed in light, attests to his love of classical design, whilst the Egyptian pyramid in the distance calls attention to the evolution of architecture and the resurrection, in new forms, of ancient styles.

In the left third of Cole's picture, shrouded in relative darkness, is a Gothic cathedral. Surrounded by a northern European forest, it is reminiscent of Caspar David Friedrich's (1774–1840) paintings of Gothic ruins set in darkly romantic German forests. It is also cast in the model of Salisbury Cathedral, with its famous spire, the largest in England, thrusting skyward, reaching the highest point in the painting. Although he was a proponent of neoclassicism, Cole's admiration for Gothic is very much in line with Ruskin's. In his 'Letter to the Publick on the Subject of Architecture' (written in the late 1830s), Cole views Grecian temples as examples of 'unsurpassed beauty.' Yet Gothic 'aspires to *something beyond [the] finite perfection*' of classical architecture:

> *Partaking of the Genius of Christianity it opens a world beyond the visible in which we dwell ... All is lofty, aspiring and mysterious. Its towers and pinnacles climb toward the clouds like airy fabricks. Ever hovering on the verge of the impossible, on it the mind does not dwell ... but takes wing & soars into an imaginary world. The longings, the imaginings, the lofty aspirations of Christianity have found expression in stone* [my emphases].

As with Ruskin's writing, the language here is reminiscent of Gothic literature; in this case romantic novels and poems that turn away from Enlightenment rationality toward the invisible and the unknowable. The mysterious deeds and secret longings of S.T. Coleridge's enigmatic Ancient Mariner, Byron's tortured Manfred or John Keats's mysteriously seductive Belle Dame – half human, half spirit – are called to mind. The same expressions that were written on the stones of Gothic buildings were inscribed on the pages of Gothic romance.

RESURRECTIONS
Religion, Politics and Architecture

Cole's identification of 'the Genius of Christianity' as the beginning of Gothic greatness, reminds us of the importance of religion to the history of architecture. The classical/Gothic divide was also drawn on religious and ideological lines. In an oft-quoted 1859 statement, Lord Acton defined the classical and the Gothic as 'two great principles that divide the world,' and he insisted that all 'political as well as religious questions' could be reduced to that 'great dualism.'[8] More recently, J. Mourdant Crook has reiterated this seeming overstatement on slightly different terms: he likewise identifies 'a geological fissure' running 'through the whole of nineteenth century thought';

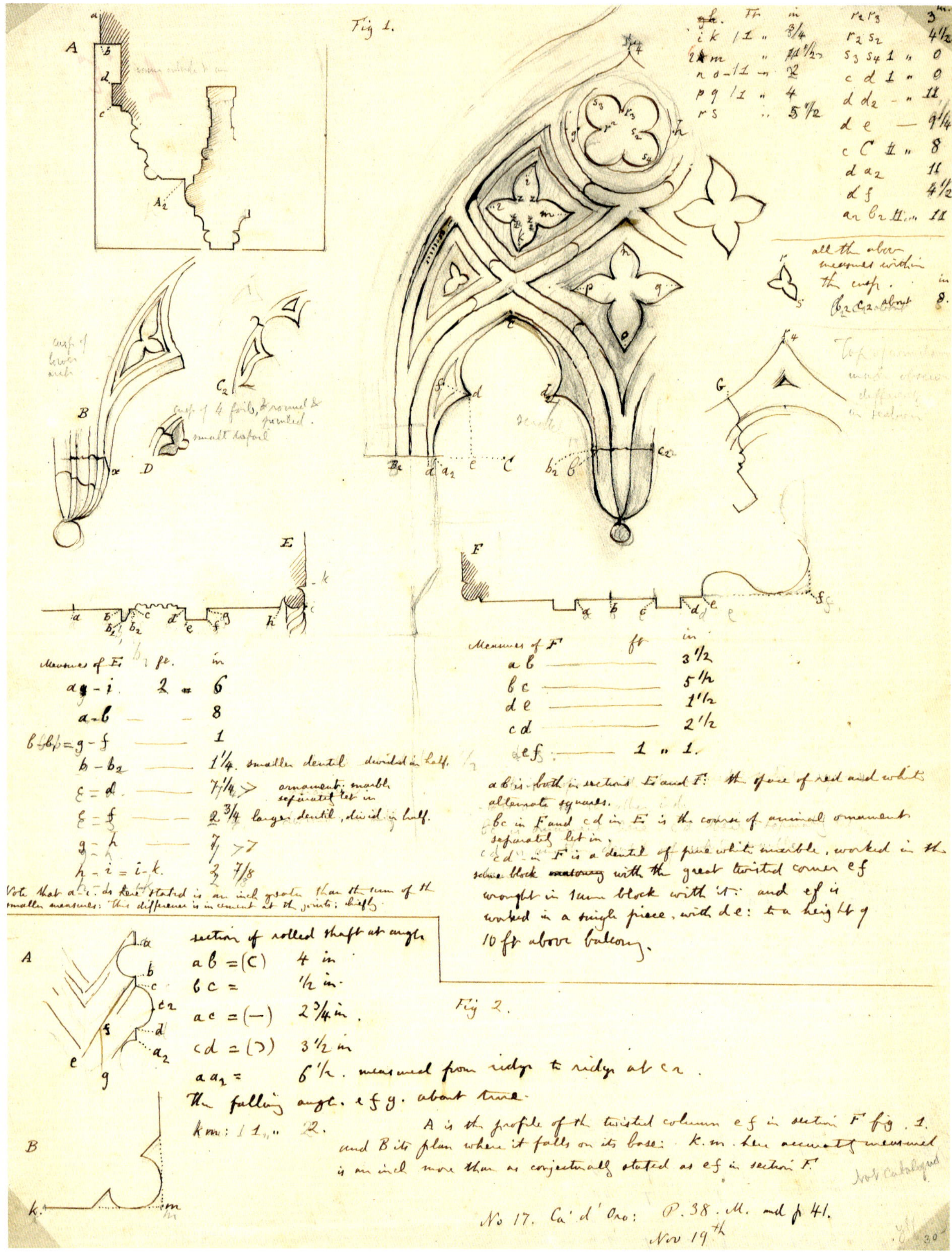

Fig. 21 / Cat. 30

Venice worksheet No 17: Notes on the Casa d'Oro 19 Nov. 1849

John Ruskin

1849 / pen over pencil

however he labels one side 'Fluent Benthamites' and the other, 'muddled Coleridgeans.'[9] His Benthamite camp is headed, as one might guess, by the utilitarian philosophers Jeremy Bentham, and James and John Stuart Mill. Its members include pragmatic politicians, writers, and theologians who tended to promote an individualistic and libertarian society. They preferred to deal in the material and the concrete, and thus inclined toward the uncluttered and modern-looking lines of the neo-classical. Ranged against them were the romantics who, like Coleridge, were visionaries, utopians and idealists. Sometimes they were paternalistic Tories and other times they were socialists whose design allegiances leaned towards the Gothic.

Politics affected the fortunes of Gothic architecture in strikingly material ways. When in 1843 Eugene-Emmanuel Viollet-le-Duc and Jean-Baptiste Lassus began to restore Paris's Notre-Dame Cathedral, they had to address the effects of a tumultuous political history. In 1771 the sculptures over the cathedral's central doorway, of figures rising from their graves, had been removed in order to allow entrance for the royal canopy. Twenty years later, during the radically anti-religious phase of the French Revolution, the cathedral was transformed from a place of worship to a temple of reason, as befitted the new secular republic. Features deemed to signify religious irrationality or social inequality were stripped out, including 28 monumental statues from the gallery of kings.

Britain may not have had a revolution, but it was deeply affected by events in France and the rise of working-class radicalism at home, and this at least partially determined architectural questions. When the fire of 16 October 1834 effectively destroyed the Houses of Parliament, people assumed the buildings would be reconstructed according to classical principles. After all, recent work – John Soane's additions to the old Westminster Palace and the construction of the New Royal Gallery – had been in that style. Moreover, the newly rebuilt and extended White House had received accolades for its classically Vitruvian and Palladian design. True to its form, the American President's official residence expressed rationality, fraternity, democracy, and secularism. For the British, these qualities were too closely associated with the republican ideals of the French revolutionaries – not a good thing for a constitutional monarchy anxious to inspire patriotism and loyalty! As a result, in June 1835, the Royal Commission for the rebuilding of the Palace announced in the House of Lords that 'the style of the buildings should be either Gothic or Elizabethan'.

In fact, the most influential early advocate of Gothic revival, the architect, antiquary and critic A.W.N. Pugin

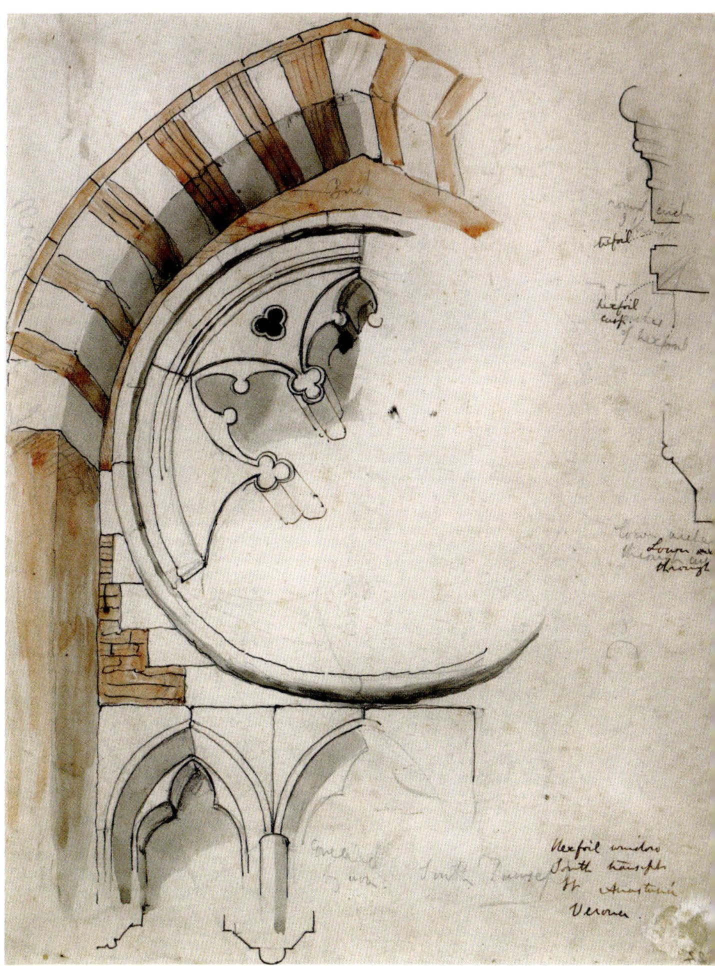

Fig. 22 / Cat. 22
Worksheet: window at Sant' Anastasia, Verona
John Ruskin

probably 1851–52 / pencil, black ink, ink wash and watercolour
© Ruskin Foundation (Ruskin Library, Lancaster University)

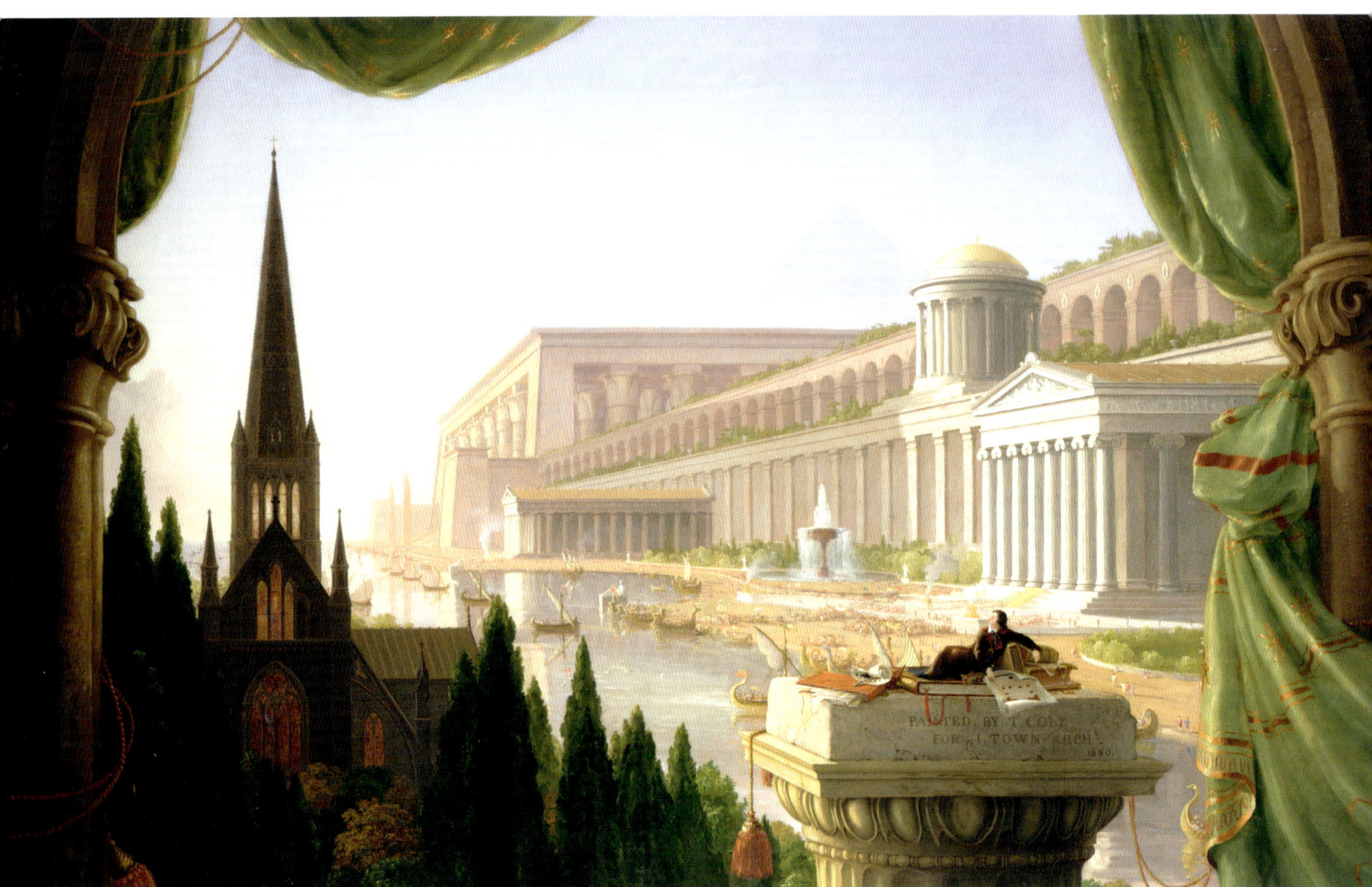

Fig. 23
The Architect's Dream
Thomas Cole

1840 / oil on canvas
© Toledo Museum of Art (Toledo, Ohio);
purchased with funds from the Florence Scott Libbey Bequest
in memory of her father, Maurice A. Scott: 1949.162.

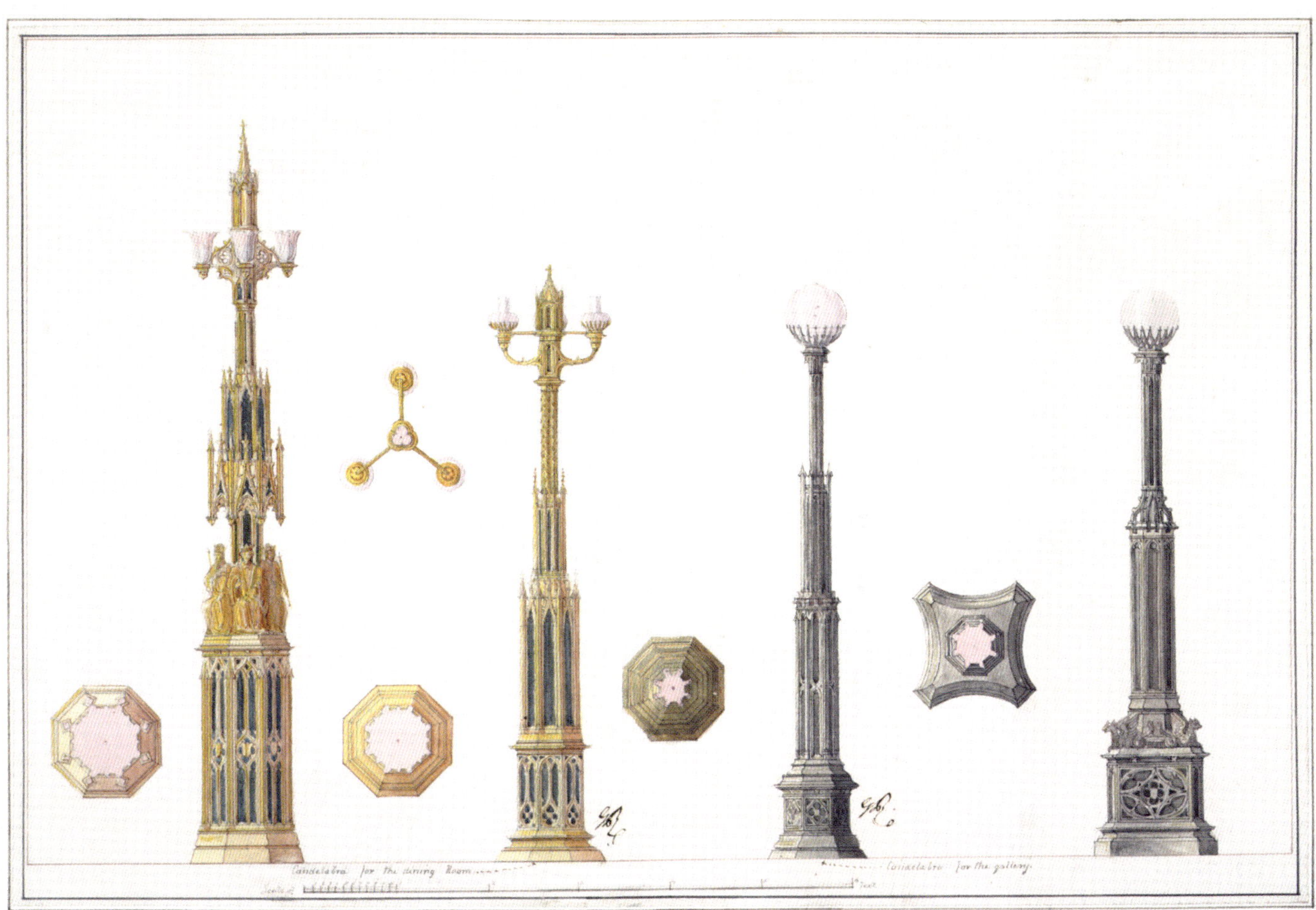

Fig. 24 / Cat. 8
Design for furniture and fittings in the Apartments of George IV
Augustus W.N. Pugin

1827 / pencil, pen, ink and watercolour on paper
© Victoria and Albert Museum, London

Fig. 25 / Cat. 14
Chalice
Augustus W.N. Pugin and John Hardman & Co.
1849–50 / silver and silver-gilt
© Victoria and Albert Museum, London

was thrilled to watch John Soane's neo-classical designs go up in flames, leaving the Gothic Westminster Hall standing triumphant. This 'glorious sight' he called a 'miraculous' sign from God.'[10] In his hugely influential design treatise *Contrasts* (1836) – often identified as the catalyst of nineteenth-century Gothic revivalism – Pugin minces no words: 'Everything glorious about the English churches is Catholic, everything debased and hideous, Protestant.'[11] Britain's Catholic progenitors of the thirteenth- and fourteenth-centuries had taken the nation 'from pagan obscurity' to cultivated greatness, and their architecture reflected that. It was 'the faith, the zeal, and above all, the unity of our ancestors,' Pugin wrote, 'that enabled them to conceive and raise those wonderful fabrics that still remain to excite our wonder and admiration'.[12] Ancient Britons developed a collective, harmonious society because they shared one God, one faith and one nation.

However, modern Britons lived with the legacy of a Reformation that had abolished their rites and destroyed their architecture, and so they lived in a radically different world. Nineteenth-century buildings were 'meagre and poor in the extreme' and society was divided by sectarianism, greed, disparity, and the ethos of individualism.'[13] No wonder modern Britons were attracted to classical design, Pugin snapped, for it was foreign and pagan and artificial.

Pugin's impassioned polemic underscores how profoundly the Gothic revival could be embroiled in debates over beliefs, principles, and politics. One particularly vexing question was how to reconcile modern individualism with the wider circles of community. Some of the favourite words of Gothic revivalists – unity, kinship, spirit, imagination, and liberty – reveal the tensions between individual desires (imagination, liberty) and the larger social group (unity, kinship). Gothic revivalists weighed the difference between, on the one hand, freedom from constraint and on the other hand, freedom from care. 'Fluent Benthamites' emphasized the exercise of free will, but the romantic Tories – the Coleridgeans – advocated a freedom that came from a class-based but interdependent society, in which workers laboured for landowners who, in turn, were duty bound to benevolently care for and defend their workers and dependents.

This was a feudal idea of liberty, and it underpinned

the Tory humanism of the influential Young England Movement of the 1830s and 40s. This group of politically-minded, pedigreed Eton and Oxbridge-educated men included the politician George Smythe, 7th Viscount Strangford, and the poet and statesman Lord John Manners, 7th Duke of Rutland. Their leader, neither aristocratic nor educated at Oxford or Cambridge, was the novelist, politician and eventual Prime Minister Isaac Disraeli. The Young England group sought a paternalistic society with a strong monarchy supported by philanthropic aristocrats and a unified national church. These socially conscious conservatives campaigned against rampant individualism, the alienating effect of urban industrialisation, and the perceived cold rationality of the Benthamite liberals. Although they never achieved a popular base of support, the Young England Tories held seats in government, influenced legislative decisions and shaped the tenor of political debate.

The religious counterpart to the Young England Movement was the Oxford (or Tractarian) Movement, headed by John Henry Newman. They argued that the Anglican Church was a branch of the One, Holy, Catholic and Apostolic Church. As the Gothic revival in the sphere of aesthetics reacted against classicism, the Oxford Movement reacted against liberalism, secularism and non-conformism in religion; it revolted against what was seen as the dry rationalism and emotionless restraint of a church infected by Enlightenment. Religious emotion was re-inspired through the beauty of medieval liturgy and the splendour of Gothic parish churches, many of which were restored and conserved by another branch of this Anglo-Catholic revival, the Cambridge Camden Society. There has sometimes been a tendency to categorise Gothic revivalists as Anglo-Catholic conservatives who were nostalgic and reactionary, and indeed some were. But it is worth repeating that the religious and political views of Gothic revivalists were – like their architecture – varied and often conflicted. So for instance, the medievalist polemicist and conservative Thomas Carlyle was schooled in Calvinism, but rejected religious orthodoxy, while the designer, poet and artist William Morris was a socialist and self-confessed atheist. As the Victorian architect Robert Kerr said of the most well-known of his architect contemporaries: 'Butterfield was High Church, Scott was Low Church, and Burges no church

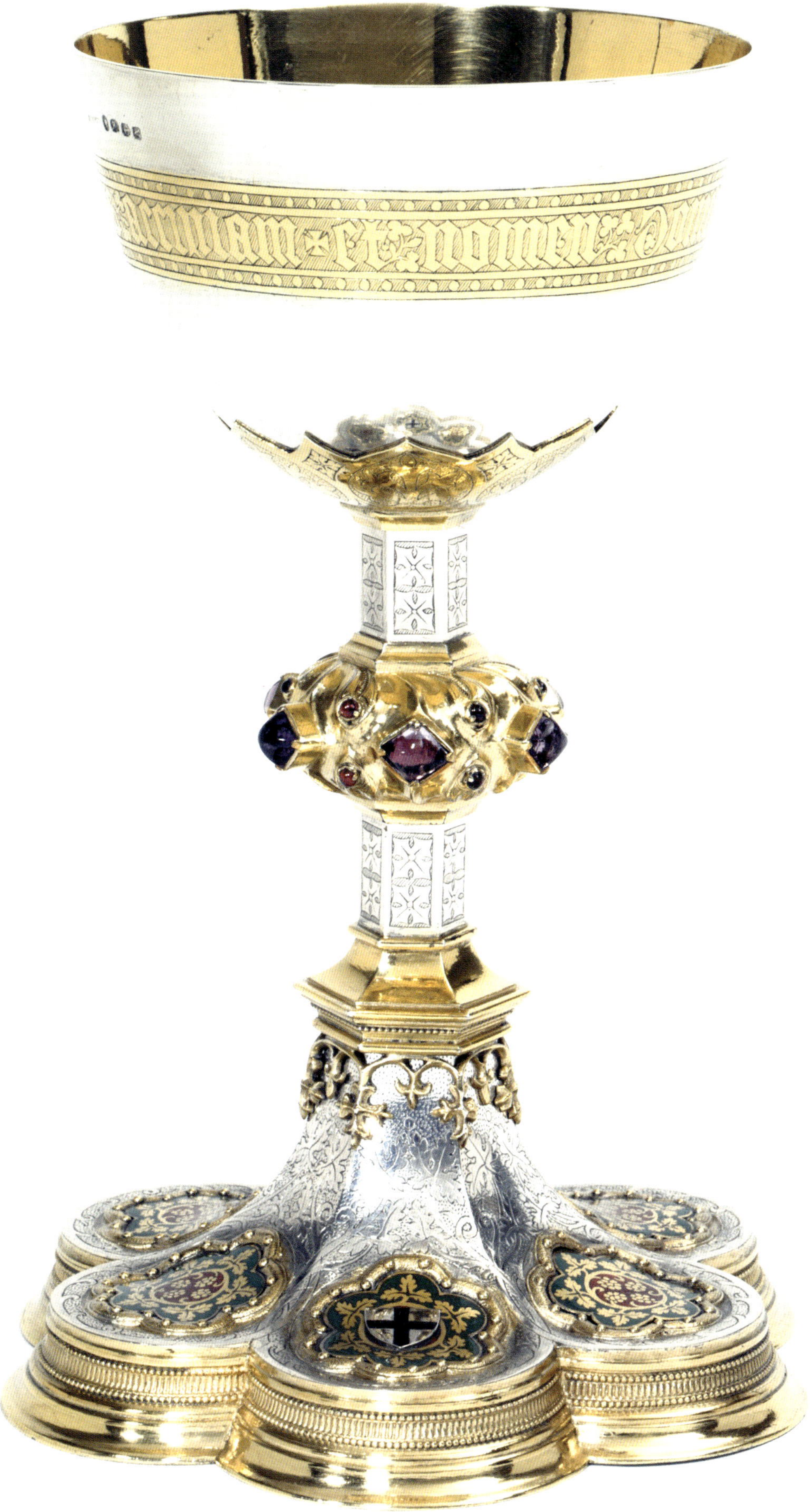

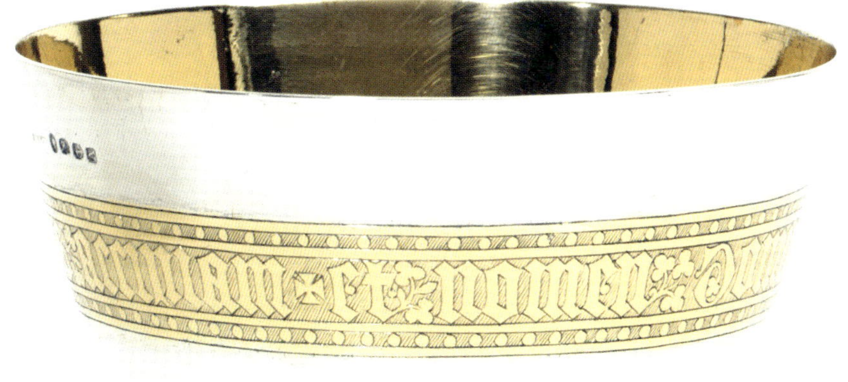

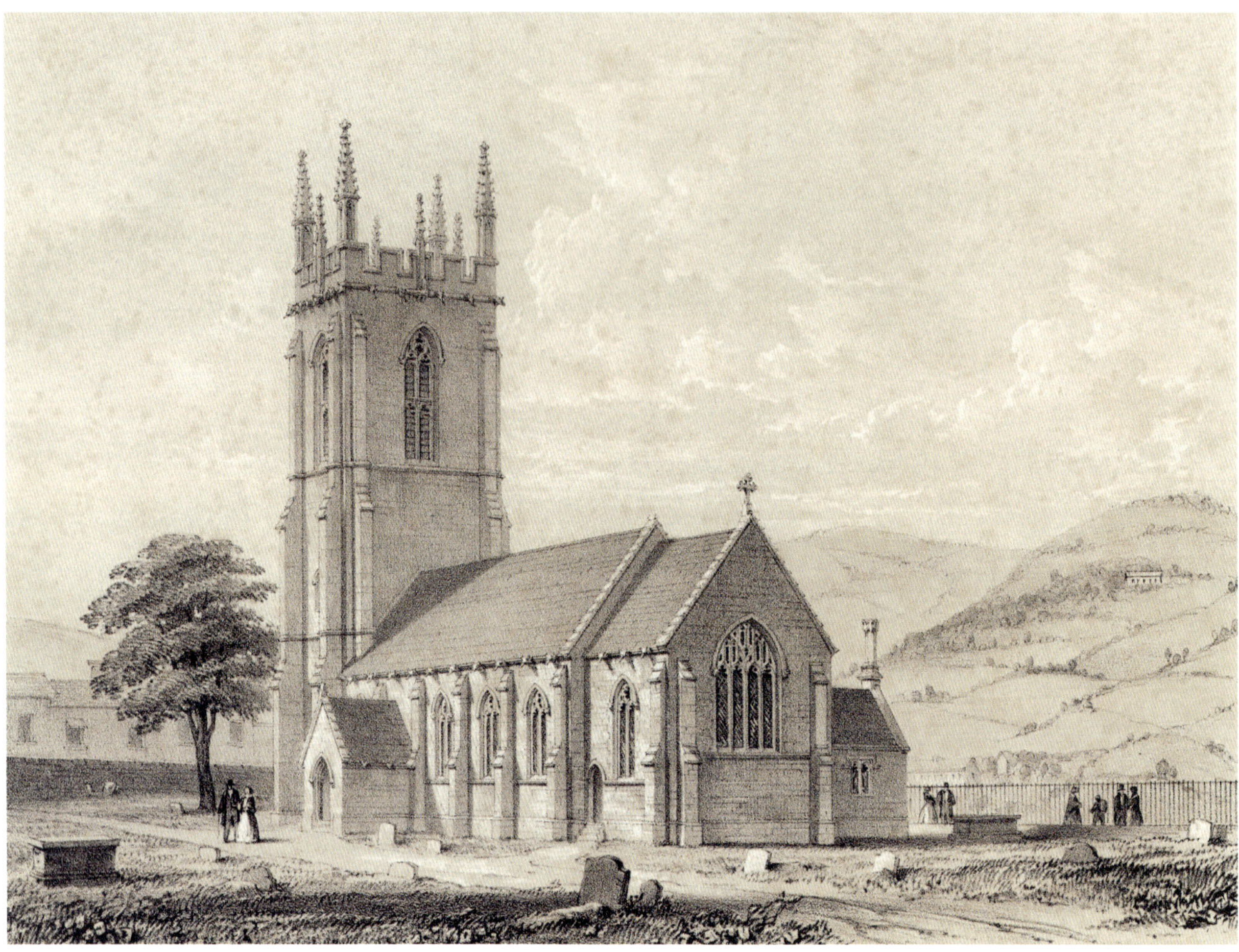

Fig. 26 / Cat. 51
Allhallows on the Walls, Exeter
R.K. Thomas (engraver)

*c.*1850 / lithograph on paper / a church by the architect John Hayward,
who built his reputation on commissions for churches in the South West
in the 1850s and 1860s
© Royal Albert Memorial Museum & Art Gallery, Exeter City Council

at all'.[14] William Butterfield, Sir George Gilbert Scott and William Burges were all advocates of the High Victorian Gothic style, and all inspired powerfully by Ruskin, yet on matters of religion and politics, like other Gothic revivalists, they were divided.

Case Study
VICTORIAN SOCIAL QUESTIONS
AND PUGIN'S *CONTRASTS*

Pugin may not have formulated a comprehensive social or political programme, nor did he expand on social issues anywhere near as extensively as Thomas Carlyle, John Ruskin or William Morris. Yet, in some of the illustrative plates of *Contrasts*, Pugin presented what might be called ideological landscapes. In the first of these, which represents two images of the same town, one in 1440 and one in 1840, he targets modern utilitarian design and the principles that support it, including liberalism, individualism and laissez-faire economics. In the upper image, Pugin portrays the imaginatively recreated fifteenth-

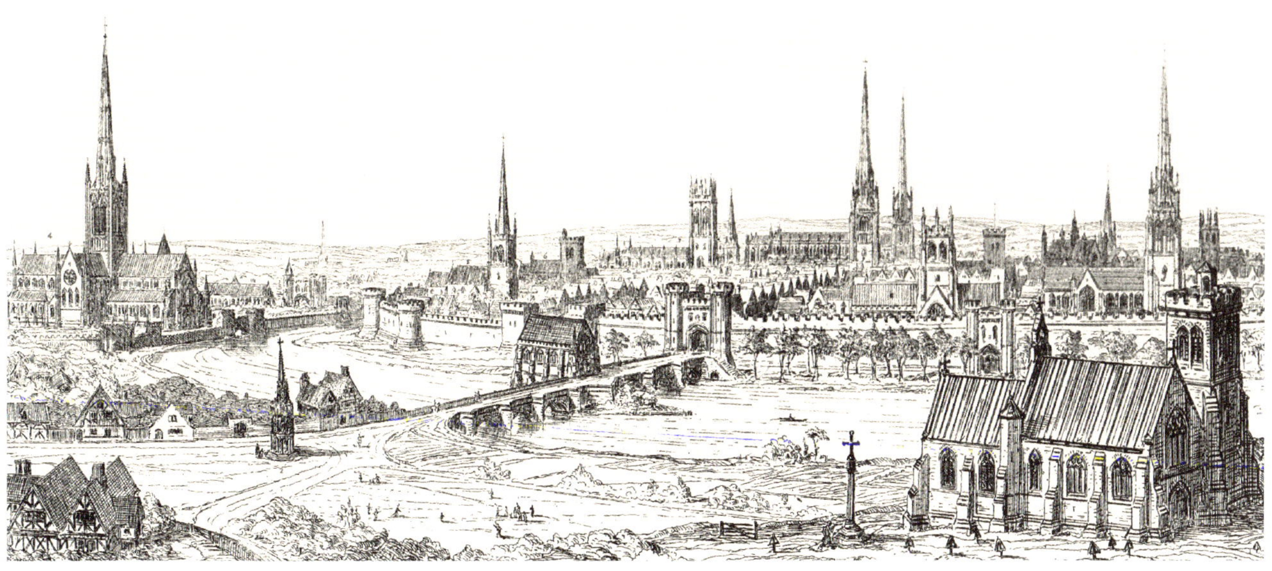

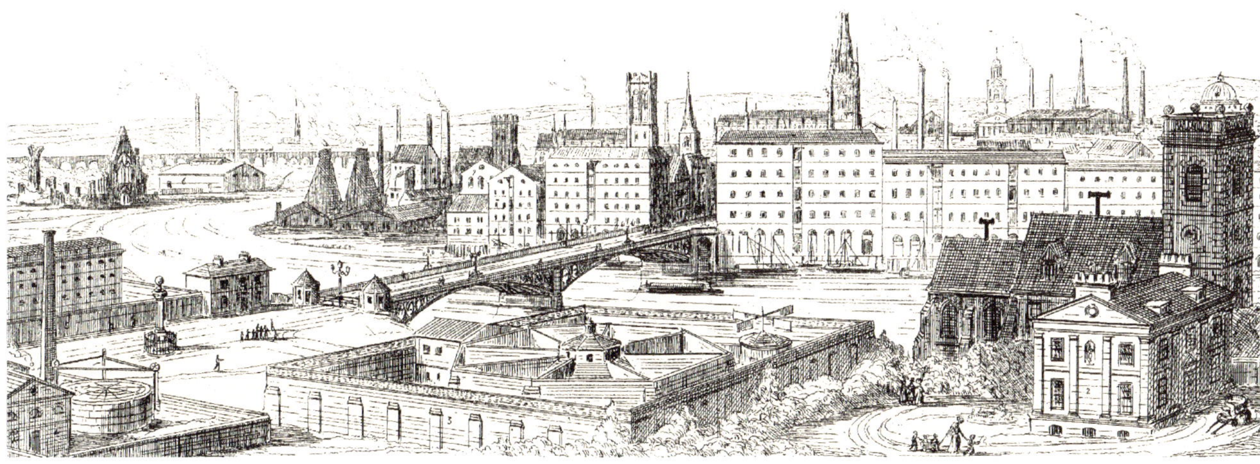

Fig. 27 / Cat. 10

A Catholic Town in 1440 [top]
A Catholic Town in 1840
Augustus W.N. Pugin

1836 / from Contrasts
© RIBA Library Photographs Collection

century Catholic town, with its abbeys, chapels, cathedrals and guildhalls, and in the lower, the contrasting modern version, in which inhabitants live in a capitalist world blighted by the spread of urban manufacture and the desire for profit. Smoke-belching iron works squat on the ruins of what was once the Abbey, surrounded by indistinct and undifferentiated modern buildings. People disperse into new boxy, unadorned chapels, each representing a different denomination, from Baptist to Unitarian, from Wesleyan to Quaker – or leaving God out, they congregate in the Socialist Hall of Science. Modern architecture represents the paradoxical nature of modernity: the homogeneous fronts of buildings signify equality and tolerance, but behind them lurks a deeply divided society.

Most problematically, and taking centre stage, is the New Jail of 1840, a perfectly symmetrical building modelled on the philosopher Jeremy Bentham's (in)famous

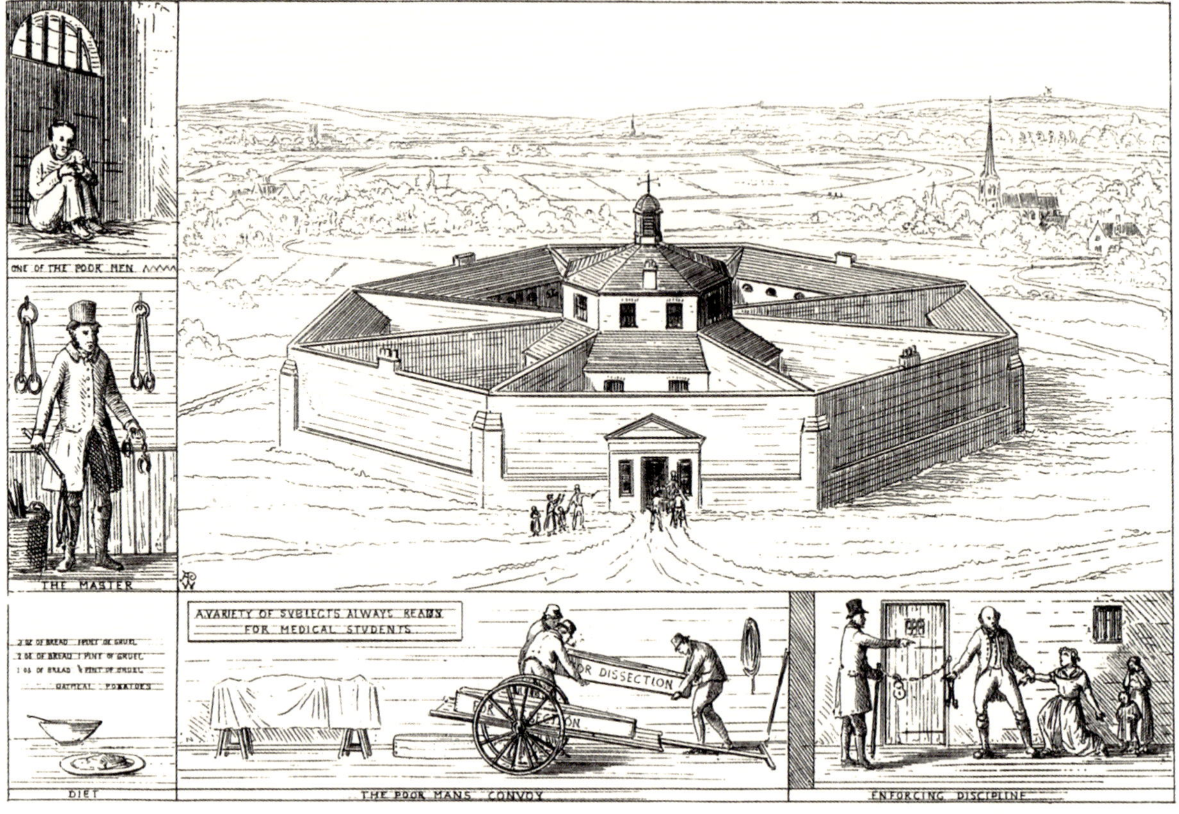

CONTRASTED RESIDENCES FOR THE POOR

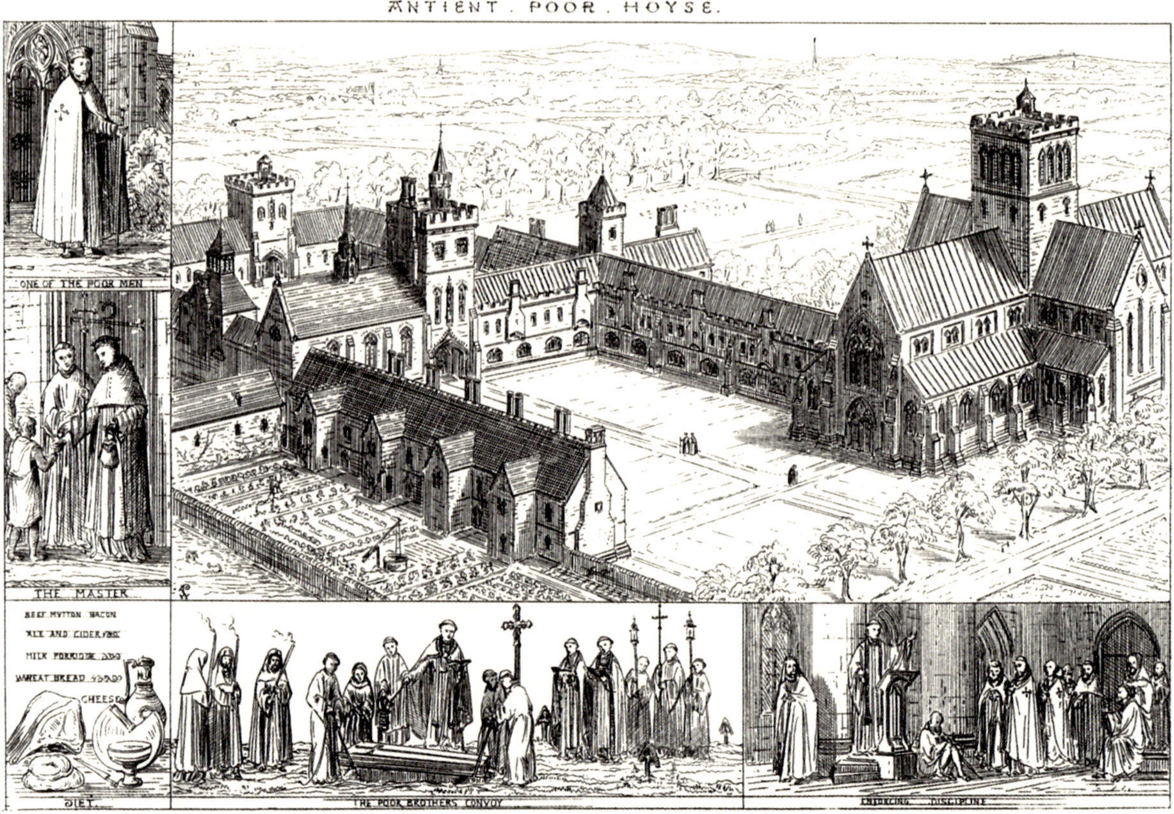

Fig. 28 / Cat. 10
Contrasted Residences of the Poor
Augustus W.N. Pugin
1836 / from *Contrasts*
© RIBA Library Photographs Collection

utilitarian architectural design, the Panopticon. In his letters on the *Panopticon; or the Inspection-House*, Bentham details the design's most identifiable features – the high central tower and the surrounding fan of peripheral cells, each of which holds an inmate. The French theorist Michel Foucault has described these cells as 'so many small theatres in which each actor is alone, perfectly individualized and constantly visible'.[15] What makes this an efficient, adaptable, and reforming design is the play of visibility. The central tower can house an authority figure or it can stand empty; it matters little, for inmates will assume they are being watched. Feeling eyes upon them, they will monitor and discipline themselves. This is an egalitarian design, for Bentham's architectural template would serve as well for prisons as factories, workhouses, poorhouses, asylums, hospitals and schools or any institution where individuals were to be kept under inspection. The design was as adaptable for 'punishing the incorrigible, guarding the insane, reforming the vicious' as it was for 'curing the sick'.[16] This is also a profoundly individualistic design, for there is little possibility of collective behaviour. Inmates are unable to communicate with one another or the outside world, for the modern design ensures that they (whether criminal, sick or poor) would be out of sight and out of mind.

In a second plate, *Contrasted Residences for the Poor*, Pugin links the modern panopticon more explicitly with social issues. The series of thumbnail illustrations bordering the two larger images reveal how a lack of compassion is easily disguised by an appeal to rationality, productivity or utility. In seclusion and authorised by authorities operating under the dictates of progress and utility, sadomasochistic disciplinarians victimise the vulnerable. The living bodies of the poor are machines of labour; the dead bodies of the poor become 'material for dissection'. This image is part of a public outcry against the illegal trade in corpses, between 'resurrectionists' who snatched them from their graves and anatomists who purchased them for dissection. It is also a reaction against the 1832 Anatomy Act. This act, largely supported by Benthamite liberal MPs and physicians, provided medical practitioners with the unclaimed bodies of the poor who died in workhouses, hospitals, or jails. Pugin targets both an economic materialism that put profit before humanity and a medical materialism that, in his view, reduced the human to a sum

of his or her parts. In this, Pugin was of the same cast of mind as the Pre-Raphaelite painter Edward Burne-Jones, who stated: 'The more materialistic science becomes, the more angels shall I paint.'[17]

REAPPEARANCES
Politics, Architecture and Gothic Literature

The issues and images raised in Pugin's plates inform a century of Gothic writing. Jails, poorhouses, sadomasochistic taskmasters and anatomists all appeared consistently in Victorian Gothic novels and short stories. They are architectural spaces in which Gothic heroes and heroines must face their fears and triumph over them or be crushed by them. Literary magazines, including *The New Monthly*, *Blackwood's* and *Fraser's* published Gothic tales and serialised novels that exploited the public fascination with real life crimes like those committed by William Burke and William Hare. In 1828, these two Edinburgh men worked as resurrectionists, but soon realized they could better meet anatomists's demands for fresh bodies. They lured vulnerable, poor people to their boarding house, plied them with alcohol, and suffocated them. In total, they delivered 16 fresh corpses to the well-known Edinburgh anatomist Robert Knox. This historical event provides a backdrop to popular tales in the 1830s, such as those published by the barrister, one-time MP and 'Master in Lunacy' Samuel Warren, whose series *Passages from the Diary of a Late Physician* raised contemporary political and ethical questions about the benefits of scientific experimentation and the value of human life. Similarly, in an introductory headnote to one 1831 anonymous Burke-and-Hare tale, the Gothic writer Edward Bulwer explained that he hoped these stories might 'swell the general desire for immediate reform in a system which most urgently and fearfully demands it'.[18] The system he referred to was the resurrection of bodies for anatomists, and the reform he sought, which came later that year, was the Anatomy Act.

As Elizabeth McCarthy rightly notes, the visually descriptive quality of Gothic literature stems from its interest in 'the unseen, the unimaginable'.[19] The practice of resurrection is one of these unseen acts; other skeletons in the closet are more overtly political in nature. The

French Revolution had made it seem as if peaceable men and women could change into monsters overnight. To observers of the Reign of Terror of 1793–94, which sent shocking numbers of citizens to the guillotine, it seemed as if republicans, who had once been motivated by high political ideals, had become cannibals. These fearful observations gave rise to Gothic narratives in which crazed mobs operated outside the bounds of reason. The scene of mob violence in Matthew Lewis's novel *The Monk* (1796) is a particularly salutary representation of revolutionary fervor. In one scene, otherwise peaceable citizens – men and women – suddenly turn on unarmed nuns in a Catholic convent and slay them in a merciless frenzy.

As the nineteenth century progressed, the mob took on a rather more modern and democratic visage. Tyranny could be exercised by a democratic majority – an issue addressed by one of the leaders of the 'Fluent Benthamites,' John Stuart Mill. In *On Liberty* he argued that in the past, kings, priests and land-owning aristocrats wielded arbitrary power over their subjects, but in the modern democratic world, it was the people who wielded influence through public opinion.[20] The fear was that the people could become so powerful and tyrannous that they would silence dissenting voices. In this light, the medieval Spanish Catholic mob in *The Monk* appears uncomfortably like modern citizens who, much closer to home, were limited by their own ignorance and unrestrained by feelings of human sympathy. If the moral structures, and the social, political and religious institutions that had developed over time were suddenly toppled, what then?

READING STONES, READING TEXTS, READING BODIES

Pugin's abhorrence of the use of the body for scientific experimentation, Burne-Jones's desire to paint angels, Ruskin's emphasis on spirit and imagination, and the Oxford Movement's emphasis on the divine may seem to indicate a rejection of the body in favour of the spiritual and the metaphysical. Indeed, the conventional narrative in the Gothic versus classical debate has it that the Greeks viewed the human body as an expression of the soul, and so it followed then that their architecture reflected this materialist view. This was why, for instance, the Doric order was aligned with the male body and the Corinthian with the female. On the flip side, this narrative suggests that medieval architects and artists (like mystics and monks) denied the body to raise the separate and privileged soul. In many ways this is something of a false division. For one thing, many Gothic and neo-Gothic buildings are decorated with the carnivalesque bodies of animal-human gargoyles. Over the centuries, architectural observers have noted that basilicas were laid out in the form of the body, and others have identified anatomical imagery in the ribbed vaults of cathedrals, which mimic the spinal cord and ribs. Stained glass has been compared to the translucent skin of the human body or parchment paper. Robert Marichal identifies striking similarities between Gothic architecture and the evolution of Gothic handwriting in eleventh-century medieval manuscript. Writing took on a physical shape that resembled 'the intersection of the ribs of a vault' or the footing of the groined vault' of cathedrals.[21] Breaks in Gothic letters appeared simultaneously with similar breaks in stone.

These are intriguing analogies, which reveal how features of Gothic buildings acted as symbolic bridges between the materiality of everyday experience and the spiritual or unseen world. The medieval world did not have the same boundaries between the real and imaginary, or the material and the metaphysical as developed in the post-Enlightenment world. The idea of architecture as a text was vitally important to Gothic revivalists. In his 1832 novel *Notre Dame de Paris*, Victor Hugo includes an essay in which architecture is described as our most longstanding system of writing. A Gothic cathedral recorded human ideas and emotions in 'a universal form of writing': it was a 'book of granite' that begins in the Orient, and evolves through Hindu, Egyptian, Greek, Romanesque and Medieval styles.[22] Using similar terms, but advocating the idea of a European Catholic tradition distinct from foreign styles, Pugin describes Britain's glorious ancient religious history as 'written on the wall, on the window, on the pavement, by the highway'.[23] In *The Nature of Gothic* (1853) (see pp. 58–59), John Ruskin sets out a method for judging buildings, which is 'conducted precisely on the same principles as that of a book.' If a building's sculpture or carvings are 'legible' then they are 'worth reading', but interpreting meaning depends 'on knowledge, feeling, and not a little on the industry and perseverance of the reader'.[24] So we are to turn the same critical, analytical eye toward buildings as we would the poetry of Coleridge, Tennyson or Browning.

The art historian Barbara Stafford reminds us that visualisation was absolutely 'central to the processes of enlightening'.[25] This emphasis on visuality is also apparent in the development of eighteenth- and nineteenth-century science. Physiognomy – the reading of character by the face – and phrenology, the method of reading personality and intelligence via the shape and size of the skull, are two of the most obvious examples. These sciences aimed to reveal truths about the self by reading the external body. In the Victorian era, evolutionary theory, degeneration theory and the emergence of the science of criminology, as well as the development of microscopes, cameras, and all kinds of optical instruments, placed even greater emphasis on sight as the way of knowing the otherwise obscure. In light of these aims, it is perhaps not surprising that Gothic literature – which is also tremendously concerned with the relationship between the body and soul or mind – engages intertextually with scientific writing.

Indeed, Gothic characters often employ the 'visual sciences' and technological tools to make sense of their worlds. In Stoker's *Dracula*, for instance, Jonathan Harker observes Count Dracula's 'very marked physiognomy' and describes how:

His face was a strong – a very strong – aquiline, with high bridge of the thin nose and peculiarly arched nostrils; with lofty domed forehead, and hair growing scantily round the temples but profusely elsewhere. His eyebrows were very massive ... The mouth ... was fixed and rather cruel-looking, with peculiarly sharp white teeth; these protruded over the lips, whose remarkable ruddiness showed astonishing vitality in a man of his years.[26]

According to physiognomical principles, we understand that the lofty forehead denotes intelligence and the aquiline nose signals determination and power. This description is also informed by evolutionary ideas and degeneration theory, for the hairy face and sharp teeth denote an animal-like cunning. Thus, the Count is a throwback to an earlier time – an atavistic creature who displays characteristics that have been bred out of civilised people – yet, he is also a modern-day aristocratic degenerate who is ruled by selfish desires to consume. Above all, then, Count Dracula unsettles categories: he is both man and animal; civilised and uncivilised; European and foreign; of this world and of a mysterious other.

REFORMING SPACE
Healthy Homes, Healthy Bodies, Healthy Lives

When Victorian Gothic revivalists surveyed their communities, they saw a paradox. Scientific progress and economic advancement also produced greater privation, pollution and disease. In Victorian Britain, the ills associated with rapid urbanisation and industrialisation were legion: overcrowding, poverty, filth, crime and the rapid spread of disease are just a few. An increasingly mobile world was hit with yellow fever and typhus epidemics, and parts of Britain were horribly affected by the cholera pandemics of 1832, 1848 and 1854. The year after the first cholera outbreak, Pugin was preparing sketches for his 1836 *Contrasts*, three of which concerned wells and water conduits. From these he created the plate *Public Conduits* for the published book (see p. 60). The modern side of this dual image demonstrates how, as the grip of capitalism intensified, even basic needs like water were increasingly determined by utility. Here a massive lock bars public access to the conduit at St Annes Soho, signalling the civic abandonment of the lower orders. A policeman, with truncheon in hand, refuses water to a child whilst a 'gentleman' looks on with indifference. In place of decoration, the neo-classical police station contains only a pasted-up notice. In contrast, the Gothic West Cheap Conduit, with its vertical lines and heavily decorated iconographic style attests to the interconnectedness of design and material conditions. Care of the body and care of the soul are one here.

Case Study
WATER, EXETER AND REGIONAL GOTHIC

The cholera epidemics that decimated many areas of Britain highlighted the need for the reform of public areas and resources. There is an important regional story here, recorded by Dr William Shapter, physician to the Devon and Exeter Hospital, in *The History of the Cholera in Exeter in 1832*. This book not only records how politicians, physicians and the clergy collaborated to combat a disease, but also how they transformed an ancient city ('Old Exeter') into a modern one.[27] Early nineteenth-century Exeter relied on medieval modes of sewage removal via medieval gutters and an inadequate public water supply, consisting of an overburdened waterworks, a few public pumps, and an ancient conduit in South Street.

In the 1830s and 40s, people were still unaware that cholera was a water-borne disease. They generally believed it was miasmic, that is, that it originated from unwholesome, filthy or infectious areas in an unseen mist. Yet water was at the centre of disease prevention because the Exeter Board of Health (formed in 1831) aimed to cleanse and purify the city. They appointed a committee of Commissioners of Improvement who set about covering drains, digging sewers, increasing scavenging, creating more public pumps and re-opening the closed ancient public conduits. In spite of this, cholera travelled to Exeter in 1832. In the aftermath, work commenced on a pumping station upstream from the city at Pynes, which began

most enduring and beneficent effect on his contemporaries, and will have through them on suc-
ceeding generations. ❡ John Ruskin the critic of
art has not only given the keenest pleasure to
thousands of readers by his life-like descriptions,
and the ingenuity and delicacy of his analysis of
works of art, but he has let a flood of daylight into the cloud of sham-technical twaddle which was
once the whole substance of "art-criticism," and
is still its staple, and that is much. But it is far
more that John Ruskin the teacher of morals and
politics (I do not use this word in the newspaper
sense), has done serious and solid work towards
that new-birth of Society, without which genuine
art, the expression of man's pleasure in his handi-
work, must inevitably cease altogether, and with
it the hopes of the happiness of mankind.

WILLIAM MORRIS,
Kelmscott House, Hammersmith.
Feb 15th, 1892.

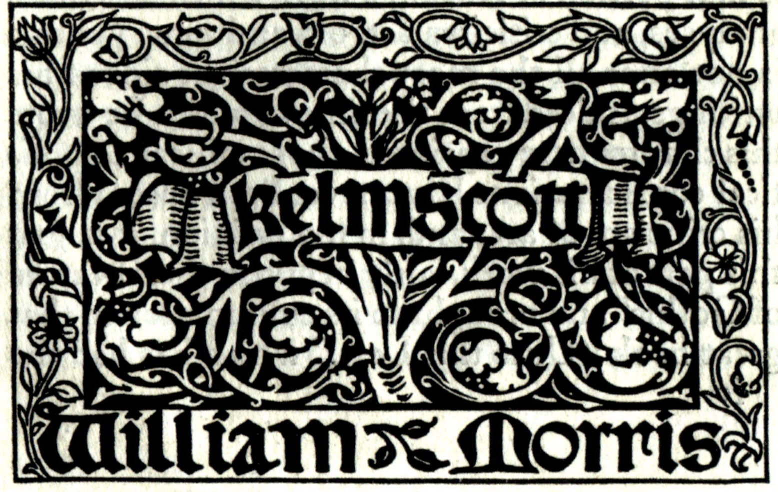

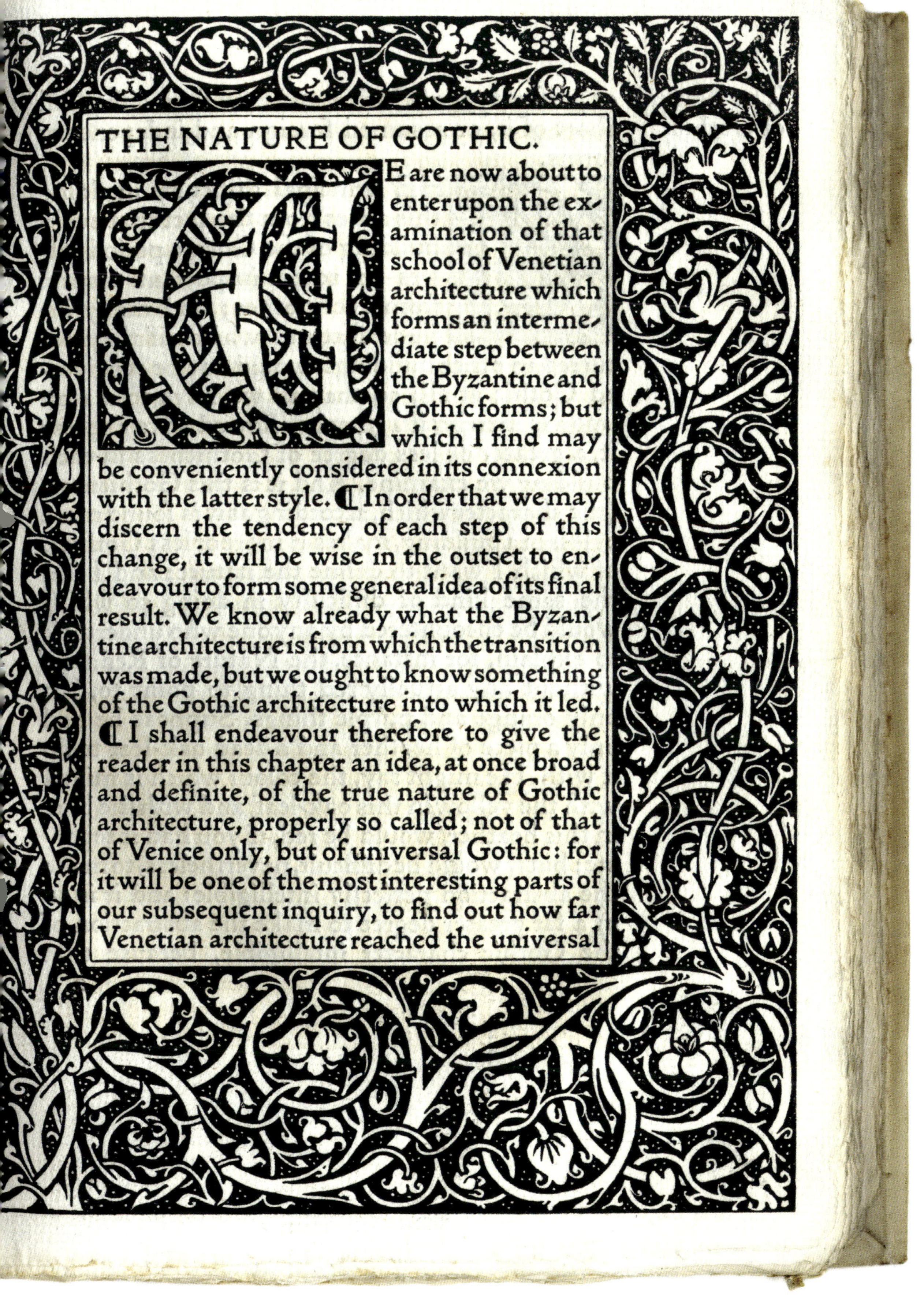

THE NATURE OF GOTHIC.

WE are now about to enter upon the examination of that school of Venetian architecture which forms an intermediate step between the Byzantine and Gothic forms; but which I find may be conveniently considered in its connexion with the latter style. ❡ In order that we may discern the tendency of each step of this change, it will be wise in the outset to endeavour to form some general idea of its final result. We know already what the Byzantine architecture is from which the transition was made, but we ought to know something of the Gothic architecture into which it led. ❡ I shall endeavour therefore to give the reader in this chapter an idea, at once broad and definite, of the true nature of Gothic architecture, properly so called; not of that of Venice only, but of universal Gothic: for it will be one of the most interesting parts of our subsequent inquiry, to find out how far Venetian architecture reached the universal

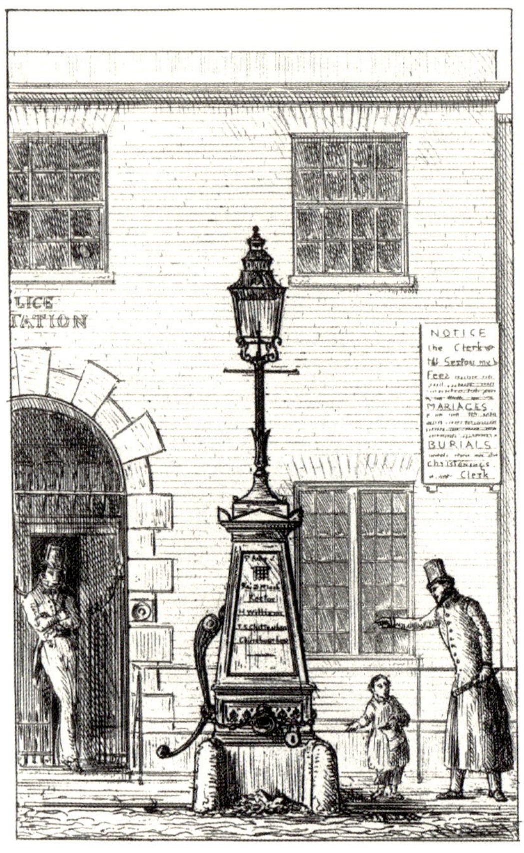
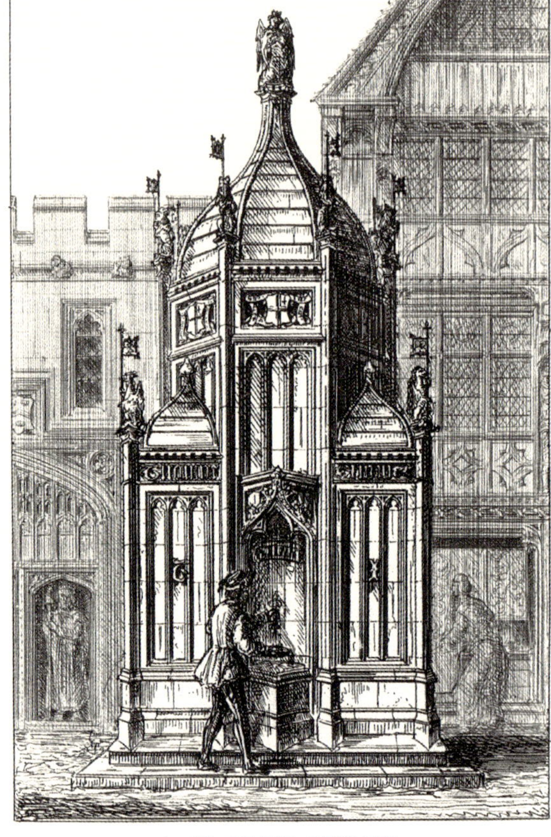

Fig. 30 / Cat. 10

Contrasted Public Conduits

Augustus W.N. Pugin

1836 / from *Contrasts*
© Courtauld Institute of Art

pp. 58–59

Fig. 29 / Cat. 27

The Nature of Gothic

1892 / a chapter from *The Stones of Venice* by John Ruskin
published by the Kelmscott Press
© Ruskin Foundation (Ruskin Library, Lancaster University)

providing unpolluted drinking water in 1834. William Cheeseman's painting of the station (c.1856) combines a pastoral Devon landscape with Gothic architecture, but also, as the smokestack and the train in the lower right side indicate, with industry, engineering, modernity, and progress. The pumping station was built in Norman or English Romanesque style of the eleventh or twelfth-century, as is indicated by the simple geometry and the rounded arches over the windows and doors. There is a further medieval twist to the story. A new water-holding reservoir was also built at nearby Danes Castle, so that the water was held right over the castle. When this reservoir was drained in the 1990s, and archaeologists had a chance to examine the fortress, they discovered that it was actually English. King Stephen, grandson of William the Conqueror, built the castle in 1136 when he held Baldwin de Redvers under a three-month siege at Rougemont Castle. In this case, there was more continuity between the medieval past, Victorian social problems, modern science, and Exeter Gothic revivalist architecture than was assumed.

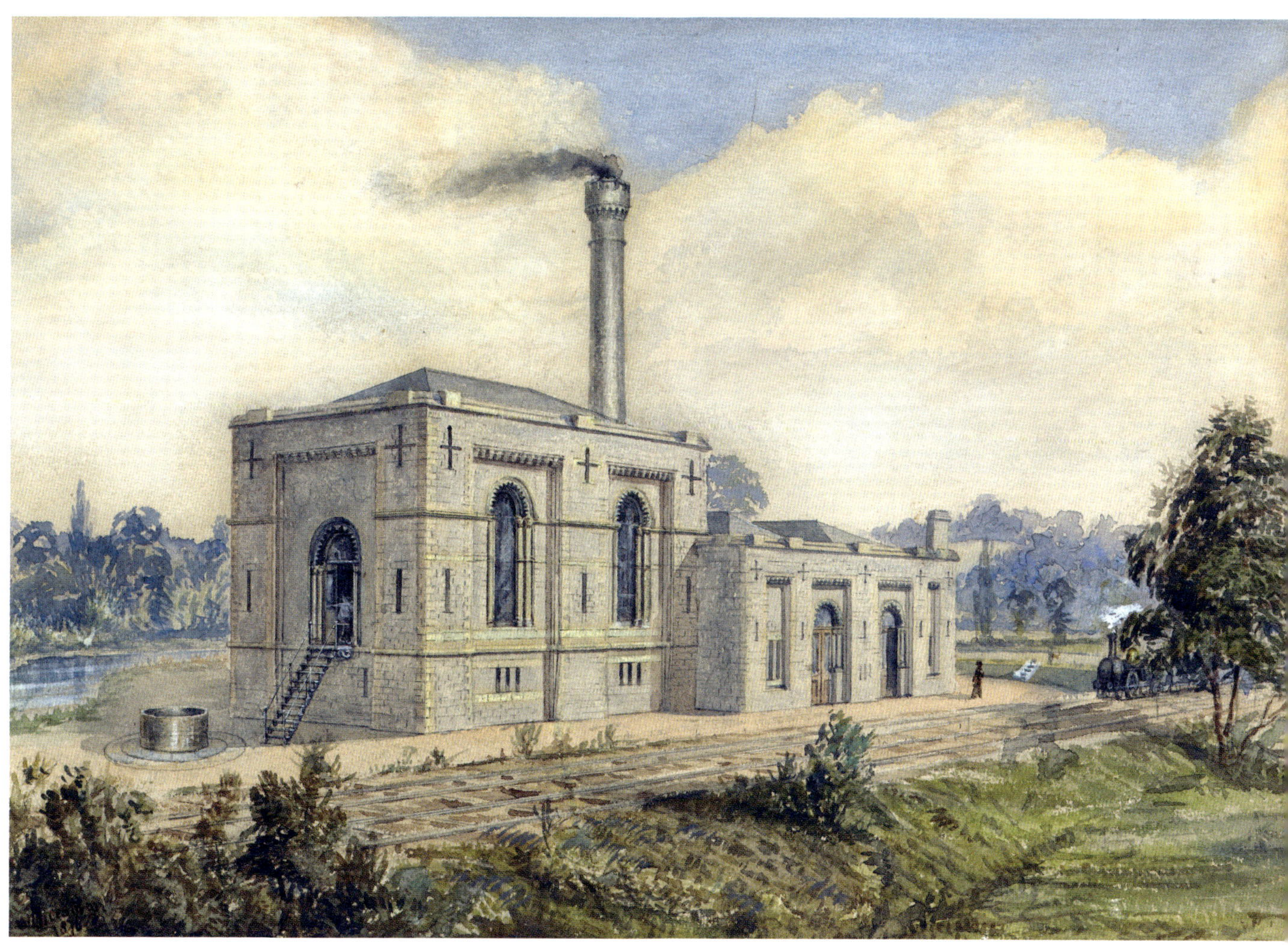

Fig. 31 / Cat. 68
The Old Pumping Station of the Exeter Water Company near St David's Station, Exeter
William Cheeseman
1876 / watercolour on paper
© Royal Albert Memorial Museum & Art Gallery, Exeter City Council

The symbiotic relationship that emerged between water, disease, urban reform and design in Exeter is a pattern for similar developments in other parts of the nation. In London the expedience of the times encouraged civil engineers, architects, designers, doctors and social reformers to work in a collaborative and what we would now term a multi-disciplinary way. So for instance, as chief engineer of London's Metropolitan Board of Works, Sir Joseph Bazalgette oversaw the creation of London's sewer network, but also consulted with Dr John Snow, one of the first physicians to recognize cholera was a waterborne disease. With designer Charles Henry Driver, renowned for his ornamental iron work, Bazalgette collaborated on designs for the Thames Embankment project (1862–74) and London's pumping stations at Abbey Mills and Crossness. Significantly, these stations look more like miniature medieval palaces than functional sewerage works. Gothic design turned the most quotidian items and the most utilitarian of spaces into objects of great beauty.

These Gothic masterpieces are testaments to how

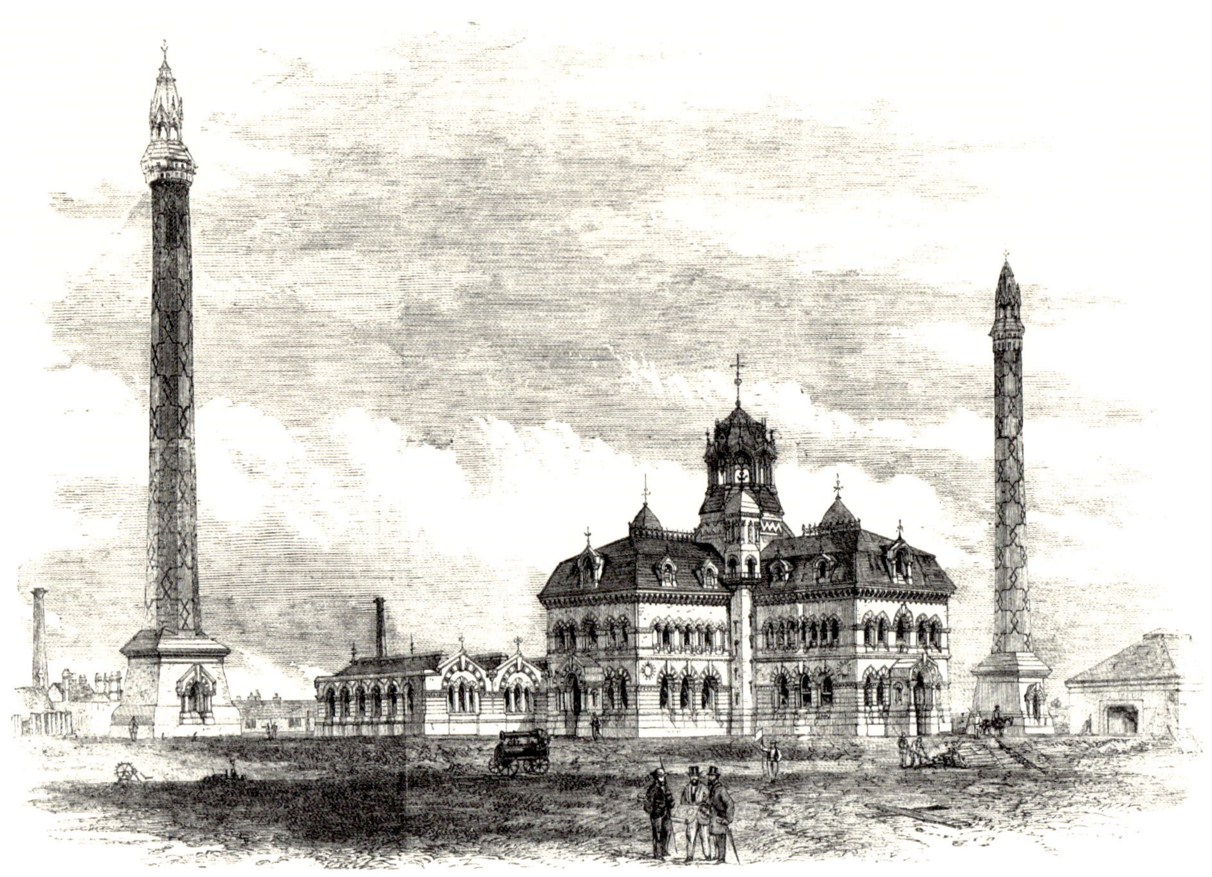

Fig. 32
*Bazalgette's Abbey Mills Pumping Station,
Stratford, London*

1868 / from *The Illustrated London News*
© Science Museum/Science & Society Picture Library

Victorian Gothic revivalists viewed the reform of cities, the health of bodies, and the beautification of living space as intimately connected. Sanitary reformers and public health officers espoused many of the same things as Gothic architects. They advocated quality construction and the use of locally sourced materials. Their construction also reflected new modern, urban living conditions, which linked individuals in new ways. In his 1862 book *Underground London*, John Hollingshead observed that:

> *the sewerage system...has linked the whole metropolitan public together by vast underground chains, and has taught them that they are all suffering, enduring brothers. In this joint-stock company, some few members have the upper hand, and they lean very heavily on those below them.*[28]

Filth, contamination and material need had shackled urban dwellers in disagreeable ways. Nevertheless, those who anticipated, or were schooled in the arguments of Ruskin, Carlyle and Morris sought to make those chains velvet. Above ground, beautiful Gothic buildings reminded Britons of their shared history, and spoke to them of their common values. Those reforming architects, designers and engineers sought too, to make human connections as different from the self-interested ties of a joint-stock company as possible.

William Morris was only born in 1834, two years after the first cholera outbreak, yet his aesthetic philosophy is marked by it. At the end of the century, he would articulate clearly the centrality of the home in the relationship between the health of art and the health of the nation:

> The contrast between past art and present, the universal beauty of men's habitations as they WERE fashioned, and the universal ugliness of them as they ARE fashioned, is of the utmost import to civilisation ... it expresses no less than a blind brutality which will destroy art at least, whatever else it may leave alive: art is not healthy, it even scarcely lives; it is on the wrong road.[29]

His use of the term 'art' refers to fine art, but also encompasses domestic objects and designs. A healthy civilisation required that no one should be consigned to a life of monotonous banality, surrounded by cheap and ugly objects, but that they have access to beauty. Significantly, Morris articulates his argument in a vocabulary that combines aesthetic and corporeal terms. Bad art and shoddy design is bound up with blindness, health, life and death.

Indeed Morris identified important continuities between art and the body. In an 1889 lecture 'How Shall We Live Then?' he insisted that

> We shall not be happy unless we live like good animals, unless we enjoy the exercise of the ordinary functions of life: eating sleeping loving walking running swimming riding sailing we must be free to enjoy all these exercises of the body.[30]

In the twenty-first century, many people see the arts as separate from, or having little to offer science or medicine. But Victorian Gothic revivalists instigated urban reform projects that addressed the minds and bodies of average citizens. They promoted the idea that one's morality, lifespan, health, level of productivity and general degree of happiness *depended* on things like the literature one read, the art one had access to, the style of one's household goods, and the spatial layout of one's home and neighbourhood. Public health reform entailed clean water, medical treatment, the construction of sewerage systems and other public works, but it also required tastefully designed civic and domestic buildings and access to art.

The rise in the global circulation of exotic goods and foreign diseases ('Asiatic' cholera was believed to have originated in the Bay of Bengal) focussed attention on the relationship between the local and the foreign in new ways. Pugin did not need an epidemic to make him suspicious of anything foreign. One of the reasons he deplored neo-classicism was that it was an imported style from a radically different climate, landscape and culture. The flat roofs of Greek buildings were fit for the sun-baked Mediterranean but northern European roofs needed to be pointed to survive winter snowfalls. Classical friezes were decorated with the heads of sheep or oxen, to signify animal sacrifice to foreign gods. Christian churches had towers to house the bells that called the community to worship.[31] Pugin deplored the popular taste for exotic eyesores. One could find, he raged, 'a Moorish fish market with a literary room over an Egyptian marine villa' or 'a gin temple in the baronial style' or monuments in the 'Hindoo style.'[32] Buildings that spoke a babel of languages produced feelings of estrangement, isolation and disconnection.

Clearly, Pugin had distinct ideas about national architecture, matched in strength by his anxieties about 'foreignness.' What he seems not to have had was a strong notion of regional differences in style. If architecture embodied the distinct character of a people and a landscape, then there should be evidence of regional variations of the Gothic style. Is there such thing as, say, a Cornish or a Devonian Gothic style, which expresses a distinctly local sense of place? The rest of this section maps some of the ways later revivalists negotiated regionalism, national identity and a taste for the foreign.

Case Study
WILLIAM BURGES AND THE SOUTH WEST

Although a Londoner, the architect and designer William Burges left his mark on Devon. Like other revivalists we've encountered thus far, he deplored neo-classical architectural styles, industrialisation and what he saw as the wretchedly dull spirit of his age. His Gothic was romantic, fantastical, extravagant, and it was borne in the thirteenth century. Along with his Pre-Raphaelite friends, Burges archaeologised the past to revive a romanticism that countered mechanism. But Burges also looked forward. With the Arts and Crafts movement he revived the applied arts, creating domestic objects – ceramics, glass, fur-

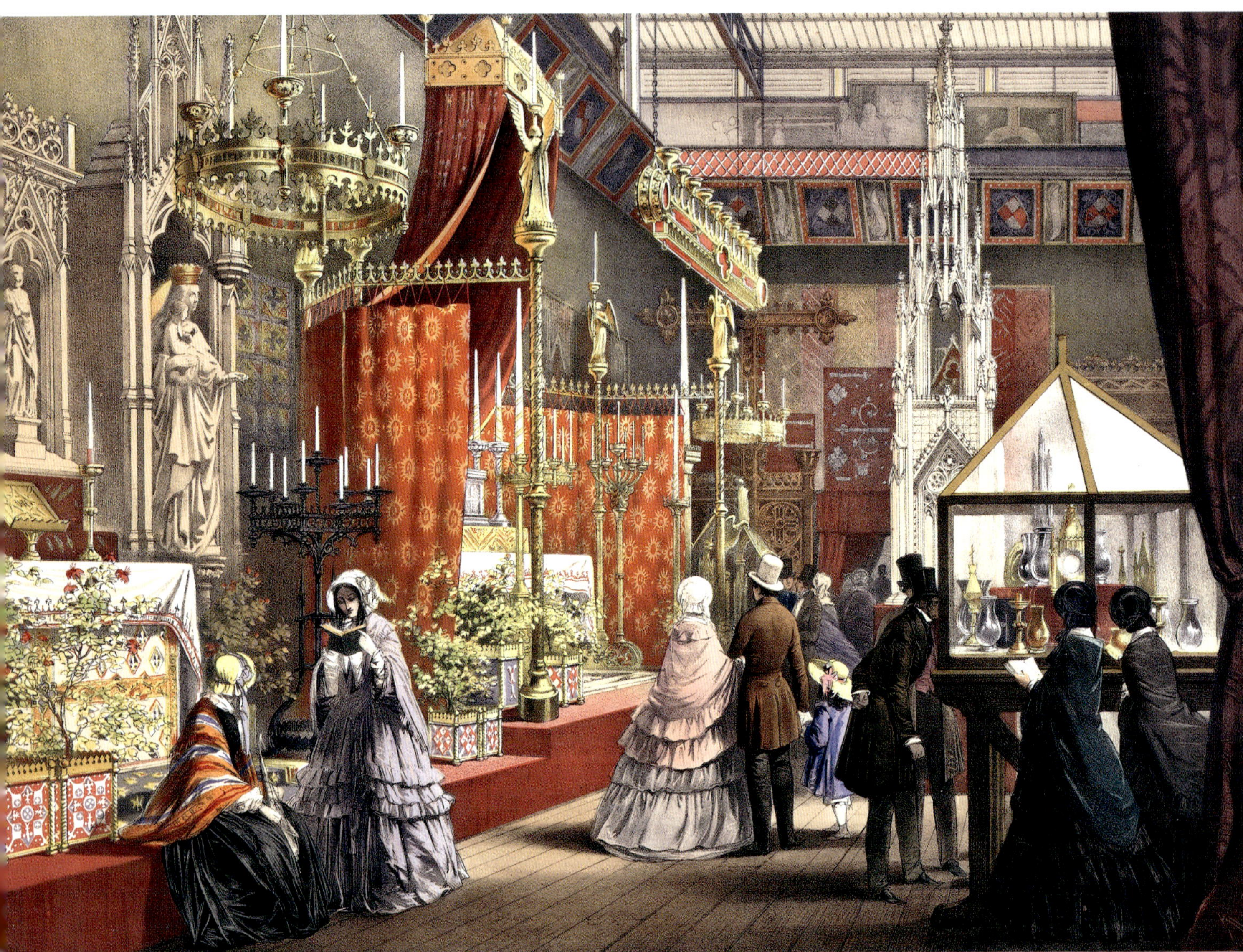

Fig. 33 / Cat. 16
The Medieval Court
W.R., L.C. and G.B. Dickinson

1854 / lithograph / from Dickinsons *Comprehensive Pictures of the Great Exhibition of 1851*
© Victoria and Albert Museum, London

niture, metalwork — that would infuse living spaces with life. 'The best way of advancing' domestic art, Burges argued, 'is to do our best in our houses,' so that if we have 'art and colour in our sitting rooms ... the improvement may gradually extend to our costume, and perhaps eventually to ... architecture'.[33] This statement, from a series of lectures entitled *Art Applied to Industry* expresses Burges's desire to create beautiful everyday objects through design reform, particularly in the case of industrially manufactured goods. His lectures were part of a wider aesthetic movement inspired by The Great Exhibition of 1851, which promoted the basic principles of good design in an industrial world.

In 1873 the Royal Archaeological Institute commissioned Burges to design the Exeter mayoral chain, which he did in 1874 (see p. 68). The gold ceremonial chain incorporates the motifs of the triple-towered castle alternating with the crowned letter X. The badge contains the city's arms. These livery collars or chains of office were made and worn in the Middle Ages as insignia or marks of fealty. The mayoral chain was one of only a few of Burges's secular commissions at the time, but his aim was to move away from ecclesiastical work toward domestic design. He aimed, to use William Morris's phrase, to bring 'universal beauty to men's habitations'; or to use Burges's own words, he sought 'to do single-handed what the entire Gothic revival had failed to do: to conjure up, in Victorian terms, the artistic spirit of a medieval house'.[34]

In Devon and Cornwall, Burges turned his hand to his domestic project. Retired Col. Charles Lygon Somers's Tudor Gothic mansion Treverbyn Vean (c.1858–62) was built at St Neot, near Liskeard, Cornwall. The exterior was designed by the Gothic revivalist, George Gilbert Scott, who would go on to design London's Albert Memorial, the Midland Grand Hotel at St Pancras, and Lanhydrock House, Bodmin. Burges was hired to do much of Treverbyn Vean's interior, parts of which reveal a commendable sensitivity to regional history, myth and landscape. He designed a monumental chimneypiece on the theme of the legend of the little-known Cornish saint St Neot, a monk who was described in Asser's ninth-century manuscript *Life of King Alfred*. With his sculptor, J.B. Philip, Burges created a chimneypiece with figures in chase, which bulge dramatically out of the stone. Treverbyn Vean reflects a passion for Gothic; as J. Mourdant Crook points out, 'even the mustard pot and sugar castor were Gothic.'[35] And yet, in the photographic records we have of the now dismantled chimneypiece, we can also see 'Jacobean' chairs, Flemish tapestries and Turkish hangings.[36] This is a domestic interior that valorizes the local and the particular, and has Cornish

Gothic as the centrepiece, but it is also an eclectic celebration of foreign craftsmanship and design.

In 1867, Burges began plans for the Gothic country house, Knightshayes Court near Tiverton, Devon. This commission proved to be one of his unrealised dreams. He fell out with the owner, Sir John Heathcoat Amory, with the result that most of his designs went unexecuted and the furniture unconstructed. Much of the work he did do was covered over by subsequent generations who deemed them too fanciful, too fantastical, too Gothic. Today, very little remains of Burges's dream of conjuring the artistic spirit of a medieval house at Knightshayes. The few Burges pieces on display have been brought in from the outside, including the Golden Bed (owned by the V&A), which was originally from Burges's own showpiece home, Tower House. Other pieces have been loaned by Led Zeppelin guitarist Jimmy Page, who is the current owner of Tower House.

Burges's presentation album, which is on display at Knightshayes, is our best look at the magnificent world he had in mind. The pages reveal a plethora of influences, from fairy-tales to Chaucer to Tennyson; more than that, his intertextual designs are transformations of myths and poetry into hybrid, eclectic narratives. They embody Burges's passion for flair and a lust for colour, which counteracted Victorian monotony and industrial smog. In many ways, these designs are distinctly English: the theme of the drawing room was to have been chivalry, with a chimneypiece titled 'Assault on the Castle of Love'. In other ways, this is a foreign fantasy: the walls and windows of that same drawing room also glow with the classical legends of Pyramus and Thisbe, Jason, Medea and Paris. The carpets were to have been of 'Turkish, Persian, Indian or other Eastern production, copied perhaps from a carpet in a picture by Van Eyck'.[37] And what would have been a horror for Pugin, a secret passage was to have 'the various conditions of life offering their hearts to Cupid' (see overleaf).[38]

Burges's South West designs are far from 'pure' or authentically regional; rather they are hybrids, fusions of a variety of styles, periods and cultures. Knightshayes is a Devon house, created by local craftspeople and formed out of local materials (including the red stone used in construction of the house). But its exterior is French in style and its interior would have been a highly individual expression of a plethora of influences, objects, and narratives — local, national, and foreign. Burges's method of synthesis is borne of Victorian curiosity; he is a product of an empire peopled by travellers, collectors and cataloguers.

Earlier architects, such as Pugin, had travelled through England to see the medieval churches of Durham,

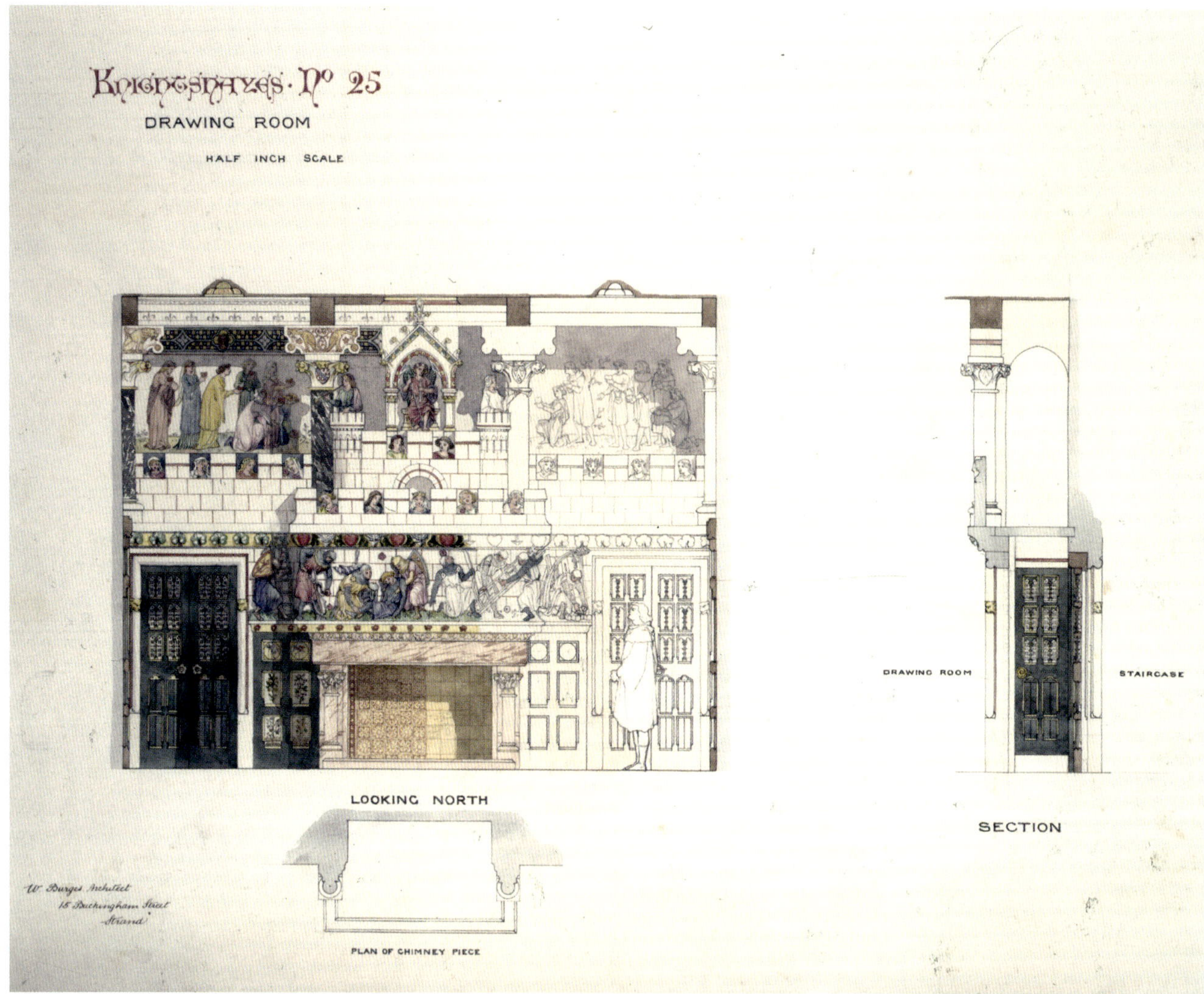

Fig. 34 / Cat. 59
Design for the Drawing Room
William Burges and assistants

early 1870s / from *Decoration for Knightshayes Court*, an album of watercolour designs
© National Trust Images/Lynda Aiano

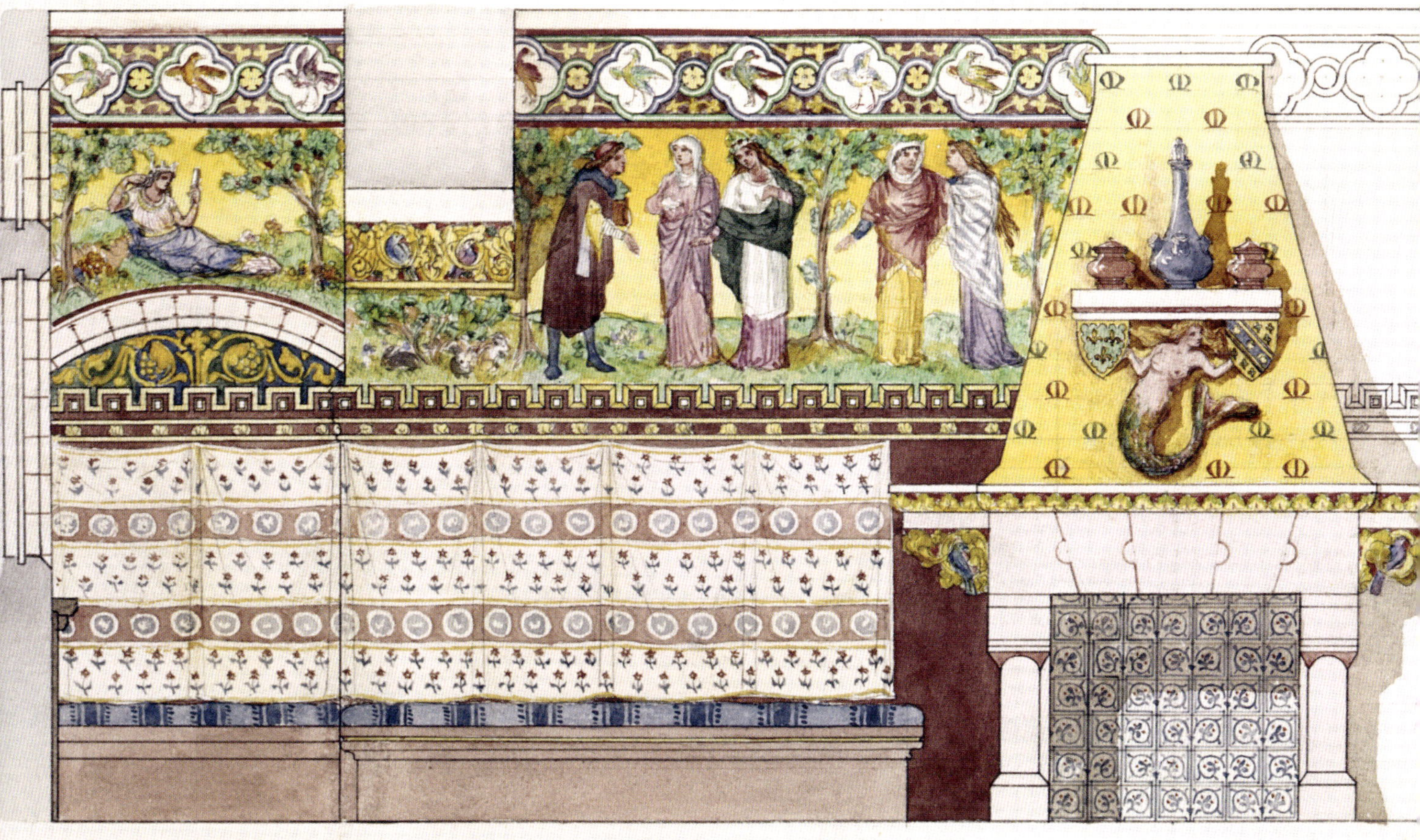

Fig. 35 / Cat. 59
Design for the Boudoir fireplace
William Burges and assistants

early 1870s / from *Decoration for Knightshayes Court*, an album of watercolour designs
© National Trust Images/John Bethell

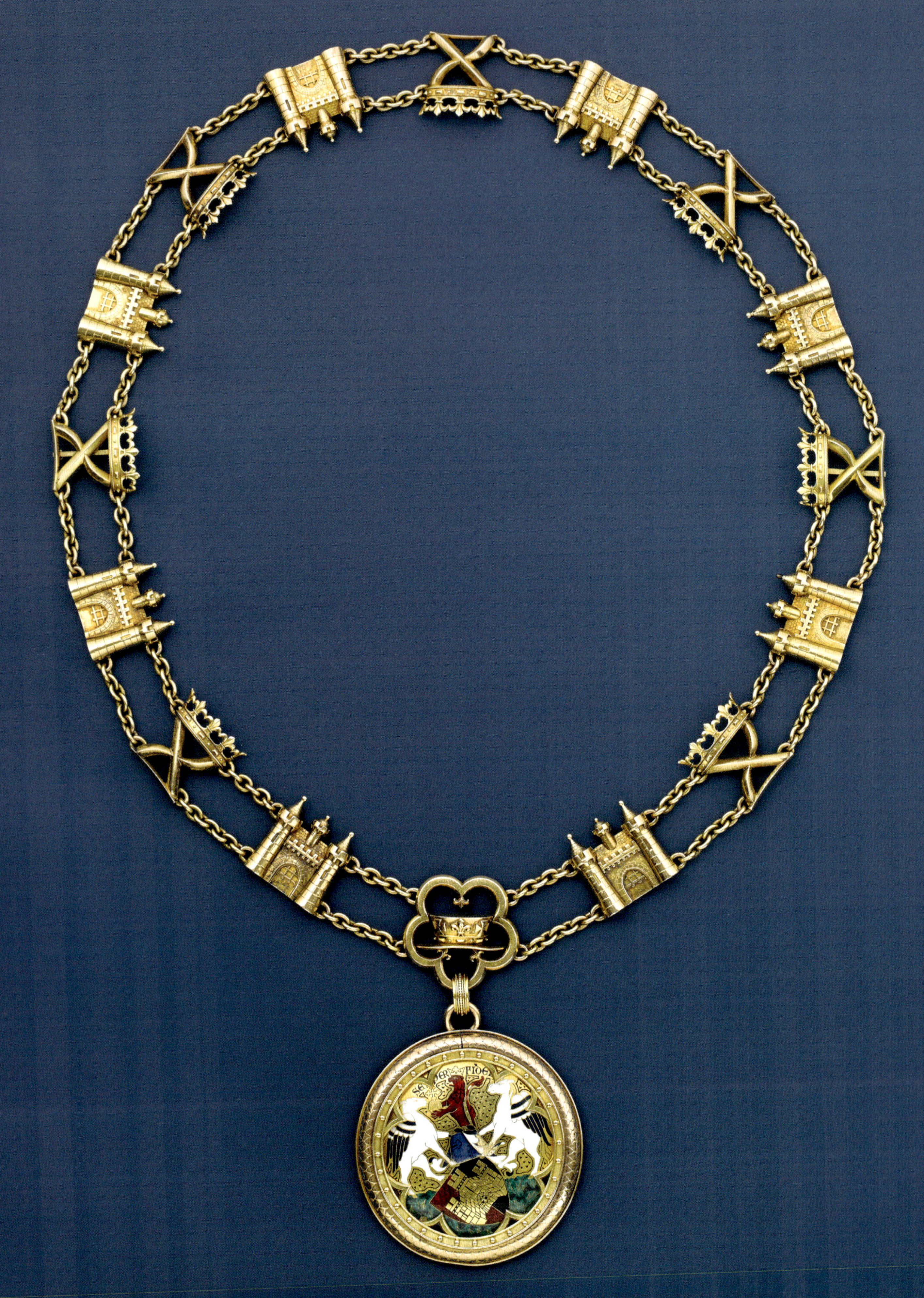

Fig. 36 / Cat. 63
Exeter Mayor's chain
William Burges (designer) and Parker & Stone (maker)
1874 / gold, with enamel badge of office
© Exeter City Council

Lincolnshire, Northampton, Yorkshire, the east coasts, Warwick, Oxford, and Devon. Perhaps they went to France, and maybe Germany. But Burges's architectural education took in extended trips to France, Belgium, Germany, Switzerland, Spain, Portugal, Italy, Sicily, Greece, and Turkey. Turkish art and architecture was of especial interest because it linked East and West, and would prove formative in the development of his style. Indeed, Burges was consistently inspired by foreign design. In a report on the International Exhibition for the *Gentleman's Magazine*, his focus moves from the medievalist French display to the Japanese, Chinese and Indian exhibits. 'Truly the Japanese Court is the real medieval court of the Exhibition,' he pronounces, 'for at the present day the arts of the Middle Ages have deserted Europe, and are only to be found in the East'. Besides admiring the Japanese ivories and coats of mail, he found that:

> *Egypt and India also exhibit the most beautiful stuffs woven with gold thread, some of the* kinkhab *of the latter country strongly reminding us, by the fineness of the work and the comparative smallness of the pattern, of those few tissues of the twelfth and thirteenth centuries which have been rescued from the shrines of the saints or the sepulchres of the rich.*[39]

In textiles, Burges identifies marked similarities between a European Gothic tradition and modern foreign arts. He uses the beauty and integrity of Eastern craftsmanship to chastise the cheap 'rubbish' produced by European makers. When 'we leave the Asiatic departments and enter the European … we have left the Middle Ages, and are in the midst of the worst rococo style. Nothing can possibly be more dreary…'[40]

Case Study
HARRY HEMS

The Victorian stone sculptor and woodcarver Harry Hems left a much wider mark than Burges on the South West landscape. Although a transplant from the metropolis, Hems became one of Exeter's local heroes (his name still graces the city's popular Harry's restaurants, one of which occupies his old workshop). Hems was a self-promoter with a fiery temper, a flamboyant character with a staunch work ethic, and a collector with a seemingly boundless curiosity. He had a passion for his vocation and an eye for business. Like Ruskin and Morris, Hems identified continuities between his aesthetics, his workshop, his politics and his community. Artisanal labour was a deeply ethical enterprise, which produced designs that embodied the vitality and honour of their makers. Politically, Hems was an old-school paternalist who supported local hospitals and care homes, and treated Exeter's elderly poor to a Christmas meal each year. Yet he could also be characterized as a right-wing radical. Refusing to pay taxes he deemed unfairly high, he had his goods auctioned off on two occasions, in 1888 and 1907. According to local newspapers, those goods included a large statue of St Matthew the Tax-gatherer (1888) and three 'second-hand tombstones (slightly damaged) … suitable for the graves of Income Tax Commissioners or other Revenue Officials' (1907).[41] When he ran for a seat on the Exeter City Council, he was a non-partisan supporter of the working classes who refused to sign up with the conservatives but pitted himself against the Liberals.[42]

So what then is regionally distinctive or authentic about Hems's use of Gothic? Part of the answer to that question stems from his self-education in the medieval archaeology and Gothic architecture of the South West. He collected hundreds of fifteenth-century ecclesiastical carvings and architectural fragments, gathered mostly it seems, from church restoration projects in Devon and Cornwall. This collection, which is held at RAMM, is significant and distinctive for its sheer size, diversity and antiquity. If we could trace the origins of many of these pieces, they could tell us much about the landscape, culture and social configurations of the communities that produced them. Hems embarked on research of local history, much of which was published in various magazines. Whilst William Morris's researches ranged to Icelandic sagas and the ancient Greek myth of the hero Jason and his quest to find the Golden Fleece, Hems investigated the local history of common fleece. Or, at least he was interested in how, in Exeter's golden age of woollen goods' production, wooden 'tillet blocks' had been used to mark the wrapping or 'tillet' around a bale of new wool cloth.

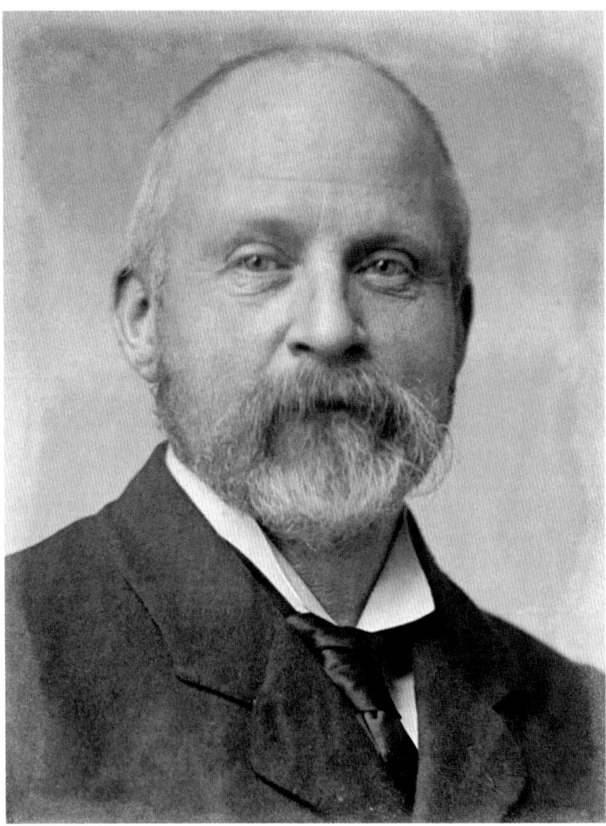

Fig. 37
Portrait of Harry Hems
© Sands Civil & Structural Chartered Engineers

This was a hallmark identifying the maker and quality of the 'fleece.' Hems wrote into the *Western Antiquary* of 1882 to share prints of his tillet blocks and the findings of his research — 'eight out of every ten citizens' were connected with the woollen goods trade. He also noted that RAMM held five such blocks.[43]

Contemporary reports reveal Hems's keen interest in recovering old methods of craftsmanship and in using time-honoured, local materials (like Beer limestone). His carvings and stonework were traditional and used established regional symbols and designs, and seem to indicate a desire to represent local history. At least this was how many contemporaries interpreted his work. *The Western Times* of 11 August 1874 lauded Hems 'of the Ever-Faithful City' for his work on the newly resurrected Plymouth Guildhall. Hems's contribution included stone and wood carving and a colossal statue of Edward the Black Prince (copied from the statue in Canterbury). With glowing civic pride, the paper praised:

> *The grotesque figures, the shields bearing arms of the West of England towns – we are all up in arms with Plymouth – the armorial bearings of the old Devon and Cornish families have all had the master hand of our townsman [Hems] in the execution. To do the work ... he has had a church-going fit, having visited from time to time most of the great Cathedrals of France. Suffice it to say that Plymouth has got a noble edifice.*

The mention here of the fashion for local insignia indicates a wider interest in regional medieval history and a Victorian expectation that regional medieval histories would be incorporated into modern neo-Gothic buildings. Interestingly, however, the writer doesn't find it incongruous that Hems goes to French cathedrals for creative inspiration.

In language echoing Pugin's, the *Western Morning News* report of 13 August 1874 railed against the historical 'vandalism' that destroyed 'the romantic old Guildhall' and its subsequent replacement, the 'abortion, which has haunted the dreams of every art-loving Plymothian, like a hideous nightmare'. But in a writing style not unlike that of restaurant reviewer and cultural critic A. A. Gill, the journalist takes a long while to address the actual buildings. 'It cannot be said of Plymouth', he writes,

> *as Palgrave said of Exeter, that she was a free republic ere Anglo Saxon king wore crown or bore sceptre. She cannot claim with Barnstable to date back her civic lineage to Athelstan, the Saxon con-*

queror of the West. She is not credited in Domesday Book, like Lydford, with the same immunities and privileges as London. But she is one of the very few towns whose history commences, earlier still than either, with myth and mystery. In the famous legend of Brute the Trojan, Plymouth is joined with Totnes in an antiquity to which no other towns in England could lay claim; and the Gog and Magog of London Guildhall simply hand down the memory of the great conflict on the Plymouth Hoe between Corinaeus and Goemagot, chief of the Cornish giants, with which the mythical history of Plymouth begins, recorded for more centuries than we can count by a rude sculpture of the struggle on the green turf of the Hoe itself.

Like a Victorian A. A. Gill, this writer is interested in the wider cultural significance of the Plymouth buildings, and wants to situate the object of his analysis in a geographical and historical trajectory. There is a connection between the new Guildhall and the legendary Trojan Brute, supposed founder and first king of Britain. The building reminds modern Plymothians of a heritage that includes the Trojan Corineus, who arrived in England and conquered Cornwall when he killed the last of the Cornish Giants, Goemagot in a wrestling match on the Hoe. London's two symbolic guardians – Gog and Magog – are simply derivatives of Goemagot, and so the metropolis borrows from the history of Plymouth.

I have quoted these newspaper passages at length as they provide a sense of what is at stake in this rage for regional Gothic. It is a way of defining communal identities against the metropolitan centre. These passages also reveal the region-centric criteria against which Hems's work was evaluated. But, like Burges, Hems was also something of a 'bricoleur' who borrowed from a wide variety of sources, and brought things together in new combinations. Much of his award-winning furniture design, which thrilled the judges at world exhibitions in America and Paris, innovated on established styles. As the critic for *Harper's Weekly* expressed it in one of the rave reviews of the carved oak chest that Hems exhibited at the 1878 Paris Exposition: 'The chest is not a copy of an existing antique work,' but an 'ideal' taken from various preserved pieces from the Middle Ages.[44] Hems's brand of Gothic could not help but combine the local with the global, for whilst his workshop did restorations all across the South West, far too numerous to mention, he also won medals at the 1876 Philadelphia Centennial International Exhibition as well as prizes at the 1893 Chicago World Fair and the 1894 Antwerp Exhibition. His work took

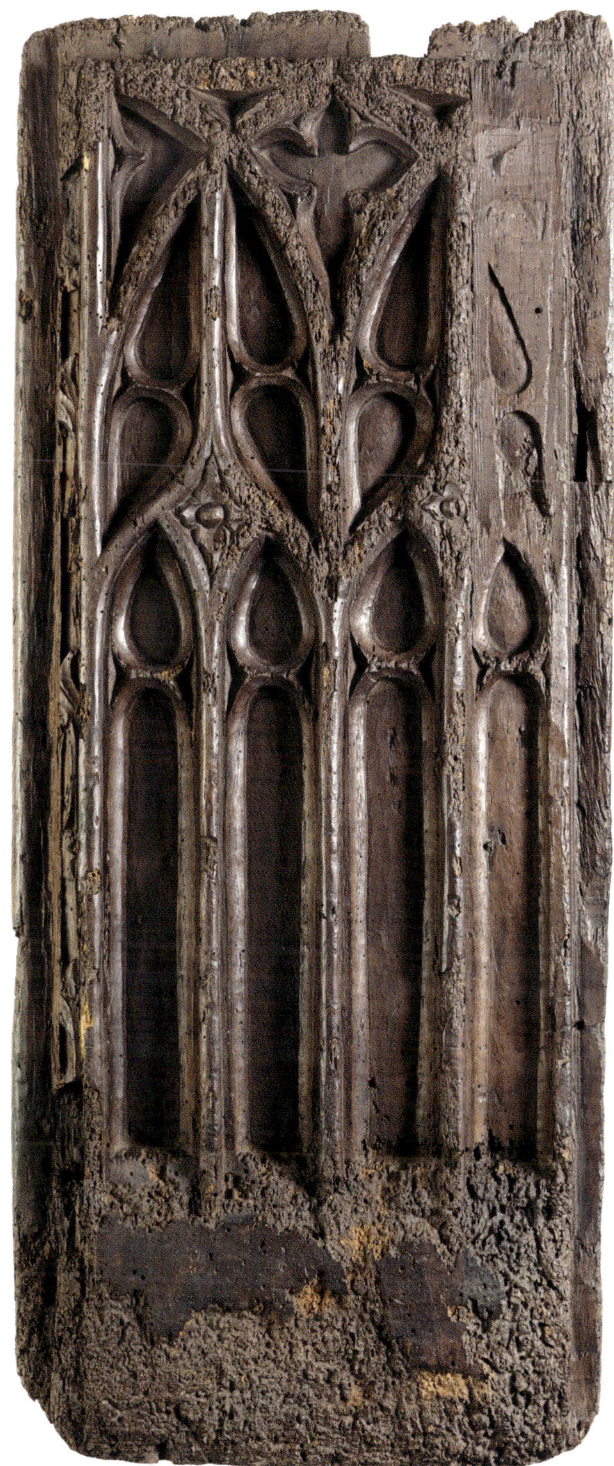

Fig. 38 / Cat. 46
Bench end

shortly after 1500 / carved oak / removed from the Church of St George, Dunster around 1838 and collected by Harry Hems around 1875
© Royal Albert Memorial Museum & Art Gallery, Exeter City Council

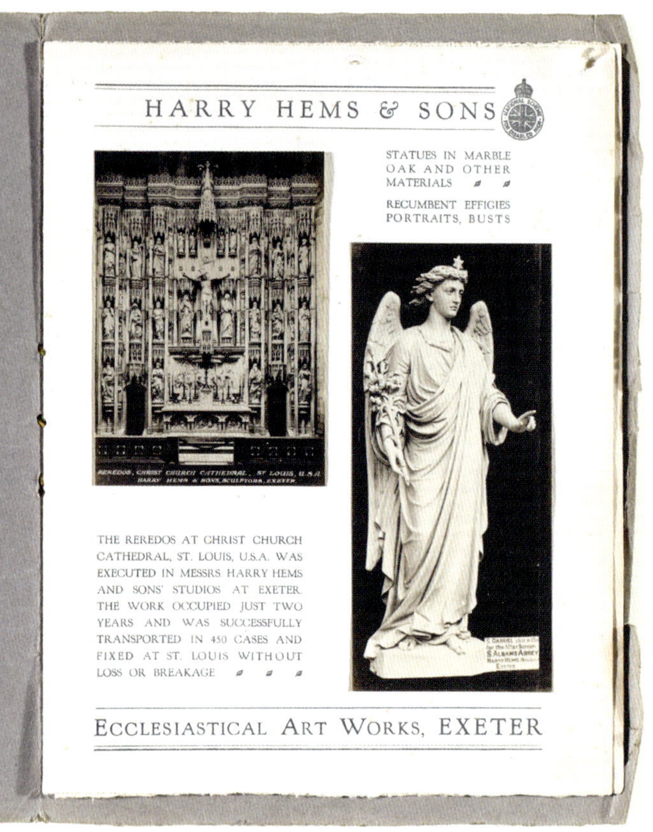

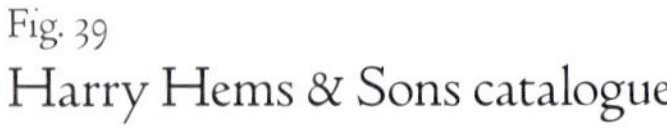

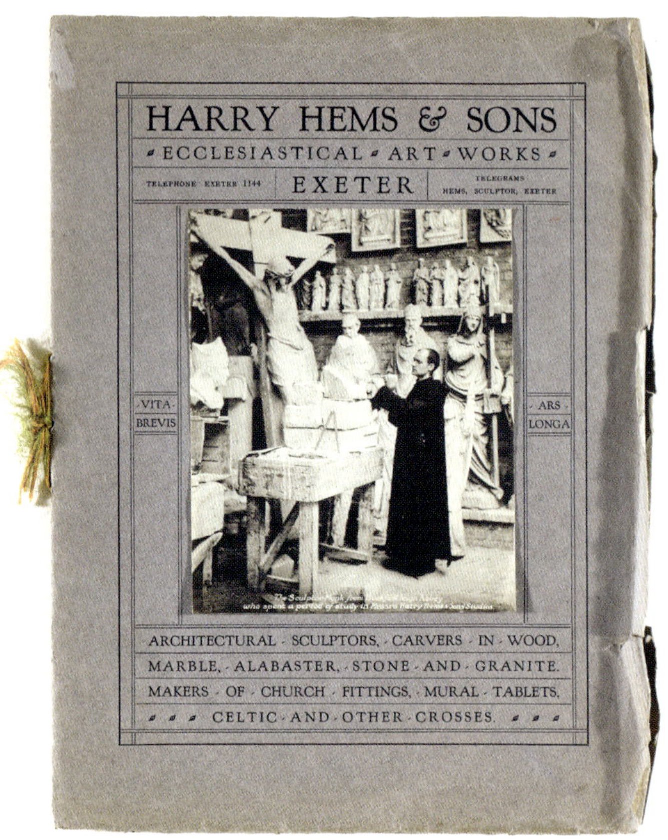

Fig. 39
Harry Hems & Sons catalogue
page: depicting Reredos from Christ Church, St Louis, c.1900
cover: depicting the Sculptor Monk from Buckfastleigh Abbey, c.1900
© Royal Albert Memorial Museum & Art Gallery, Exeter City Council

him from Hessenford, Cornwall, where he did the reredos in St Ann's Church (1883) to his home in Exeter, where he produced the memorial tablet and window commemorating novelist R.D. Blackmore for Exeter Cathedral (1901–4). In between, he produced designs for buildings in Australia and Africa.

REGIONALISM, FOREIGNNESS AND GOTHIC LITERATURE

For many Victorians, foreignness did not only originate in Africa or Asia. It could be found much closer to home, in Cornwall. Both familiar and alien, Cornwall was a place peopled by inhabitants who were not really English. Cornwall was a borderland cut off geographically from the rest of the country, a sort of liminal place, caught between England proper and her colonies across the seas. The way that Gothic writers responded to the unique position of Cornwall reveals insights about regional, national and global identities in the Victorian period.

There were two main conceptions about Cornwall that circulated in print culture. The first was to see the Cornish as a less civilised race, borne of a wilder, less developed region. The study of the medieval roots of

English institutions and customs emphasised the evolution of a progressive people; in contrast, as historian James Vernon notes, the same types of studies cast the Cornish as occupying 'a lower point on the evolutionary scale, being part of a "Celtic" people who were driven back to the peripheries of Britain by the racially superior Anglo-Saxons'.[45] In his 1885 study *The Races of Britain*, John Beddoe wrote of his worry that with increased mobility, the Cornish, who were 'decidedly the darkest people in England' might 'swamp the blond Teutons of England by a reflux migration'.[46] The devastating effects on the Teutonic English would include, he suggests, biological and cultural degeneration.

But this was a two-way street. The second and competing view represented England as an invading force, which threatened to subsume Cornish distinctiveness and to change the landscape irrevocably. As Vernon points out, this idea informed the findings of the Ethnographic Survey of the British Isles (1893). The report expresses concerns that the racial purity of the Cornish, heretofore protected by its geography, could be diluted, either by English tourists who were newly arriving via rail, or from external contact with foreign invaders, as in the 'intermixture of Spanish blood from the Armada'.[47]

Internal contact via the new railway links created another kind of fissure that divided society. The narrator of Thomas Hardy's 'The Fiddler of the Reels' (1893) describes how the opening of a new train line into a previously isolated area produced 'what one might call a precipice in Time.' This 'geological "fault"' suddenly brought 'ancient and modern into absolute contact'.[48] Ancient meets modern as the Home Counties encounter the nation's periphery.

Observers were anxious about the homogenizing effects of cultural contact, and the resulting degeneration of art and society. In his 1867 essay, 'On the Study of Celtic Literature,' Matthew Arnold worried that the increased mobility and the exchange of goods would create 'the fusion of all the inhabitants of these islands into one, homogenous, English-speaking whole'. Similarly, the Anglican priest and hymn-writer John Jason Neale produced a 300-page account of the travels of two fictional characters on a tour of Britain's Gothic ecclesiastical architecture. At one point, the two men arrive at a railway station to begin a new leg of their journey. As they await the train, the character 'Catholicus' observes:

How lamentably unromantic is every thing and every one becoming! We must … submit to be whirled on with the rest of the world. What a completely nineteenth-century look have these stations! Our forefathers would no more have thought of running up these lather-and-plaster things, than they would of going to sea in a sieve. But see to what the love of money – nay, worse than that – the grasping after an immediate return – can lead!

The striking differences between the Gothic architecture they have just seen and the cheaply built modern rail station is matched by an anxiety about the circulation of people via the new transport. The 'immense moral mischief the railroads have caused and will cause to England' would be responsible for:

amalgamating into one senseless heap the various usages of different localities – mixing … local habits, feelings, prejudices, affections into one colourless and monotonous mass – cutting up by the root hearty old English associations, superstitions, attachments, and, by weakening patriotism on a small scale, weakening it also on a larger; thus turning us into cosmopolites, most odious name!

These comments convey wider fears about the relationship between degeneration and evolution, technology and mobility, national progress and national regress. The circulation of people, and their customs and traditions, led to the more serious destruction of the regional, communal identities that make up the social fabric. Not only that, fears of cultural degeneration went all the way down to biology, to apprehensions about the intermixture of blood and racial miscegenation.

These fears are manifested in Victorian Gothic literature, which is replete with images of circulation, contagion, poison and the contamination of blood. One only needs to survey the literature of vampires – who are often, as in the case of Bram Stoker's famous *Dracula*, cast as foreigners. The fear of contamination also underwrites Stoker's 1903 Gothic novel, set in Cornwall, *The Jewel of Seven Stars*. The narrative concerns an archaeologist, Egyptologist and collector, Abel Trelawny, who has ambitions to resurrect an Egyptian mummy named Queen Tera. Obsessed with the idea of historical progress and scientific advancement, Trelawny is motivated in part by his belief that the ancient Egyptians were more evolved than modern Britons. In the *Jewel of the Seven Stars*, Cornwall becomes a conduit through which the spectre of the foreign (as represented by the Egyptian mummy) enters the nation. Cornwall's geographical distance from the centre and its peripheral cultural status means it is more vulnerable to foreign invasion and occupation.

Trelawny's collection is fed by the overseas plundering of an impressively educated agent named Corbeck, a man whose Egyptian adventures have turned him 'brown as a coffee-berry'. His neck is 'an intricate surface of seams and wrinkles, and sun-scarred with the burning of the Desert'.[49] In other words, his body has been altered – inscribed, one might say – by a foreign climate, so that he resembles the mummies he trades. Contact with the exotic results in both visible and invisible changes. The plundered goods that enter England and circulate between collectors cause sometimes undetectable transformations—but those transformations are always irrevocable.

There is an important historical and aesthetic context to this type of literature. The goods that Burges admired at the Great Exhibition and the Egyptian mummy in Stoker's novel are products of British cultural imperialism. From the colonies came artefacts, which then filled houses, private collections, museums and auction rooms. The 1882 occupation of Egypt, coinciding with the professionalisation of archaeology and the mania for collecting, stimulated the public taste for the exotic. Out of this context emerged a literary genre Patrick Brantlinger describes as 'imperial Gothic', a genre that expresses doubts about British pre-eminence by raising the spectre of the occult.[50] Queen Tera is a material embodiment of 'reverse colonization' since her resurrection – at English hands – represents an invasion from a previously invaded foreign nation. She represents strange, unknown dangers, for

you may put a mummy in a glass case and hermetically seal it...but all the same it will exhale its

odour....these smells remain, and their secrets are unknown to us. Today they are as much mysteries as they were when the embalmers put the body in the bath of natron.[51]

That odour is miasmic: undetectable and unseen it infiltrates Trelawney's house on the seaside Cornish cliff, and it penetrates the nostrils of his estranged daughter and their English visitors, recalling ancient secrets and inspiring contemporary fears.

This may seem a strange place to conclude. The subject of the mummy, carefully crafted into an immortal artifact by hallowed hands only to be resurrected on British soil by a mad scientist may seem a long way off from earlier sections of this essay. But the fact that the mummy, a relic from a mysterious past, had such a hold on the Victorian imagination speaks to many of the issues and ideas raised here. The mummy emerged in Gothic literature as a response to rapid and anxiety-producing changes in modern society. It is a spectre raised by other spectres: materialism, mechanisation, industrialisation, empire – to name a few. Critic Aviva Briefel argues that the literary appearance of ominous objects such as mummy hands is symptomatic of the cultural anxieties about the loss of artisanal methods of production (a loss bemoaned by Ruskin and Morris).[52] Historical objects and collected relics – no matter what they are – are cultural resurrections. They are indicative of the enduring hold of the past over the present, as well as the overriding investment we moderns have had – and continue to have – in our shared past, whether regional, national or global.

1. John Ruskin, *On the Nature of Gothic Architecture: An Herein of the True Functions of the Workman in Art* (London: Smith, Elder & Co, 1854), p. 2.

2. Martin Myrone, 'Gothic and Eighteenth-century Visual Art,' in *The Gothic World*, ed. Glennis Byron and Dale Townshend (London: Routledge, 2014), pp. 323-340, 323.

3. Lewis Melville, *The Life and Letters of William Beckford of Fonthill* (London: William Heinemann, 1910), p. 299.

4. Nicole Reynolds, 'Gothic and the Architectural Imagination', *The Gothic World*, pp. 85-97, 92.

5. When Walpole wrote these words he had been overseeing the 'Gothicization' of his Twickenham villa, Strawberry Hill for about ten years and he was two years away from publication of *The Castle of Otranto*. *The Works of Horatio Walpole, Earl of Orford* (London: G. G & J. Robinson, 1798), p. 94.

6. *Nature of Gothic*, p. 19.

7. William Cullen Bryant, *A Funeral Oration, Occasioned by the Death of Thomas Cole* (New York: George S. Appleton, 1848), p. 27.

8. The source of this epigraph is an unpublished paper, which Lord Acton wrote about 1859; it was printed in Herbert Butterfield, *Man on His Past* (Cambridge: CUP, 1955), p. 212.

9. J. Mourdant Crook, *William Burges and the High Victorian Dream* (London: Francis Lincoln, 2013) p. 23.

10. A.W.N. Pugin, *The Collected Letters of A.W.N. Pugin*, vol. 2, ed. Margaret Belcher (Oxford: OUP, 2003) p. 42.

11. A.W.N. Pugin, *Contrasts: or, A Parallel between the Noble Edifices of the Middle Ages, and Corresponding Buildings of the Present Day*, 2nd ed. (Leicester and New York: Humanities Press, 1969) p. 51.

12. A.W.N. Pugin, *Contrasts*, pp. 21, 26.

13. A.W.N. Pugin, *Contrasts*, p. 43.

14. Qtd. in *The Builder*, vol. 46, 1884, p. 714.

15. Michel Foucault, *Discipline and Punish: the Birth of the Prison* (1975), trans. Alan Sheridan (New York: Vintage, 1977; rpt. 1995) p. 200.

16. Jeremy Bentham, *Panopticon: Or, the Inspection-house: Containing the Idea of a New Principle of Construction Applicable to Any Sort of Establishment, in which Persons of Any Description Are to Be Kept Under Inspection* (Dublin: Thomas Byrne, 1791), p. 2 and see title-page.

17. Oscar Wilde stated this in his lecture on 'The English Renaissance of Art,' in New York on 9 January 1882; see Fiona McCarthy, *The Last Pre-Raphaelite: Edward Burne-Jones and the Victorian Imagination* (London: Faber & Faber, 2012), p. 333.

18. *The New Monthly Magazine* (December 1831), vol 32: p. 132.

19. Elizabeth McCarthy, 'Gothic Visuality in the Nineteenth Century,' *The Gothic World*, pp. 341-365, 342.

20. John Stuart Mill, *On Liberty*, 2nd ed. (London: John W. Parker & Son, 1860).

21. Trans. and qtd. in Bruce Holsinger, *The Premodern Condition: Medievalism and the Making of Theory* (Chicago: Chicago UP, 2005), p. 236.

22. Victor Hugo, *Notre-Dame de Paris*, trans. Alban Krailsheimer (Oxford: OUP, 2009), p. 198.

23. A.W.N. Pugin, *An Apology for the Revival of Christian Architecture in England* (London: John Weale, 1843), p. 49.

24. J. Ruskin, *Gothic*, p. 48.

25. Barbara Maria Stafford, *Body Criticism: Imaging the Unseen in Enlightenment Art and Medicine* (Cambridge, MA: MIT Press, 1991), p. 2.

26. Bram Stoker, *Dracula* (New York: Norton, 1997), p. 23.

27. Thomas Shapter, *The History of the Cholera in Exeter in 1832* (1849; Wakefield: S.R. Publishers, 1971), p. ix.

28. John Hollingshead, *Underground London* (London: Groombridge & Sons, 1862), p. 86.

29. William Morris, 'The Prospects of Architecture in Civilization' (1881) in *William Morris on Art and Socialism*, ed. Norman Kelvin (Mineola, NY: Dover, 1999), p. 58.

30. William Morris, 'An Unpublished Lecture of William Morris,' ed. Paul Meier, *International Review of Social History*, 16 (1971), p. 261.

31. A.W.N. Pugin, *The True Principles of Pointed or Christian Architecture* (1841, intro. Timothy Brittain-Catlin (Reading: Spire Books, 2003), pp. 45-50.

32. See Pugin's plate 'The Trade' in *Contrasts*.

33. William Burges, *Art Applied to Industry* (Oxford and London: John Henry and James Parker, 1865), p. 92.

34. Burges qtd. in Orby Shipley, *The Church and the World in 1868*, vol. 3 (London: Longman) pp. 596-87. Also qtd. in J. Crook, *William Burges*, p. 299.

35. J. Crook draws this observation from the John Hardman designed items listed by Christie's in 1986. See note 97, *William Burges*, p. 395.

36. J. Crook, *William Burges*, p. 300.

37. *Knightshayes Album* [1873], I. See 234A and 234B.

38. *Knightshayes Album*, pp. 28 et seq.

39. William Burges, *Gentleman's Magazine*, vol. 12 (1862), pp. 10-11.

40. W. Burges, *Gentleman's Magazine*, p. 12.

41. 'Mr Hems and the Income-tax,' *Western Times*, 26 September 1888, 2; 'Income-tax Raid,' *Western Times*, 30 April 1907, p. 8.

42. Much of the information about Hems comes from his voluminous scrapbooks, containing mostly newspaper clippings but also political posters. The 19 out of 22 surviving books are held at the Devon Heritage Centre (formerly the Westcountry Studies Library).

43. Harry Hems, 'Four Old Tillet Blocks,' *The Western Antiquary* (July 1882), pp. 69-70.

44. 'The Cenennial: A Carved Oak Chest,' *Harper's Weekly: Journal of Civilization* (October 14, 1878), vol. 20, p. 1033.

45. James Vernon, 'Cornwall and the English Imagi(nation),' *Imagining the Nation*, 156. See also John Beddoe, *The Races of Britain: a Contribution to the Anthropology of Western Europe* (London: 1885), pp. 258, 270.

46. John Beddoe, *The Races of Britain: a Contribution to the Anthropology of Western Europe* (Bristol: J. W. Arrowsmith, 1885), p. 298; also qtd. in Vernon, p. 157.

47. 'Ethnographic Survey of the United Kingdom. First Report of the Committee,' in *Report of the British Association for the Advancement of Science 1893* (London, 1894), p. 623; qtd. in Vernon, p. 159.

48. Thomas Hardy, 'The Fiddler of the Reels' (1893), in *Life's Little Ironies and A Changed Man*, ed. by F.B. Pinion (London: Macmillan, 1977), pp. 123-38, 123. On more, see Paul Young, 'Rambles Beyond Railways: Globalised Space and Gothicised Place in Victorian Cornwall,' *Gothic Studies*, 13: 1 (2011), pp. 55-74.

49. Bram Stoker, *The Jewel of the Seven Stars* (New York: Dover Publications, 2009), p. 58.

50. Patrick Bratlinger, *Rule of Darkness: British Literature and Imperialism, 1830-1914* (Ithaca, NY: Cornell UP, 1988) p. 227.

51. Bram Stoker, *Jewel*, p. 207.

52. Aviva Briefel, 'Hands of Beauty, Hands of Horror: Fear and Egyptian Art at the Fin de Siècle,' *Victorian Studies* 50:2 (2008) pp. 263-271; see also Nicholas Daly, 'That Obscure Object of Desire: Victorian Commodity Culture and Fictions of the Mummy,' *Novel*, 28: 1 (1994), pp. 24-51.

THE GOTHIC REVIVAL IN THE SOUTH WEST
Places to Visit …

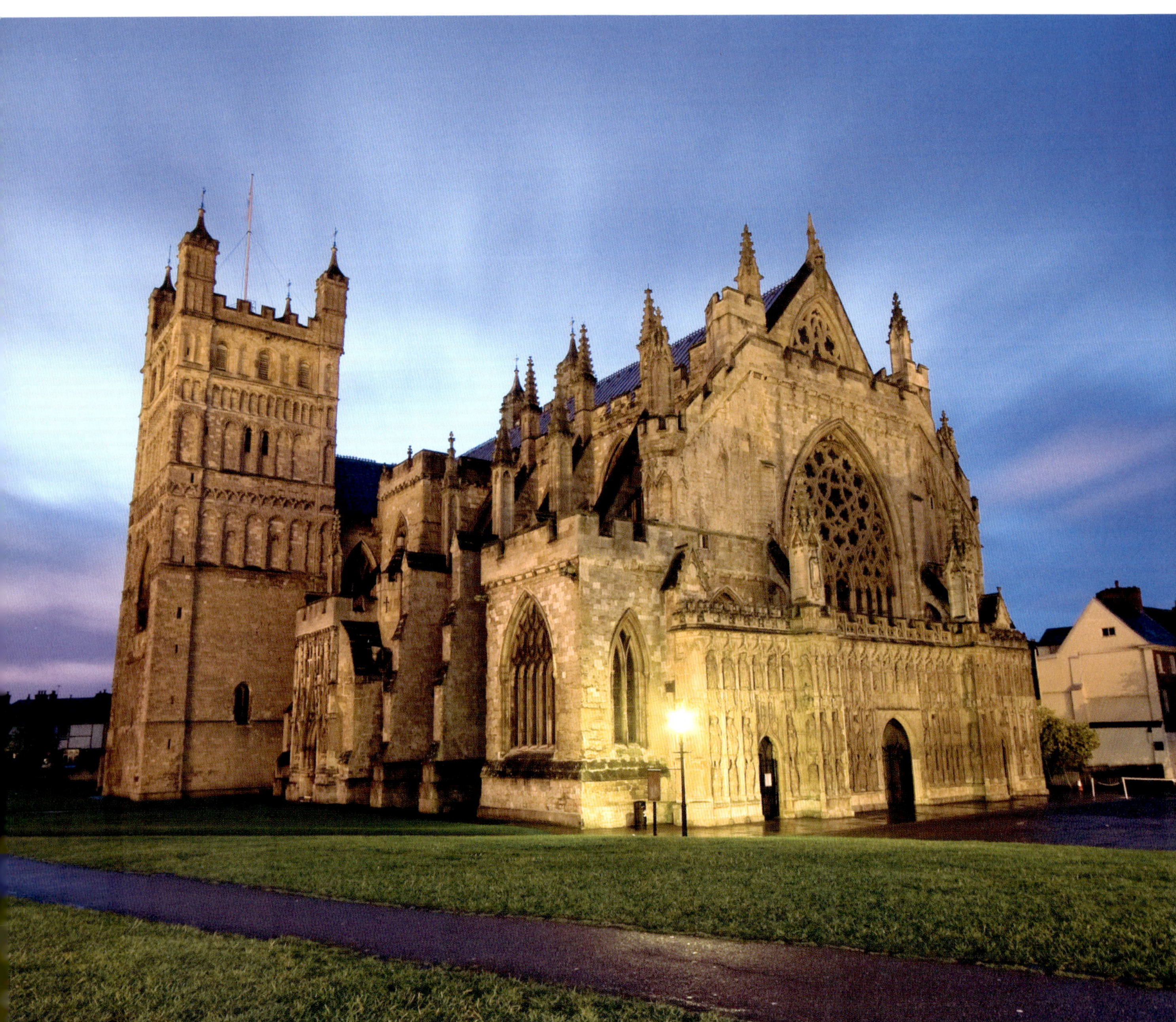

Fig. 40
Exeter Cathedral
© Dean and Chapter of Exeter

EXETER CATHEDRAL

Exeter Cathedral was one of at least 25 cathedrals restored in the nineteenth century by the Gothic revival architect Sir George Gilbert Scott who was also responsible for designing the Albert Memorial, the main building of Glasgow University, and the Midland Grand Hotel which fronts St Pancras Station. Today it is a fine example of Gothic revival restoration work.

When Gilbert Scott began work in Exeter in 1871, the Cathedral (like many others at that time) had suffered centuries of neglect and deliberate damage. From the Reformation onwards, Gothic decorations had been obliterated, inappropriate furnishings had been introduced, chapels had been abandoned and become overwhelmed by monuments, and the Cloisters had been demolished. From 1657 until 1660, moreover, Exeter Cathedral had been divided into two sections for separate use by Presbyterians and Independents. To provide the Presbyterians with access to 'Exeter East', a doorway had been inserted in the eastern wall of the Speke Chantry Chapel. Scott reconstructed this wall of the chapel. He also completed the painted decoration that can be seen today in the vaults of the Chapel of St John the Evangelist and the Chapel of St Gabriel, which was based on fragments of medieval decoration uncovered during cleaning and restoration.

Medieval-style encaustic tiles [painted with hot wax] of many different designs can be found in Exeter Cathedral. Many of these were reproduced for Scott by William Godwin of Lugwardine, Herefordshire. Scott used the reproductions in several of the cathedral's chapels. The most interesting place to view them is on the altar platforms in the Chapel of St Andrew, where Scott's tiled floors appear alongside genuinely medieval tiles. In other areas, too, Scott's work blends with the medieval parts of the cathedral. His choir stalls were designed to harmonise with the magnificent early-fourteenth-century Bishop's Throne Canopy. Their decorative carvings illustrate the text of the Benedicite – the Song of Creation, from the service of Morning Prayer. The stalls integrate medieval material – the back row incorporates the oldest complete set of misericords in England, dating from the mid-thirteenth century.

Scott's work at the cathedral finished in 1877, but ten years later the south-eastern corner of its Cloisters was reconstructed by John Loughborough Pearson. Essentially a Victorian creation, this building is divided into bays based on the spacing of the medieval cloister bays and incorporates several medieval bosses from the original structure. It was clearly hoped to extend the project

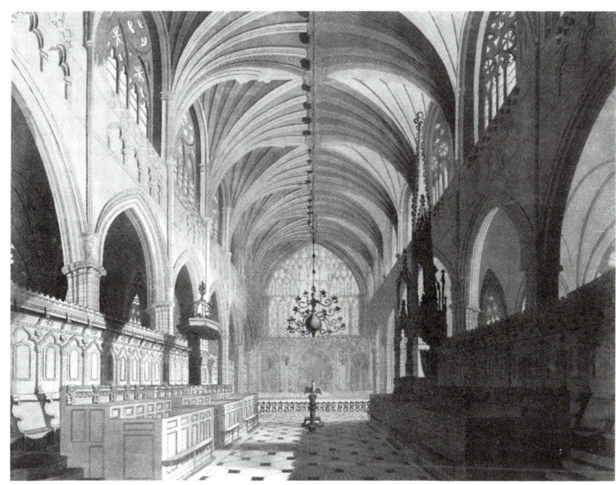

Fig. 41 / Cat. 56
The Choir of the Cathedral Church of St Peter's Exeter
John Pierce Snr (artist) / F. Jukes (engraver)
1801 / aquatint on paper
© Royal Albert Memorial Museum & Art Gallery, Exeter City Council

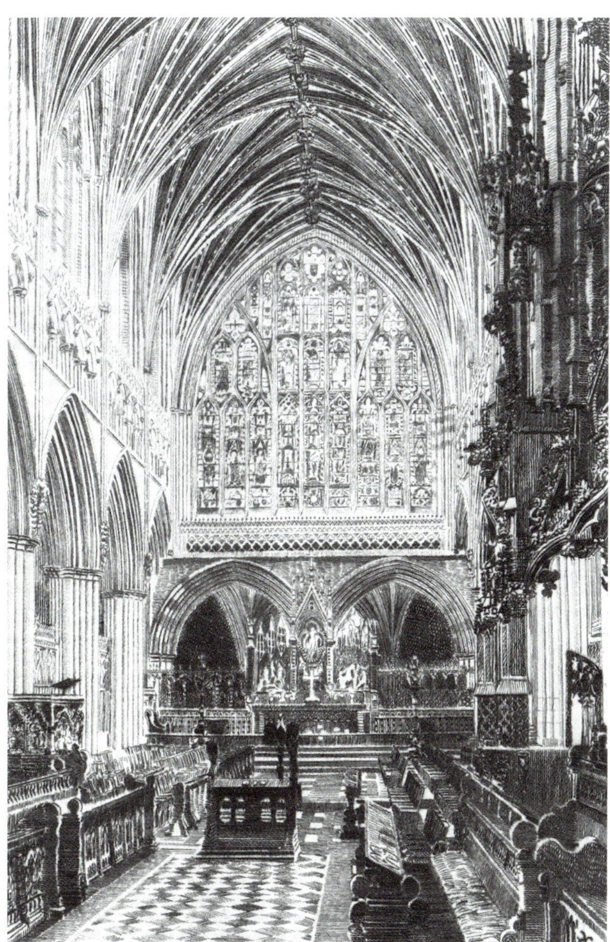

Fig. 42 / Cat. 57
Exeter Cathedral – the Choir
c.1880 / etching on paper
© Royal Albert Memorial Museum & Art Gallery, Exeter City Council

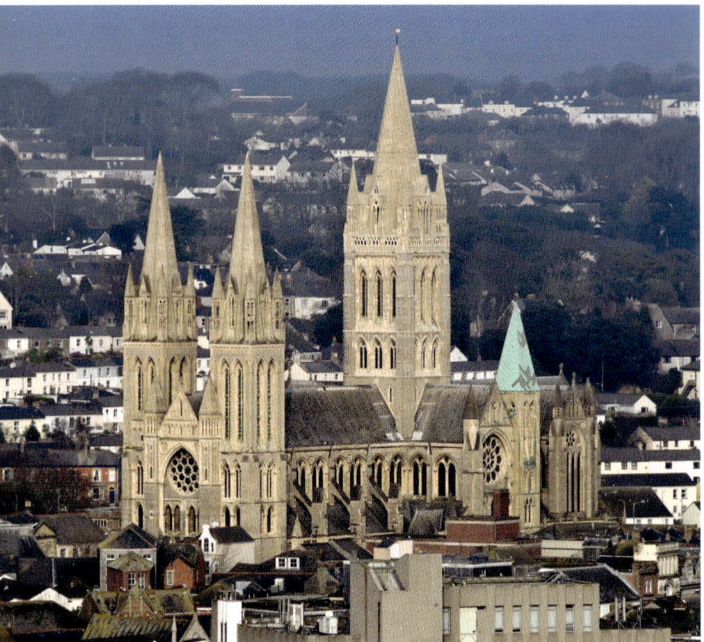

Fig. 43
Truro Cathedral
Paul Richards

— externally, springing has been left ready for the work to continue northwards. The ground floor of Pearson's building now houses the Cathedral's café.

Diane Walker/Joanne Parker

TRURO CATHEDRAL

When the foundation stone of Truro Cathedral was laid on 20 May 1880, the edifice became the first Anglican cathedral to be built on a new site since the construction of Salisbury had begun in 1220. Until the project began, Cornwall had not had its own cathedral. Its parishes had been under the care of a Cornish bishop, based at St Germans, until 1050. However, that year the Cornish 'diocese', or grouping of parishes, was amalgamated with the Devon Diocese, under the jurisdiction of the Bishop of Crediton. This was the situation for more than 800 years. In 1877, however, after 30 years of intense lobbying, the Cornish Diocese was re-established at Truro — paving the way for the creation of a new cathedral there.

The building of the cathedral was therefore a grand assertion of regional pride — as was so much medievalism in south west England in the nineteenth century. Like other expressions of Victorian medievalism, the creation of the new cathedral was also an elaborate marriage of the old and the new. Since at least 1259 there had been a

parish church of St Mary in the centre of Truro. When the city was chosen for the site of the new cathedral, it was assumed that the parish church would be completely demolished to make way for it. However, the architect John Loughborough Pearson argued and eventually gained permission to keep at least part of the old parish church. He cleverly incorporated its south aisle into his design for the new Cathedral, so that symbolically and physically the Mother Church of the Diocese has a protective arm around one of her daughter churches. Building a new Gothic cathedral was such an audacious act in 1880 that nobody was entirely confident that the project would ever be completed — after all, no one had attempted to emulate the great cathedral builders of the medieval era for over 650 years. As well as placing a foundation stone in the building's north east corner, therefore (as tradition dictated) a second stone was also placed in what was then the churchyard of St Mary's — as an act of faith that the cathedral would one day reach that far. Today that stone forms one of the pillars in the nave of a cathedral that attracts 200,000 visitors a year.

With its pointed arches, built using modern techniques, Truro Cathedral is arguably the pinnacle of Gothic revival architecture. A particular highlight of the building is its huge 'reredos' or altar screen, intricately carved from Bath stone and depicting the crucified Christ and other figures associated with the theme of sacrifice. With its Anglo-Catholic baptistery and hanging pyx (a sacrament holder that was suspended in many medieval churches), the cathedral is also of interest as one of the most remarkable products of the Anglo-Catholic movement that began with the medievalist Oxford Movement of the 1830s. And its fantastic stained glass — arguably the finest set of Victorian windows in the world — also represents the apex of the Victorian project to self-consciously revive that craft, which began in the workshops of William Morris.

Colin Reid/Joanne Parker

CASTLE DROGO

Castle Drogo, near the Dartmoor village of Drewsteignton, claims to be 'the last castle built in England'. Reminiscent of a medieval fortress, with its impregnable position, austere materials and distant echoes of the Norman Conquest, it represents one of the most remarkable twentieth-century fruits of the Victorian Gothic revival, and a fantastic expression of the romantic fascination with castles that began in Gothic literature and developed through the work of Sir Walter Scott.

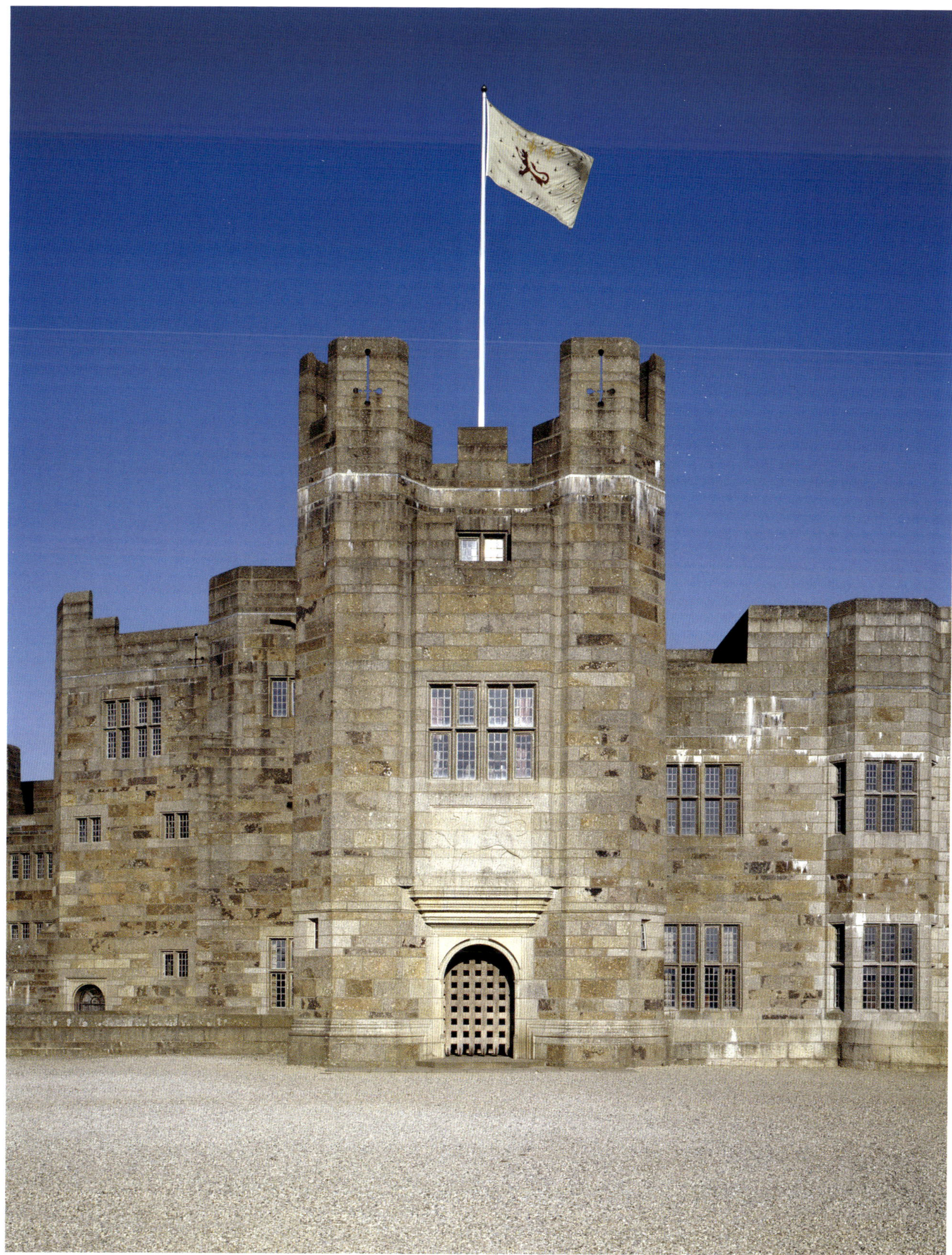

Fig. 44
Castle Drogo
© National Trust Images/Chris Gascoigne

Castle Drogo was designed by one of the leading British architects of the first half of the twentieth century Sir Edwin Lutyens, for one of the wealthiest entrepreneurs in Britain, Julius Drewe – founder of the successful Home and Colonial Stores chain of shops. In the spirit of much Victorian medievalism, Lutyens cleverly integrated eight centuries-worth of historical and stylistic design into his plans for the castle. Building began in 1911 and was completed 20 years later. Lutyens' practical skills combined with his romantic vision made him the perfect architect for Julius Drewe. Like many Victorian entrepreneurs before him, who rediscovered or created family coats of arms, or added moats and Gothic windows to family homes, what Drewe wanted was the type of ancestral pile that providence had omitted to provide him with.

Castle Drogo is undoubtedly a masterpiece – an intricate fantasy in three dimensions. The interior design of the castle reflects Lutyens's dream of creating an authentic castle, with its working portcullis, beautifully carved granite blocks to match the exterior, vaulted domed ceilings, and beautifully carved oak panelling and doors. In this sense, the building represents the epitome of the Gothic revival. However, following in the spirit of Gothic railway stations and water-works, the castle was also furnished with every modern convenience available, to transform what could have been an austere building into a comfortable family home.

At present, there is a unique opportunity to visit Castle Drogo as the building undergoes a huge renovation to make it watertight for the first time in its history. The castle is staying open to the public throughout the project – though covered in scaffold surrounded by white shrink wrap – and the National Trust is taking the opportunity to use a very different style of interpretation inside the building, while also offering visitors the opportunity to climb the viewing platform to see the building works in progress.

Lucinda Heron/Joanne Parker

KING ARTHUR'S GREAT HALLS

King Arthur's Halls in Tintagel is perhaps the most remarkable early-twentieth-century legacy of the Victorian fascination with King Arthur. It also contains some of the best post-Pre-Raphaelite artwork, in the form of one of the most impressive twentieth-century fruits of the revival in stained glass production that began in the 1860s at Morris, Marshal, Faulkner and Co.

The building that is now the halls began life as Trevena House – a substantial family home built in Tintagel in the 1860s for the newspaper editor John Douglas Cook. In the early 1920s, however, it was acquired by the custard-magnate Frederick Thomas Glasscock (co-founder of Monk and Glass Custard, and the reputed inventor of hundreds and thousands). On the sale of his company to Birds, Glasscock retired to Tintagel, taking a large library of Arthurian literature with him. Employing a small team of builders and stonemasons, Glasscock had walls and floors removed from much of Trevena House to create within it a large, medieval-style hall with a barrel-vaulted ceiling.

The hall was decorated with wall hangings, flags, shields and heraldic standards, and in 1928, Glasscock also commissioned the aging artist William Hatherell to produce a series of ten paintings of the Arthurian legend for it. The room was to serve as the Council Chamber of the 'Fellowship of the Knights of the Round Table of King Arthur', a masonic-style fellowship that Glasscock founded in 1927. By the early 1930s, it had an international membership of 17,000 and work began to create a larger meeting hall in the back garden of Trevena House, which was opened in a grand ceremony in June 1933.

The 'Hall of Chivalry' as it became known is decorated with a huge granite throne and with 73 'post-Pre-Raphaelite' stained glass windows that Glasscock commissioned in 1930 from Veronica Whall, a pupil of William Morris and the daughter of the late Victorian glass-maker Christopher Whall (whose work appears in Gloucester Cathedral). The windows included two sets of triptychs depicting the Arthurian myth, and the collection is widely regarded as some of the best twentieth-century stained glass in the world.

After Glasscock's death his Fellowship dissolved and the halls were returned to his family, but in 1952 they were acquired by the Freemasons of Tintagel to use as a masonic hall. In the 1990s they began to open to the public and are now open every day except Christmas Day.

Joanne Parker: with reference to Don Hutchinson's One Man's Dream: The Story of King Arthur's Great Halls, Tintagel, Cornwall, England, (Tintagel: privately printed, [n.d.])

TYNTESFIELD

Tyntesfield is a Victorian Gothic revival house and estate near Wraxall, North Somerset, England. The fortunes of Tyntesfield changed as dramatically as those of its owner, the enterprising Victorian businessman William Gibbs.

Gibbs's father was a merchant in Exeter's woollen cloth trade, his grandfather was chief surgeon at the

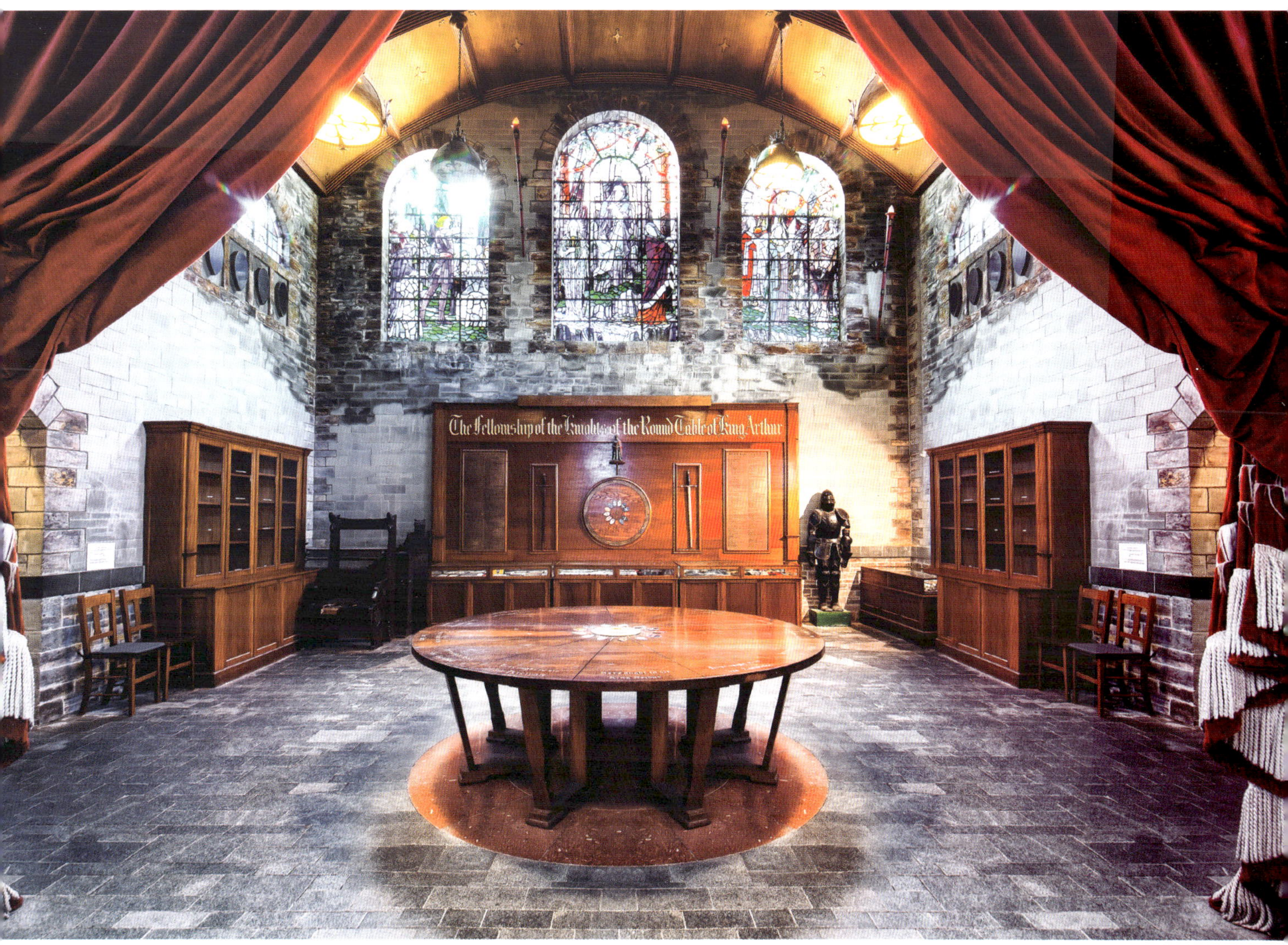

Fig. 45
King Arthur's Great Halls, Tintagel
© Joe Daniel Price

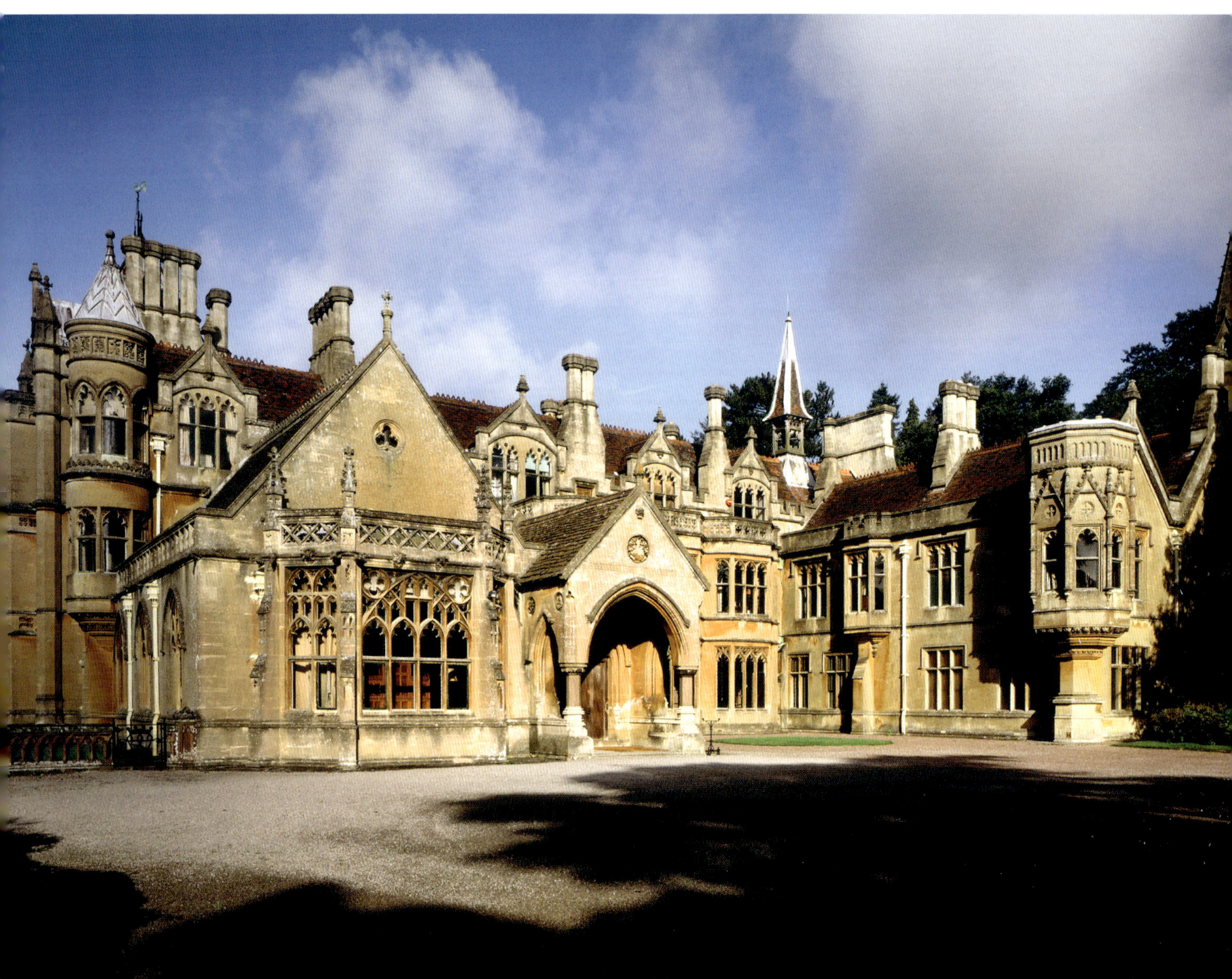

Fig. 46
Tyntesfield

Royal Devon and Exeter Hospital, and his uncle Vicary Gibbs co-defended the radicals John Horne Tooke, Thomas Hardy and John Thelwall at the treason trials of 1794. Vicary became something of a celebrity when the radicals were acquitted; he went on to be knighted and became Attorney-General. William Gibbs eventually took over the Spanish branch of the family trading business, which was often on shaky financial ground. The mixed fortunes of the business changed when he imported nitrate-rich guano, or hardened bird droppings, from uninhabited islands off South America. Gibbs cleverly promoted guano to farmers as fertilizer, and the business took off. He rapidly became, according to newspaper reports, the richest commoner in England.

Three years after the guano venture, William and his wife Blanche purchased a country estate they renamed Tyntesfield, and within a few years, they began a programme of remodelling and enlarging. In the 1850s the designer John Gregory Crace remodelled the existing interior, and signs of his links with the Gothic revivalist A.W.N. Pugin are clear to see in furniture, such as the richly ornamented oak sideboard in the dining room; when the house was enlarged, Pugin-styled caustic tiles and chandeliers were added.

The much more substantive changes to Tyntesfield began in earnest in 1863, under the direction of the Bristol architect John Norton, an understudy of Pugin's friend and fellow 'Goth' Benjamin Ferrey. Essentially, Norton wrapped a new – and much more striking – house around the existing one. He quite seamlessly mingled differing periods, styles and influences, but all the elements spoke a shared Gothic language.

Working with the builder George Plucknett, the men added an extra floor, two new wings and towers. The end result is highly romantic, picturesque, and above all, Gothic. Turrets stab skyward and chimneys thrust above steeply sloping and irregularly pitched roofs. The highest point of the building is a tower with tourelles or turrets, and a gaslight-illuminated chiming clock. The Gothic style is continental, but also reminiscent of the Ruskinian Gothic of the Oxford Museum. There are also Oriel windows and others with tracery; there are blind arches (arches on outer walls) and an arcade. Ruskin's influence can be seen on the exterior ornamental stone carving, which combines nature with imagination in the decorative animals, birds, branches and fantastical gargoyles.

The Gothic idiom continues inside the house, in the ironwork, glass, mosaics, furniture and walls. There are several star pieces of Gothic design, collected in the height of Victorian Gothic revival and later, including the extraordinary throne chair, of solid bronze with crystal

finials to the arms, designed on an engraving by French Gothic revivalist Eugène Viollet-le-Duc.

As the two essays in this catalogue show, design is never separate from religion and politics. The Gothic style of Tyntesfield is reflective of the Gibbs's Anglo-Catholicism and their connection to the Oxford Movement. Indeed, Blanche's cousin, the novelist Charlotte Mary Yonge described the house as 'like a church in spirit'. These religious allegiances are most obvious in the monastic-style chapel (1872–77), modelled on Paris's Sainte-Chapelle. Other buildings in the area were conserved through Gibbs's support and the work of Gothic revivalist architects such as George Gilbert Scott, William Butterfield and others. These include St Michael and All Angels at Clifton Hampden, the Exeter Free Cottages in Exwick, and renovations of both the Bristol and Exeter Cathedrals.

Corinna Wagner

KNIGHTSHAYES

Knightshayes is a rare example of a William Burges domestic building in the picturesque Gothic style. In a circuitous way, machine-breaking Luddites had a hand in its existence.

John Heathcoat invented a bobbin that revolutionised his lace manufacturing business, but also caused envy among his fellow Loughborough producers. Perhaps because of this, Luddites destroyed Heathcoat's manufacturing works. He packed up and moved home, business and many of his workers to Tiverton, Devon. He went on to have, for a period of time, the largest lace-producing factory in the world.

His grandson and heir John Amory (who became Sir John Heathcoat Amory) purchased land to build a country house in 1867, and by 1874, Knightshayes was complete. William Burges was originally commissioned for the job but most of his designs went unexecuted and the furniture unconstructed. Heathcoat Amory balked at the cost of what he saw as Burges's overly fantastical style. Burges was dismissed and replaced by the interior designer John Dibblee Crace, who had completed design plans for the British Museum, the National Gallery and the Royal Academy (Crace's father headed the design work at Tyntesfield).

The form and exterior of Knightshayes is largely Burges's. The principal block of the house – consisting of hall, drawing room, morning room, library and billiard room – is fairly straightforward and the exterior is relatively restrained. Burges's plans to build a massive med-

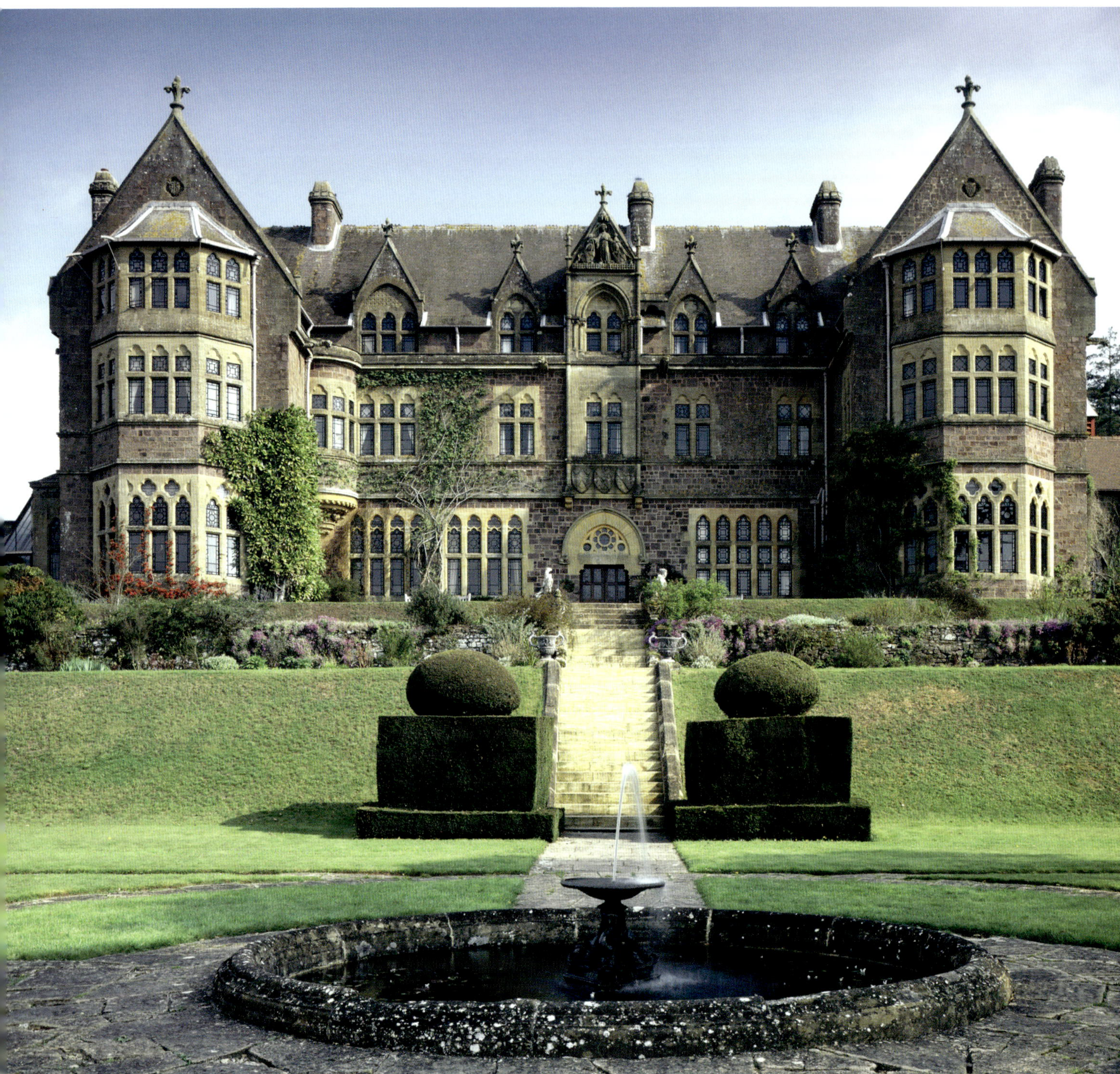

Fig. 47
Knightshayes
© National Trust Images/Rupert Truman

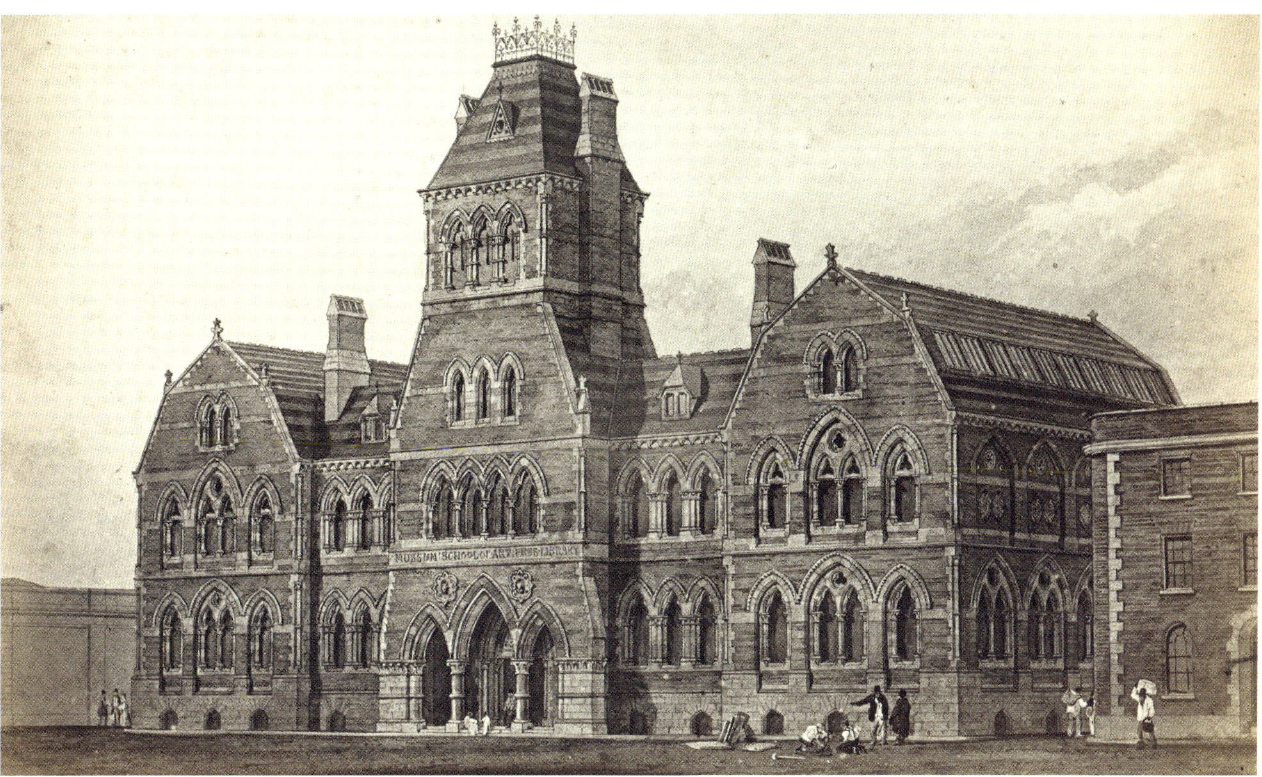

Fig. 48 / Cat. 31
The original competition design for the Albert Memorial Museum
John Hayward (1807–91)
© Royal Albert Memorial Museum & Art Gallery, Exeter City Council

ieval-styled tower were never realized, nor his elaborate and romantically eccentric interior designs. Most of the interior is Crace's, but Burges's conception can be seen in the most imaginatively romantic of the rooms, the medieval great hall. It has a gallery with a pierced stone balcony and Gothic arches supported by great marble columns. Burges also created a wonderfully detailed presentation album, which showcases his thematic designs, in colour, for walls, fireplaces, and other interior features of the house's rooms. This album can be seen, on display, at the house.

Knightshayes provides visitors with the opportunity to see conservation in action. Old photographs and surviving materials have provided a blueprint for a restoration that has brought the work of both Burges and Crace back to life. The National Trust is also restoring some particularly unusual Burges features that had been covered over, including 'sparkling' ceilings in the drawing room. In addition, there are some wonderful pieces on display, including a few from Burges's own Westminster home, Tower House, some of which are on loan from current owner, guitarist Jimmy Page. There is also a marble fireplace from Burges's Worcester College,

Oxford redecoration. In 'The Burges Room' the National Trust presents a vision of what a completed Burges decorated room would have looked like.

Corinna Wagner

ROYAL ALBERT MEMORIAL MUSEUM

The Royal Albert Memorial Museum & Art Gallery is a product of several things: the emergence of various branches of the natural sciences in the Enlightenment, the Georgian project of creating public museums, galleries and libraries, the nineteenth-century passion for collecting, and the spirit of Victorian philanthropy. It is also a manifestation of the Victorian love of the medieval past and the rage for neo-Gothic architecture.

In 1813, the Devon and Exeter Institution opened. With the aim of promoting local history and bringing about 'the general diffusion of Science, Literature and Art', they created a library and gathered artefacts. It was not until 1861, however, that the idea of the museum came to fruition. Sir Stafford Northcote of Pynes (later 1st Earl of Iddesleigh) was a Devon MP and President of the

Exeter School of Art. When Queen Victoria's consort Prince Albert died in 1861, Northcote proposed that a memorial to him should be established in Exeter, and a committee was formed. They created the Devon and Exeter Albert Memorial Institution, which was to house a museum, art gallery, public library, a school of art, and a mechanical institute.

The project was inspired in general by a culture of Victorian altruism and national pride, and it drew impetus from London's Great Exhibition of 1851, which showcased design and goods from around the world. The crowds that poured into the Crystal Palace produced revenue for the creation of public educational institutions such as the Albert Hall, the Science Museum, the Natural History Museum and South Kensington Museum, which would become the Victoria and Albert Museum. As one of Prince Albert's secretaries for the exhibition, Northcote had seen the possibilities for Exeter.

The committee collected about £15,000 in public subscription funds for the construction of the Memorial Institution. A Gothic revivalist, John Hayward won the architectural competition, with a design modelled on the University Museum in Oxford and informed by the Early English architectural style of the thirteenth century. Building began in 1865 and finished in 1868.

The building's Gothic details include a large ecclesiastical-styled rose window, arched windows with tracery and also trefoil-headed windows. The Gothic building houses a notable archaeological, anthropological, and natural history collection, as well as an impressive art collection. These became the basis of RAMM, when in the first half of the twentieth century, the library and other departments were transplanted to new homes. From the beginning, under the first curatorship of William Steward Mitchell D'Urban (1884–95), the collections expanded and space was a perennial issue. Over the years, this led to various building extensions.

RAMM underwent a major redevelopment from 2001 to 2011, funded by Exeter City Council, the Heritage Lottery Fund and others. This allowed for integration of the extensions, repair to structural damage, and expansion. In 2012, the success of this project was acknowledged with the Art Fund's Museum of the Year award.

Corinna Wagner

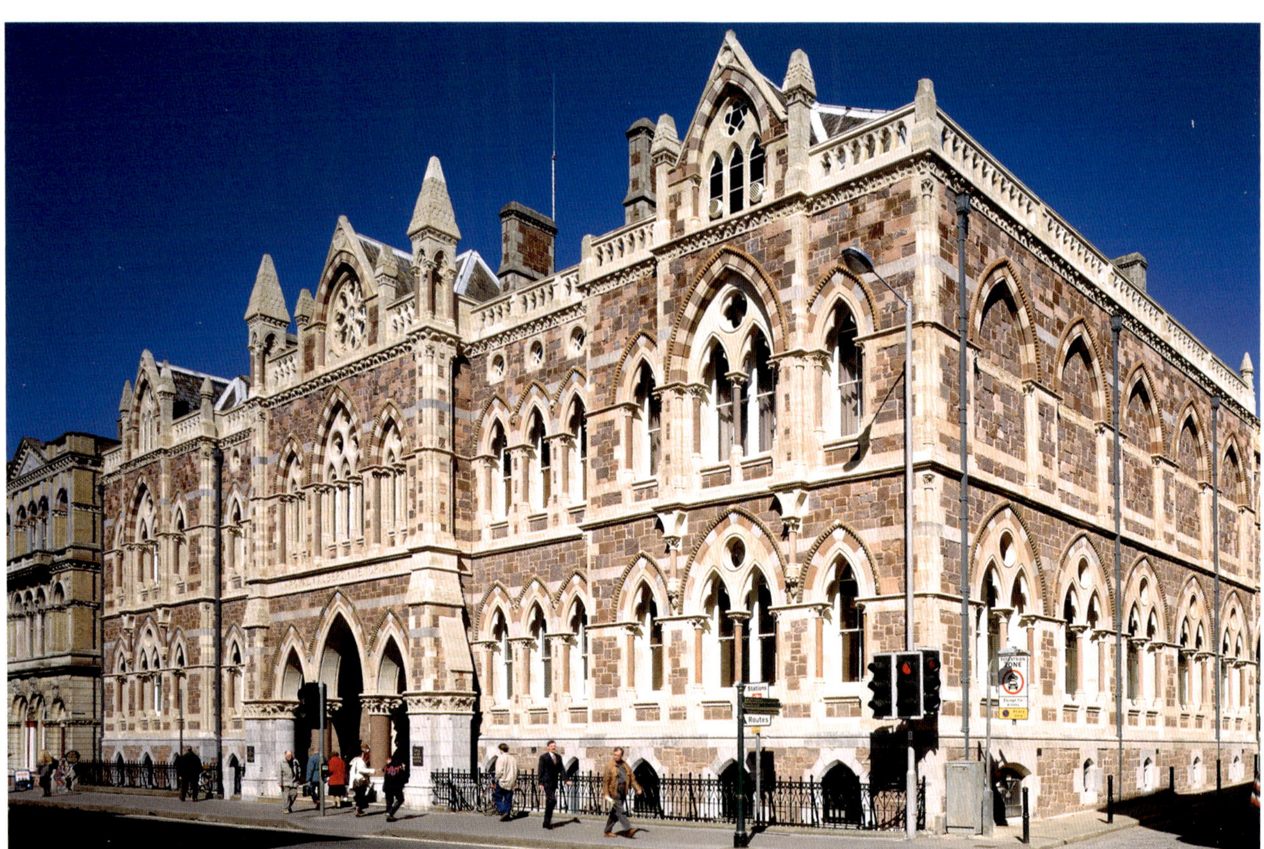

Fig. 49
Royal Albert Memorial Museum

CATALOGUE

Catalogue of exhibits on display in 'Art & Soul:
Victorians and the Gothic' at the Royal Albert
Memorial Museum & Art Gallery, Exeter,
22 November 2014 to 12 April 2015.

INTRODUCTION

Cat. 1 (see p. 24)
The Ruins of Glastonbury Abbey
George Arnald (1763–1841)
c.1810 / oil on canvas
Museum of Somerset

Cat. 2 (see p. 10)
The Seeds and Fruits of English Poetry
Ford Madox Brown (1821–93)
1853 / oil on canvas
Ashmolean Museum

Cat. 3 (see p. 15)
*Queen Victoria and Prince Albert
at the Bal Costumé of 12 May 1842*
Sir Edwin Landseer (1802–73)
1842–46 / oil on canvas
Lent by Royal Collection Trust on behalf of
Her Majesty the Queen

Cat. 4
*The Queen receiving the Sacrament
at her Coronation*
Charles Robert Leslie (artist); Samuel Cousins
(engraver); F.G. Moon (publisher)
1843 / engraving on paper
Royal Albert Memorial Museum & Art Gallery

Cat. 5 (see p. 21)
*Edward III Conferring the Order of the Garter
on Edward the Black Prince*
Charles West Cope (1811–90)
c.1847 / oil on canvas
Museums Sheffield

Cat. 6
*Programme for the Celebrations of the Marriage
of the Prince and Princess of Wales, Exeter,
March 10 1863*
John Gidley
1863 / printed on paper
Royal Albert Memorial Museum & Art Gallery

Cat. 7
The Houses of Parliament
Lucien (engraver);
Hildesheimer & Co Ltd (publisher)
1890s / etching on parchment
Royal Albert Memorial Museum & Art Gallery

Cat. 8 (see p. 49)
*Design for furniture and fittings
in the Apartments of George IV*
Augustus W.N. Pugin (1812–52)
1827 / pencil, pen, ink and watercolour on paper
Victoria and Albert Museum

Cat. 9
*Examples of Gothic Architecture selected
from various Ancient Edifices in England
(Volume I of III)*
Auguste-Charles Pugin (1762–1832)
1831 / book
Devon & Exeter Institution

Cat. 10 (see pp. 53, 54 and 60)
*Contrasts, or a parallel between the noble edifices
of the 14th and 15th centuries and similar buildings
of the present day: shewing the present decay of
taste / by A.Welby Pugin*
Augustus W.N. Pugin (1812–52)
1836 / book
University of Exeter, Heritage Collections

Cat. 11
*The true principles of pointed or Christian
architecture: set forth in two lectures delivered
at St Marie's, Oscott / by A.Welby Pugin*
Augustus W.N. Pugin (1812–52)
1841 / book
University of Exeter, Heritage Collections

Cat. 12
Glossary of Ecclesiastical Ornament and Costume
Augustus W.N. Pugin (1812–52)
1846 / book
Devon & Exeter Institution

Cat. 13
Candelabrum
Augustus W.N. Pugin (1812–52)
and John Hardman & Co.
c.1846 / wrought brasswork
Victoria and Albert Museum

Cat. 14 (see p. 51)
Chalice
Augustus W.N. Pugin (1812–52)
and John Hardman & Co.
1849–50 / silver and silver-gilt
Victoria and Albert Museum

Cat. 15
Floriated Ornament: A Series of Thirty-one Designs
Augustus W.N. Pugin (1812–52)
1849 / book
Devon & Exeter Institution

Cat. 16 (see p. 64)
*The Medieval Court from Dickinsons Comprehensive
Pictures of the Great Exhibition of 1851*
W.R., L.C. and G.B. Dickinson
1854 / lithograph
Victoria and Albert Museum

Cat. 17
The Grammar of Ornament
Owen Jones (1809–74)
First published 1856 / book
Royal Albert Memorial Museum & Art Gallery

Cat. 18 (see p. 31)
Tapestry panel: Pomona
Edward Coley Burne-Jones (1833–98);
Morris & Co. (weaver)
c.1900 / wool and silk on cotton warp
Victoria and Albert Museum

Cat. 19
Wallpaper design: Acanthus
William Morris (1834–96)
1874 / pencil, watercolour and bodycolour
Victoria and Albert Museum

Cat. 20
Textile design: Rose and Thistle
William Morris (1834–96)
c.1882 / charcoal and watercolour
Victoria and Albert Museum

Cat. 21
Design for a Tapestry
William Morris (1834–96)
1880s / pencil, watercolour and bodycolour
Victoria and Albert Museum

RUSKIN AND RAMM

Cat. 22 (see p. 47)
Worksheet: window at Sant' Anastasia, Verona
John Ruskin (1819–1900)
Probably 1851–52
pencil, black ink, ink wash and watercolour
The Ruskin Library (Lancaster University)

Cat. 23
Worksheet: window at Sant' Anastasia, Verona
John Ruskin (1819–1900)
Probably 1851–52
pencil, black ink, ink wash and watercolour
The Ruskin Library (Lancaster University)

Cat. 24
*Study of the North Gable of the Tomb of Mastino
II della Scala, Verona*
John Ruskin (1819–1900)
1852 / pencil and watercolour
Ashmolean Museum

Cat. 25
The Seven Lamps of Architecture
John Ruskin (1819–1900)
1849 / book
Devon & Exeter Institution

Cat. 26
The Stones of Venice Volume II
John Ruskin (1819–1900)
1853 / book
Devon & Exeter Institution

Cat. 27 (see pp. 58–59)
*The Nature of Gothic:
a chapter of The Stones of Venice (Kelmscott Press)*
John Ruskin (1819–1900)
1892 / book
The Ruskin Library (Lancaster University)

Cat. 28
Poetic obituary to Albert Prince consort:
Albert the Good
F. Warner Jones
1861 / pen and ink
Royal Albert Memorial Museum & Art Gallery

Cat. 29
The Queen and Prince Albert 'The Parting'
From the statue by William Theed
c.1897 / photogravure
Royal Albert Memorial Museum & Art Gallery

Cat. 30 (see p. 46)
Venice worksheet No 17: Notes on the Casa d'Oro
19 Nov. 1849
John Ruskin (1819–1900)
1849 / pen over pencil
The Ruskin Library (Lancaster University)

Cat. 31 (see p. 85)
The original competition design for the
Albert Memorial Museum
John Hayward (1807–91)
Early 1860s / print
Royal Albert Memorial Museum & Art Gallery

Cat. 32
Ground Floor Plan of the Albert Memorial Museum,
Exeter
Hayward & Son
early 1860s / ink and wash on paper
Royal Albert Memorial Museum & Art Gallery

Cat. 33
Upper Floor Plan of the Albert Memorial Museum,
Exeter
Hayward & Son
early 1860s / ink and wash on paper
Royal Albert Memorial Museum & Art Gallery

Cat. 34
Interior of the Royal Albert Memorial Museum from
the Ethnography Gallery to the Upper Landing
Frances Marjorie Hayman (c.1900–1982)
c.1925 / watercolour,
Royal Albert Memorial Museum & Art Gallery

Cat. 35
Interior of the Royal Albert Memorial Museum
(Rowley Gallery)
Frances Roberts (1895–1980)
c.1927 / watercolour
Royal Albert Memorial Museum & Art Gallery

Cat. 36
Interior of the Royal Albert Memorial Museum
(Main Staircase)
Frances Roberts (1895–1980)
c.1927 / watercolour
Royal Albert Memorial Museum & Art Gallery

MAKERS WITH SOUTH WEST CONNECTIONS

Cat. 37
St Anne's Chapel, Barnstaple
William R. Lethaby (1857–1931)
early-to-mid 1870s / pen and ink on paper
Museum of Barnstaple & North Devon

Cat. 38.
Old House in Exeter
William R. Lethaby (1857–1931)
1879 / pen on paper
Museum of Barnstaple & North Devon

Cat. 39
A House of the Learned Societies: perspective aerial
William R. Lethaby (1857–1931)
1879 / pen and ink on paper
Athenaeum, Barnstaple

Cat. 40
Sideboard / kitchen dresser
William R. Lethaby (1857–1931) (designer)
1898–99 / oak with ebony, sycamore and
mahogany inlay
Victoria and Albert Museum

Cat. 41
Sideboard
Shapland and Petter Ltd, Barnstaple
c.1900 / oak with beaten copper panels
Royal Albert Memorial Museum & Art Gallery

Cat. 42
The History of Reynard the Fox by F.S. Ellis
Walter Crane (1845–1915) (illustrator);
Omar Ramsden and Alwyn Carr (silversmiths)
published 1897 / vellum bound book with
silver mounts
The Wilson, Cheltenham Art Gallery & Museum

Cat. 43 (see p. 32)
The Story of the Glittering Plain
or the Land of Living Men (Kelmscott Press)
Walter Crane (1845–1915) (illustrator)
1894 / book
The Wilson, Cheltenham Art Gallery & Museum

Cat. 44 (see p. 17)
Illustrations from Spenser's The Faerie Queene
Walter Crane (1845–1915) (illustrator)
1897 / line prints, hand-coloured by the artist
Royal Albert Memorial Museum & Art Gallery

Cat. 45
Alms Dish
W.H. and E.R. Singer (design);
Singer and Sons, Frome (manufacture)
1884 / brass, with repoussé decoration
Victoria and Albert Museum

Cat. 46 (see p. 71)
Bench end
Medieval (shortly after 1500) / carved oak
(removed from the Church of St George, Dunster
around 1838 and collected by Harry Hems, c.1875)
Royal Albert Memorial Museum & Art Gallery

Cat. 47
Bench end
medieval (around 1600) / carved oak
(removed from St James the Great Church,
Kilkhampton and collected by Harry Hems
after 1860)
Royal Albert Memorial Museum & Art Gallery

Cat. 48
Roof bosses
Medieval (15th century) / carved oak
(Harry Hems collection from Devon churches)
Royal Albert Memorial Museum & Art Gallery

Cat. 49
Prie Dieu
Pearson Barry Hayward (1838–88) (designer);
Harry Hems (1842–1916) (maker)
1878 / carved oak
Parish of St David's with St Michael
and All Angels, Exeter

SOUTH WEST PATRONS

Cat. 50
Font cover
W.D. Caroe (designer); Dart & Francis (maker)
1912 / carved oak
St Andrew's Church, Paignton

Cat. 51 (see p. 52)
Allhallows on the Walls, Exeter
John Hayward (1807–91) (architect);
R.K. Thomas (engraver)
c.1850 / lithograph on paper
Royal Albert Memorial Museum & Art Gallery

Cat. 52
Chalice, paten and salver with two ewers
from St Olave's Church, Exeter
J.B. London
1874 / silver, glass and enamel
Parish of Central Exeter

Cat. 53
Stained glass roundel of The Nativity
from the Royal Devon & Exeter Hospital chapel
Frederick Drake & Sons
1868 / glass
Royal Albert Memorial Museum & Art Gallery

Cat. 54
Stained glass roundel of The Ascension
from St David's Church, Exeter
Clayton & Bell
1862 / glass
Parish of St David's with St Michael
and All Angels, Exeter

Cat. 55
Marsh-Dunn Memorial Lectern
from St Michael's Church, East Teignmouth
1885 / brass
Parish of St Michael's, East Teignmouth

Cat. 56 (see p. 77)
The Choir of the Cathedral Church
of St Peter's Exeter
John Pierce Snr (artist); F. Jukes (engraver);
R. Pierce (publisher)
1801 / aquatint on paper
Royal Albert Memorial Museum & Art Gallery

Cat. 57 (see p. 77)
Exeter Cathedral – the Choir
c.1880 / etching on paper
Royal Albert Memorial Museum & Art Gallery

Cat. 58
Design for the Tanner Memorial Window,
south nave aisle, Exeter Cathedral
produced for the firm of Burlison & Grylls
1872 / pen and ink and watercolour on paper
Royal Albert Memorial Museum & Art Gallery

Cat. 59 (see pp. 66–67)
Decoration for Knightshayes Court
William Burges (1827–81) and assistants
early 1870s / album of watercolour designs
National Trust (Knightshayes)

Cat. 60
Exterior elevation No.6 (Knightshayes Court)
William Burges (1827–81) and assistants
c.1868 / watercolour on paper
National Trust (Knightshayes)

Cat. 61
Minstrels Gallery No.23 (Knightshayes Court)
William Burges (1827–81) and assistants
early 1870s / watercolour on paper
National Trust (Knightshayes)

Cat. 62
Staircase Designs No.5 (Knightshayes Court)
William Burges (1827–81) and assistants
early 1870s / watercolour on paper
National Trust (Knightshayes)

Cat. 63 (see p. 68)
Exeter Mayor's chain
William Burges (1827–81) (designer);
Parker & Stone (maker)
1874 / gold, with enamel badge of office
Exeter City Council, Mayor's Office

Cat. 64
Throne from Tyntesfield
Viollet-le-Duc (designer);
Barkentin and Krall (maker)
1877 / bronze and crystal
National Trust (Tyntesfield)

Cat. 65
Three-leaf screen from Tyntesfield
mid-to-late 19th century / carved oak
National Trust (Tyntesfield)

Cat. 66
Under the Iron Bridge, Exeter
(with a view of St Michael's Church)
Edna Fry (1902–1989)
1926 / etching
Royal Albert Memorial Museum & Art Gallery

Cat. 67
Architectural elevation:
St. Michael's and All Angels Church
Major Rhode Hawkins (architect)
1865 / pen and ink and watercolour on paper
Parish of St David's with
St Michael and All Angels, Exeter

SOUTH WEST COMMUNITY

Cat. 68 (see p. 61)
The Old Pumping Station of the Exeter Water
Company near St David's Station, Exeter
William Cheeseman
1876 / watercolour on paper
Royal Albert Memorial Museum & Art Gallery

Cat. 69 (see p. 34)
Plaque of Alfred the Great
produced for the West of England Fire and Life
Insurance Company
c.1840 / oil on copper panel
Royal Albert Memorial Museum & Art Gallery

Cat. 70
Bust of Alfred the Great
Andrew Patey (architect) (1783–1826);
part of the façade of the West of England Fire
and Life Insurance Company, destroyed by
German bombing 1942
1833 / carved stone
Royal Albert Memorial Museum & Art Gallery

Cat. 71
Seal of John Bull, Archdeacon of Barnstaple
George Halfhide (seal engraver)
1826 / bronze
Royal Albert Memorial Museum & Art Gallery

Cat. 72
Guild of St Sidwell ecclesiastical medal
1881–1903 / bronze
Royal Albert Memorial Museum & Art Gallery

Cat. 73
The Royal Institute of Public Health official's badge
1902 / gilt and enamel
Royal Albert Memorial Museum & Art Gallery

Cat. 74
The Constitutional Club, Exeter, 1883 medal
1883 / bronze
Royal Albert Memorial Museum & Art Gallery

Cat. 75
Exeter Middle School for Girls
perfect attendance medal
1889 / bronze
Royal Albert Memorial Museum & Art Gallery

Cat. 76
Tiverton Science, Art and Technical School
Hadow medal
1893 / silver
Royal Albert Memorial Museum & Art Gallery

Cat. 77
Primrose League General Election
Special Service badge
1900 / gilt and enamel
Royal Albert Memorial Museum & Art Gallery

Cat. 78
Primrose League Special Service badge
1896 / gilt and enamel
Royal Albert Memorial Museum & Art Gallery

Cat. 79
'Billy and Charley Medallions',
faked medieval objects
William Smith (Billy) and
Charles Eaton (Charley) (makers)
made between 1851–1870 / lead alloy
Royal Albert Memorial Museum & Art Gallery

MYTHS AND LEGENDS

Cat. 80 (see p. 29)
The Lady of Shalott
John William Waterhouse (1849–1917)
1894 / oil on canvas
Falmouth Art Gallery

Cat. 81 (see p. 28)
Figure of Guinevere
William Morris (1834–96)
c.1858, watercolour and graphite on paper
Tate, London

Cat. 82 (see p. 33)
Study of Iseult for 'The Marriage of Sir Tristram'.
Verso: Figure of Sir Tristram
Edward Coley Burne-Jones (1833–98)
c.1862 / graphite on paper
Tate, London

Cat. 83
Poems
Alfred, Lord Tennyson (1809–92);
Edward Moxon, London (publisher)
1860 / book
University of Exeter, Heritage Collections

Cat. 84
Guinevere
Alfred, Lord Tennyson (1809–92);
Edward Moxon, London (publisher)
1868 / book
University of Exeter, Heritage Collections

Cat. 85
Enid
Alfred, Lord Tennyson (1809–92);
Edward Moxon, London (publisher)
1868 / book
University of Exeter, Heritage Collections

Cat. 86
Elaine
Alfred, Lord Tennyson (1809–92);
Edward Moxon, London (publisher)
1867 / book
University of Exeter, Heritage Collections

Cat. 87
Vivien
Alfred, Lord Tennyson (1809–92);
Edward Moxon, London (publisher)
1867 / book
University of Exeter, Heritage Collections

Cat. 88 (see p. 27)
Alfred Lord Tennyson
Elliot & Fry (photographer);
McClure, Macdonald & Co. (engraver)
c.1880 / engraving on paper
Royal Albert Memorial Museum & Art Gallery

Cat. 89 (see p. 30)
Holy Grail Tapestry – Knights of the Round Table
Summoned to the Quest by the Strange Damsel
Edward Coley Burne-Jones, William Morris, John
Henry Dearle (designers); Morris & Co. (weaver)
1898–99 / wool, silk, mohair and camel hair weft
on cotton warp
Birmingham Museums & Art Gallery

Cat. 90
Stained Glass Panel – The Death of Tristram
Ford Madox Brown (designer);
Morris, Marshall, Faulkner & Co.
1862
Bradford Museums & Galleries, Cartwright Hall

SUGGESTED READING

MEDIEVALIST OR GOTHIC WORKS

Sabine Baring-Gould, *The Book of Werewolves* (London: Smith Elder, 1865).

Sabine Baring-Gould, *Curious Myths of the Middle Ages* (London: Rivingtons, 1868).

Sabine Baring-Gould, *Songs and Ballads of the West* (London: Methuen, 1891).

Eliza Bray, *Henry de Pomeroy: Or, The Eve of St John* (London: Longman, 1845).

Thomas Carlyle, *On Heroes, Hero Worship and the Heroic in History* (London: Chapman and Hall, 1840).

Thomas Carlyle, *Past and Present, in Thomas Carlyle's Works* (London: Chapman and Hall, n.d.).

William Godwin, *Life of Geoffrey Chaucer, the Early English Poet* (London: Richard Phillips, 1803).

Thomas Hardy, *A Pair of Blue Eyes* (Oxford: OUP, 1985 [1873]).

David Hume, *The History of England* (London: A. Millar, 1762).

G.P.R. James, *Forest Days* (London: Saunders and Otley, 1843).

John Keats, *Lamia, Isabella, The Eve of St Agnes and Other Poems* (London: Taylor and Hessey, 1820).

M. Lonsdale, *Sketch of Alfred the Great: Or, The Danish Invasion: A Grand Historical Ballet* (London, 1865).

David Mallet and James Thomson, *Alfred: A Masque* (London: A. Millar, 1740).

Tom Matthews, *Harlequin Alfred the Great! Or, the Magic Banjo and the Mystic Raven* (London, 1850).

Edward Montague, *The Castle of Berry Pomeroy* (London: Valancourt, 2014 [1806]).

T.C. and A.E. Mortimer, *Berry Pomeroy Castle: An Historical and Descriptive Sketch* (Totnes: Totnes Times and Western Guardian, [n.d.]).

John Newman, *Apologia Pro Vita Sua* (London: Longman, 1890 [1864]).

A.W.N. Pugin, *Contrasts: or, a Parallel between the Noble Edifices of the Middle Ages, and Corresponding Buildings of the Present Day* (Leicester: Humanities Press, 1969 [1836]).

John Ruskin, *The Stones of Venice, in The Works of John Ruskin* (London: George Allen, 1902).

Bram Stoker, *Dracula*, ed. Glennis Byron (Peterborough, ON: Broadview, 1998 [1897]).

Alfred, Lord Tennyson, *Poems*, 2 vols. (London: Edward Moxon, 1842).

Gothic Evolutions: Poetry, Tales, Context, Theory, ed. Corinna Wagner (Peterborough, ON: Broadview, 2014).

Horace Walpole, *The Castle of Otranto: A Gothic Story*, ed. Nick Groom (Oxford: OUP, 2014).

Gerrard Winstanley, *The Law of Freedom and Other Writings* (Cambridge University Press, 1983).

Mrs Henry Wood, *Pomeroy Abbey: A Romance* (London: Richard Bentley, 1898).

George Woodley, *Cornubia: A Poem in Five Cantos, Descriptive of the Most Interesting Scenery, Natural and Artificial, in the County of Cornwall, Interspersed with Historical Anecdotes and Legendary Tales* (London: Longman, 1819).

Charlotte Yonge, *The Prince and the Page: A Story of the Last Crusade* (London: Macmillan, 1893 [1865]).

STUDIES OF THE GOTHIC AND MEDIEVALISM

Marie-Francoise Alamichel and Derek Brewer, *The Middle Ages after the Middle Ages* (Cambridge: D.S. Brewer, 1997).

The Albert Memorial. The Prince Consort National Memorial: its History, Contexts, and Conservation, ed. Chris Brooks (New Haven, CT: Yale University Press, 2000).

Michael Alexander, *Medievalism: The Middle Ages in Modern England* (New Haven: Yale University Press, 2007).

Joanna Banham and Jennifer Harris, *William Morris and the Middle Ages* (Manchester University Press, 1984).

Stephanie L. Barczewski, *Myth and National Identity: The Legends of King Arthur and Robin Hood* (Oxford: OUP, 2000).

Christopher Baswell and William Sharpe, *The Passing of Arthur: New Essays in Arthurian Tradition* (London: Garland, 1988).

Chris Brooks, *The Gothic* (London: Phaidon, 1999).

Inga Bryden, *Reinventing King Arthur: The Arthurian Legends in Victorian Culture* (Aldershot: Ashgate, 2005).

Michael Camille, *The Gargoyles of Notre-Dame: Medievalism and the Monsters of Modernity* (Chicago: Chicago University Press, 2009).

James P. Carley (ed.), *Arthurian Poets: Matthew Arnold and William Morris* (Woodbridge: Boydell, 1990).

Alice Chandler, *A Dream of Order: The Medieval Ideal in Nineteenth-Century English Literature* (Lincoln: University of Nebraska Press, 1970).

Charles Dellheim, *The Face of the Past: The Preservation of the Medieval Inheritance in Victorian England* (Cambridge: CUP, 1982).

Robin Gilmour, *The Victorian Period: The Intellectual and Cultural Context of English Literature, 1830-1890* (New York: Longman, 1993).

Nick Groom, *The Gothic: A Very Short Introduction* (Oxford: OUP, 2012).

Nick Groom, *The Making of Percy's Reliques* (Oxford: OUP, 1999).

Antony H. Harrison, *Swinburne's Medievalism* (Baton Rouge: Louisiana University Press, 1988).

Ronald Hutton, *Witches, Druids and King Arthur* (London: Hambledon, 2003).

W. Mackail, *The Life of William Morris* (London: Longmans, 1907).

David Matthews, *The Invention of Middle English: An Anthology of Primary Sources* (Turnhout, Belgium: Brepols, 2000).

Rosemary Mitchell, *Picturing the Past: English History in Text and Image 1830-1870* (Oxford: Clarendon, 2000).

Dafydd Moore, *Enlightenment and Romance in James Macpherson's 'The Poems of Ossian': Myth, Genre and Cultural Change* (Farnham: Ashgate, 2003).

Gillian Naylor, *William Morris by Himself: Designs and Writings* (London: MacDonald, 1990).

Aubrey Noakes, *Waterhouse: John William Waterhouse* (London: Chaucer, 2004).

Beyond Arthurian Romances: The Reach of Victorian Medievalism, ed. Jennifer A. Palmgren & Loretta M. Holloway (Basingstoke: Palgrave, 2005).

Joanne Parker, *England's Darling: The Victorian Cult of Alfred the Great* (Manchester University Press, 2014[2009]).

Linda Parry, *William Morris Textiles* (London: V&A, 2013).

C. Poulson, *The Quest for the Grail: Arthurian Legend in British Art 1840-1920* (Manchester University Press, 1999).

Elizabeth Prettejohn, *The Art of the Pre-Raphaelites* (London: Tate, 2007).

Tison Pugh and Angela Jane Weisel, *Medievalisms: Making the Past in the Present* (Newy York: Routledge, 2013).

Clare Simmons, *Reversing the Conquest: History and Myth in Nineteenth-Century British Literature* (New Brunswick: Rutgers University Press, 1990).

Christopher Shaw and Malcolm Chase, *The Imagined Past: History and Nostalgia* (Manchester University Press, 1989).

Roger Simpson, *Camelot Regained: The Arthurian Revival and Tennyson, 1800-1849* (Cambridge: Brewer, 1990).

Roy Strong, *And When Did You Last See your Father: The Victorian Painter and British History* (London: Thames and Hudson, 1978).

Andrew Wawn, *The Vikings and the Victorians* (Cambridge: D.S. Brewer, 2000).

ACKNOWLEDGEMENTS

The Royal Albert Memorial Museum & Art Gallery gratefully acknowledges the support and assistance of the following individuals and institutions in preparing the exhibition 'Art & Soul: Victorians and the Gothic'.

INDIVIDUALS

Alun Sands and Sands Civil & Structural Chartered Engineers for permission to use the portrait of Harry Hems; Colin Reid, for information about Truro Cathedral; Lucinda Heron (National Trust, Castle Drogo); Diane Walker (Exeter Cathedral); Paul Holden (Lanhydrock); Richard Parker for information on Devon churches; Dave Allin, Jeremy Lawford, Avril Pattinson and Richard Parker for information about the Parish of St David's with St Michael and All Angels, Exeter; Revd Graham Stones and Fred Price for information on St Michael's Church, East Teignmouth; Revd Roger Carlton for information on St Andrew's Church, Paignton; Sara Currant, House Manager, National Trust (Knightshayes); Stephen Ponder, Curator, National Trust South West Region; Meghan Wilton, House and Collections Experience Manager, National Trust (Tyntesfield); David Garner, photography.

INSTITUTIONS

Ashmolean Museum, Oxford; Birmingham Museums and Art Gallery; Bradford Museums & Galleries, Cartwright Hall; Devon and Exeter Institution; Devon Heritage Services, Devon County Council; Exeter City Council, Mayor's Office; Falmouth Art Gallery; Museum of Barnstaple and North Devon; Museum of Somerset; Museums Sheffield; National Trust (Knightshayes); National Trust (Tyntesfield); North Devon Athenaeum; Parish of Central Exeter; Parish of St David's with St Michael and All Angels, Exeter; Parish of St Michael's, East Teignmouth; Royal Collection Trust on behalf of Her Majesty the Queen; Ruskin Library (Lancaster University); St Andrew's Church in the Parish of Paignton; Tate, London; The Wilson, Cheltenham Art Gallery and Museum; University of Exeter, Heritage Collections; Victoria and Albert Museum.

The Art & Soul exhibition would not have been possible without the hard work of the whole exhibition team and staff at RAMM. Additionally this publication has benefitted from the input of Kate Loubser, Helen Burbage, John Madin, Tom Cadbury and Julien Parsons.

ABOUT THE AUTHORS

JOANNE PARKER is a Senior Lecturer in Victorian Literature at the University of Exeter. She works on medievalism, and on the relationships between history, myth, place and national identity in the nineteenth century. She has written widely on the Victorian interest in stone circles, King Alfred, King Arthur, Robin Hood, and the Vikings. Her most recent book *Britannia Obscura* (Jonathan Cape, 2014) examines the history of alternative maps of Britain from the nineteenth century onwards, and her previous publications include *England's Darling: The Victorian Cult of Alfred the Great* (Manchester University Press, 2014 [2009]); *Written on Stone: The Cultural History of British Prehistoric Monuments* (Cambridge Scholars, 2009); and *The Robin Hood Classic Fiction Library* (Routledge, 2005), 8 vols., edited with Stephen Knight.

CORINNA WAGNER is Senior Lecturer in English, and a member of the History of Art and Visual Culture Department at the University of Exeter. Her interests include Victorian Gothic art and literature, and neo-Gothic architecture and design. She has published on the architect A.W.N. Pugin and has edited *Gothic Evolutions: Poetry, Tales, Context, Theory* (Broadview, 2014). Wagner is principal investigator of the Arts & Humanities Research Council project, 'Identity, Community and Victorian Medievalism in the South West'. As part of this project, she is co-editing, with Joanne Parker, the *Oxford Handbook to Victorian Medievalism* (2015). Wagner is also a specialist in the medical humanities, focusing on the relationship between medicine and the arts. Her publications on this topic include *Pathological Bodies: Medicine and Political Culture* (University of California, 2013) and *A Body of Work: An Anthology of Poetry and Medicine* (with Andy Brown, Bloomsbury, 2015).